William Roberts

The Earlier History of English Bookselling

William Roberts

The Earlier History of English Bookselling

ISBN/EAN: 9783337338411

Printed in Europe, USA, Canada, Australia, Japan

Cover: Foto ©ninafisch / pixelio.de

More available books at **www.hansebooks.com**

THE
EARLIER HISTORY

OF

ENGLISH BOOKSELLING

BY

WILLIAM ROBERTS

'A little row of Naphtha-lamps, with its line of Naphtha-light, burns clear and holy through the dead Night of the Past: they who are gone are still here; though hidden they are revealed, though dead they yet speak.'

CARLYLE.

•

LONDON
SAMPSON LOW, MARSTON, SEARLE, & RIVINGTON
Limited
St. Dunstan's House
FETTER LANE, FLEET STREET, E.C.
1889
[*All rights reserved*]

TO THE

DOWAGER LADY HATHERTON

This Volume

IS

RESPECTFULLY DEDICATED.

PREFACE.

IN planning a 'History of English Bookselling' I found myself compelled to adopt one of two alternatives. In one, the History would have consisted of a complete list of Booksellers, with exhaustive bibliographies of each, and full extracts from the Stationers' Registers, an account of the Company's Masters and other officers, and verbatim reprints of Charters granted at different times to the fraternity —to individual members as well as to the Company. Biographical data of the earlier booksellers would also have had to be considered, but it is scarcely necessary to remind those who have interested themselves in the earlier aspects of literary activity that biography is a singularly deficient element. If next to nothing is known of Marlowe and Shakespeare, their predecessors and their contemporaries, it is scarcely reasonable to expect much information about the lives of men who played a very subordinate part in general history. Some private animosity or professional jealousy often throws a little light upon their history or methods of work, but it rarely amounts to anything more than this. A 'History of Bookselling' on these lines, therefore, would not only be a portly volume, but it is difficult to see how the matter could be digested into a readable form. The appearance of Mr. Arber's unparalleled monument of single-handed labour, moreover, was another reason for discarding a scheme which could, by no possibility, be considered as enumerating every book published, for fresh books of the early printers and booksellers are constantly being discovered in public or private libraries, the auction-room or the bookshop. To attempt to say the last word on a subject with such endless ramifications, would be ridiculous.

Of the second alternative, the reader has now an opportunity of judging. I may, however, point out that the present volume only brings my scheme up to the earlier part of the last century. I have purposely omitted chapters on several interesting phases—such as Booksellers' Signs, Sale Catalogues, and Retail Catalogues, the wholesale and retail prices of certain books, Booksellers as publishers of newspapers, and many others, with which I purpose dealing fully in a future volume, should the present instalment be favourably received.

Preface.

It is rather an extraordinary fact that so interesting a section in literary history as Bookselling should have so long remained undone. My own aim has been to write a readable book on an interesting subject, taking care, at the same time, to be as accurate as possible. I cannot hope to have produced a work free of errors, which would, perhaps, be unique in literary history. Depending on statements at second-hand is too often a matter of leaning on a broken reed, but it is frequently the only one available. And even with the splendid resources of the British Museum, and a modest private collection (gleanings of several years from various sources), of Bibliopoliana, there are many points which I have not been able to clear up satisfactorily.

The books which have been consulted in the progress of the work are too numerous to be here specified, but the principal are *Notes and Queries, Gentleman's Magazine,* Nichols' 'Literary Anecdotes,' Mr. W. C. Hazlitt's admirable bibliographical works, Mr. Quaritch's equally useful catalogues, D'Israeli's works, Timperley's 'Dictionary,' the *Bibliographer,* Mr. Arber's 'Reprints,' Dunton's 'Life and Errors,' and many more to which due acknowledgment is given in the proper places. The British Museum 'Catalogue of Early English Books' has also been most useful.

Very many facts, derived from the newspapers of the earlier part of the last century, are now published for the first time in book form. I need hardly mention that I should at all times be grateful for any fresh information relative to the fraternity as a body, or to any of its individual members.

In conclusion, it may be pointed out that where the Christian names of persons incidentally mentioned are omitted in the body of the work, they will generally be found in the Index, in which, also, a few slips in the text—detected too late for correction—are rectified.

January 5, 1889.

CONTENTS.

CHAPTER I.
BOOKSELLING BEFORE PRINTING 1

CHAPTER II.
THE DAWN OF ENGLISH BOOKSELLING . . 18

CHAPTER III.
BOOKSELLING IN THE TIME OF SHAKESPEARE . . 46

CHAPTER IV.
BOOKSELLING IN THE SEVENTEENTH CENTURY . 78

CHAPTER V.
BOOKSELLING IN LITTLE BRITAIN . . . 116

CHAPTER VI.
BOOKSELLING ON LONDON BRIDGE . . . 130

CHAPTER VII.
OTHER BOOKSELLING LOCALITIES 140

CHAPTER VIII.
JACOB TONSON 150

CHAPTER IX.
BERNARD LINTOT 188

CHAPTER X.
EDMUND CURLL 215

CHAPTER XI.
JOHN DUNTON 281

CHAPTER XII.
THOMAS GUY 314

THE EARLIER HISTORY OF ENGLISH BOOKSELLING.

CHAPTER I.

BOOKSELLING BEFORE PRINTING.

CARLYLE has, truthfully we think, declared that 'ten ordinary histories of kings and courtiers were well exchanged against the tenth part of one good History of Booksellers.' In the history of the whole world no movement can be pointed at whose inception involved so many issues, or whose importance has proved so universal and so enduring, as the history of books, which is practically the history of human thought itself. Literature and its most primary cognate never had separate existences, for in ages long anterior to those of books, as we now understand the term, we shall find traces of bookselling by way of bartering one commodity for another, when money had only a comparative value, or was almost unknown.

We shall confine ourselves, however, so far as possible, in this chapter to a brief consideration of the origin and rise of bookselling in England. In the early centuries of the Christian era, men had no time, in the making and unmaking of towns, cities, and countries, to devote to literature, which indeed offered but few attractions to those who could neither read nor write. The cultivation of the soil, or the various methods of offence and defence in the event of war, were almost the only two alternatives, besides hunting and fishing, which the early inhabitants of Great Britain possessed to pass away the time. The seventh century, which both Hallam and Guizot considered as the *nadir* of the human mind in Europe, was only the intense darkness which preceded—almost heralded—a bright and luminous dawn, for the eighth century is a splendid landmark in the literary history of this country. Previous to this, the quality of the manuscripts was generally inferior, and the collectors few. Benedict Biscop (629-690), may be regarded as the first real and enthusiastic collector, and, in a sense, propagator of books. This famous person, who founded the monastery of Wearmouth in the year 674, made no less than five journeys to Rome for the almost express purpose of collecting books, besides commissioning his friends on various parts of the continent to collect others for him. The Venerable Bede (673-735), who was greatly indebted to the library formed by Benedict Biscop, was also a great patron and purchaser of books, and was instrumental in saving many a fine manuscript from destruction. Boniface (680-755), the Saxon missionary, had sufficient of the bibliomaniac element in him to make up for half-a-dozen men. His demands for books were simply insatiable, and there was scarcely any one of note from whom he had not begged copies of something. One of his most constant friends seems to have been the Abbess Eadburga, who sent him a number of books transcribed either by herself or her scholars. On one occasion he presented the Abbess with a silver pen. The century to which we are referring was productive of some very beautiful manuscripts, of which a few are still in existence. Books not only largely increased in numbers, but several libraries, private and public, sprang into existence.

The monks may be regarded as our very earliest booksellers. The preservation of literary treasures, the making and disposal of books, were for many centuries confined to the cloister. Whatever their faults may have been—and these were unquestionably numerous—it is only right and fair that we should accord them the merit of preserving much of our early literature and records. Among them were many who possessed an artistic taste at once exquisite and strangely out of harmony with the times, and an industry which completely overcame all opposition. The Benedictines more especially distinguished themselves in the beauty of their manuscripts, and to this order, which was the most widely diffused, we may attribute the preservation of many valuable works other than religious, for in exhorting his brethren to read, copy, and collect books, Benedict does not appear to have laid down any stipulation as to whether the books were to be heathen or the reverse. We may rest assured that the monks did not inquire too particularly into the question. The energy to which we have referred,—which also sometimes found a vent in the committal of original thoughts to paper, or rather parchment,—cannot be regarded as wholly satisfactory. Writing material was at certain periods both costly and difficult to obtain, and the over-zealous monks did not hesitate to erase the writing on old manuscripts and substitute their own notions. Of these palimpsests or rescripts, as they are now called, there are several in existence, and to this cause may be attributed the loss of many a classic, and the existence of many more in a corrupted condition. Boccaccio, when travelling through Apulia, found all the books in the library of Mount Cassino covered with dust, and on examining these he discovered book after book with entire sections cut out, and others without any margins. He was informed that it was the work of the monks, who did it to earn a penny, to make little psalters for children; with the white margins they made mass books for women. There can be hardly any doubt that the same or analogous causes contributed to our own losses in England.

The greater number of manuscripts written prior to the eleventh century fell into the hands of the Danes, and perished in consequence. The Danish invasions of the dying years of the tenth century resulted in the destruction of fifty-three monasteries; and William of Malmesbury alludes to the ancient libraries of conventual churches destroyed by these free-booters,— 'Ecclesiæ in quibus numerosæ a prisco bibliothecæ continebantur, cum libris a Danis incensæ.'

A number of inaccuracies and misleading statements concerning the books and literature of the 'dark ages' have been promulgated through the works of Robertson and Warton. Most of these were ably and categorically refuted by the late Rev. S. R. Maitland, in the pages of the long-defunct

Bookselling before Printing.

British Magazine. These refutations have been published in book form under the title of 'The Dark Ages.' The statements derived, by these writers, from Latin and French authors, are often twisted into meanings quite the reverse to what was originally intended; and they are, moreover, advanced as examples of a general rule. But they are purely exceptional cases. Books were, it is true, both dear and scarce, but only so in a comparative point of view. Robertson, quoting from 'Histoire Littéraire de la France par des religieux Bénédictins,' &c., states that 'the prices of books became so high, that persons of a moderate fortune could not afford to purchase them. The Countess of Anjou paid for a copy of the Homilies of Haimon, Bishop of Halberstadt, two hundred sheep, five quarters of wheat, and the same quantity of rye and millett.' And again, quoting from another source, he says, 'Even so late as the year 1471, when Louis XI. borrowed the works of Rasis, the Arabian philosopher, from the Faculty of Medicine in Paris, he not only deposited as a pledge a considerable quantity of plate, but was obliged to procure a nobleman to join with him as a surety in a deed, binding himself under a great forfeiture to restore it.' These two instances, while interesting in themselves, along with a number of others so commonly cited, really do not prove that books were so very expensive in early times, any more than certain recent purchases of single volumes at from 3000*l.* to 5000*l.* each illustrate the present prices in literature. Unique books have, and always will have, unique values. No book or manuscript volume which preceded the introduction of printing has an exact counterpart. The quality and price were more varied than is generally thought, and the subject-matter was most usually of little moment when compared with the extent to which it was illustrated or illuminated—a work of the most important and delicate nature. Many books, especially those used in the Church Service, were, observes Mr. Maitland, 'frequently written with great care and pains, illuminated and gilded with almost incredible industry, bound in, or covered with, plates of gold, silver, or carved ivory, adorned with gems, and even enriched with relics.'

The following extract from a letter of the thirteenth century, addressed to Alphonsus, King of Naples, by 'Parrome'—Antonius Bononia Becatellus—refers to the expense of books :—'You lately wrote to me from Florence that the works of Titus Livius are there to be sold in very handsome books, and that the price of each book is 120 crowns of gold. Therefore, I entreat your majesty, that you cause to be bought for us Livy, which we used to call the king of books.' Ames, the author of 'Typographical Antiquities,' possessed a folio MS. of the 'Roman de la Rose,' which was sold before the palace-gate at Paris, about 1400, for forty crowns, or 33*l.* 6*s.* 6*d.* In a blank leaf of this copy was written 'Cest lyvir cost a palas du Parys quarante corones d'or, sans mentyr.'

The value, extrinsic and intrinsic, of books during the three or four centuries previous to the invention of printing, is one of great importance and interest.

But the few and fragmentary facts which have been handed down to us preclude the possibility of drawing any very general inferences. Books in those days were treasured up as heirlooms, and duly bequeathed in a fittingly serious and even reverend manner. From one source we learn that Thomas Walleworth, a canon residentiary of York, and rector of Hemingburgh, bequeathed to his chaplain or curate, 'parvum Pontiforium meum, cum quo sepulchrum Domini nostri Jesu Christi pereyre visitavi.' The Earl of Warren, in 1347, left to his son William a bible which he had had 'made' in France. A year later, John de-Harpham, vicar of Outthorne, leaves to Nicholas, an apothecary at Beverley, 'unum librum de Phisicâ;' and in 1349, the head of the house of Percy bequeathed his daughter 'de naturâ animalium, in gallico.' Examples of the jealous care with which books were regarded can be multiplied *ad infinitum*. Warton mentions several in his 'History of English Poetry.' Among the constitutions given to the monks of England by Archbishop Lanfranc, in the year 1072, the following injunction occurs:—At the beginning of Lent, the librarian is ordered to deliver a book to each of the religious: a whole year was allowed for the perusal of this book: and at the returning Lent, those monks who had neglected to read the books they had respectively received, are commanded to prostrate themselves before the abbot, and to supplicate his indulgence. Warton alludes to this regulation as being partly occasioned by the low state of literature which Lanfranc found in the English monasteries. But, he adds, at the same time it was a matter of necessity, and is in great measure to be referred to the scarcity of copies of useful and suitable authors. The same writer points out that when a single book was bequeathed to a friend or relation, it was almost invariably with numerous restrictions and stipulations. And 'if any person gave a book to a religious house, he believed that so valuable a donation merited eternal salvation, and he offered it on the altar with great ceremony.' It was, in addition to this, quite a frequent practice to lend money on the deposit of a book, and the universities appear to have kept public chests for the reception of these books.

Comparatively few books with valuable appendages have come down to us. This fact is easily accounted for. Valuable personal property, then as now, was not regarded by everybody as sacred, and many cases of forcible robbery might be cited. These robberies were not always committed by the Philistines. Circumstances often compelled the clergy to strip their books of their valuable adornments. As, for example, the heavy tax levied by William II. to raise sufficient money to purchase Normandy. On this occasion, Godfred, Abbot of Malmesbury, stripped the valuable adornments from off twelve copies of the Gospels. And again, William de Longchamp pawned thirteen copies of the Gospels—one of which belonged to King Edgar, and was of great value—in order to contribute towards the redemption of Richard I. Fires also were the cause of much destruction, especially that of Hide Abbey, near Winchester, in 1141, when we are told that 'the monks got out of the ashes sixty pounds of silver and fifteen pounds of gold, and various other things, which they brought to the bishop.' But numerous robberies were effected by monks and Abbots.

In several monasteries the transcription of books gradually became regulated upon a strictly commercial basis. The monies derived from the sales were added to the revenues. of the Abbey, and books received in exchange were placed in the library. The practice of exchanging duplicate copies was a frequent one between the monasteries. From a statute date 1264 it would appear that the Dominicans were strictly prohibited from selling their books. The Scriptorium was an institution found in nearly every monastery: the Scriptoria were on the same principle but in smaller rooms. The monk most intimate with the particular author, whose work was being transcribed, dictated clearly and distinctly to a number of writers, from whom great diligence and care were exacted. The scribes were generally placed at stated distances from each other, on long seats fitted up for the purpose. The Armarian (*custos librorum*) was responsible for all the manuscripts; had to give out the work, and also the material, such as knives, parchment, &c. The original, or that of which copies were taken, was always retained, and usually one example at least of the 'copy.' And we can well imagine the monks, in the long dreamy summer afternoons, killing time by inscribing the names of works in their possession, and sometimes delineating a portrait of the author whom they most liked.

Transcribing by secular students dates back to the

seventh century, but it did not take a decided stand as a trade for some centuries afterwards. There were nearly half-a-dozen sections. The *stationarii* were those who copied, the *librarii* sold or lent, the *relieurs* bound, the *enlumineurs* illustrated, and the *parchemineurs* sold parchment. Competition was the cause of splitting the *stationarii* into more than one section, the more noteworthy being designated *notarii* and *antiquarii*. A strong professional jealousy was the result. The latter devoted their time more particularly to transcribing from, and renovating, old books. But they did not confine their attention to their speciality. And we learn from Astle that they deprived 'the common scriptores of a great part of their business, so that they found it difficult to gain a subsistence for themselves and their families.' In consequence of this the 'scriptores' sought more expeditious methods of transcribing books; 'they formed the letters smaller, and made use of more conjunctions and abbreviations than had been usual. They proceeded in this manner till the letters became exceedingly small and extremely difficult to be read.' Whitaker ('Ancient Cathedrals of Cornwall,' ii. 321), quoting from Gale, states that books were brought into England for sale so early as the year 705. But 'the trade' had only an abstract form of existence for a very long time afterwards, and then it was almost solely confined to the monks. In the matter of lending books, certain rules appear to have been adopted. In most cases a security exceeding the value—real or fictitious—of the book lent was insisted upon. Where a monastery possessed duplicates, it was not difficult to borrow, but if the book happened to be unique it was rarely allowed off the premises. The three most popular 'heathen' books were Boethius' 'Consolation of Philosophy,' Quintius Curtius' 'History of Alexander the Great,' and the 'Gesta Romanorum,' the last being perhaps the most widely-read of the three. Each monk had a lamp erected over his bed, so as to allow him to study after retiring to rest. We may be sure that he did not burn much midnight oil in perusing heavy doctrinal treatises.

About the middle of the twelfth century it seems that the manner of publishing new works was to have them read over for three days successively, before one of the universities, or other judges appointed by the public.

With the slow but sure march of progress, the demand for books greatly increased. The universities soon stepped in with a code of laws and regulations which reserved to themselves the immediate supervision over the public transcribers. The booksellers during the thirteenth and fourteenth centuries were necessarily men of judgment and learning, and the oath was administered to them with great solemnity. Their profits were subject to limitation. A charge of about five per cent. was made to any one connected with the university for the loan of certain books, whilst citizens not university men made at a rate of nearly one-third more. Stationers could not by any means be denounced as drinking wine out of the skulls of their authors in those times; and we learn that the prices allowed to stationers in 1303 for the use of their copies was excessively small. A treatise on the Gospel of Matthew, 37 pages, was lent for 1 sol; one on Mark, 20 pages, 17 deniers; St. Thomas on Metaphysics, 3 sols; a treatise on Canon Law, 120 pages, 7 sols, and St. Thomas on the Soul, 19 pages, 13 deniers. It may be pointed out that a sol is now equivalent to a halfpenny, and that a denier is a twelfth part thereof.

French bookselling was for a very long period in advance of that in this country. In 1259 the manuscript vendors became so numerous that special regulations were instituted respecting them. Censorship of the press antedated printing by at least a couple of centuries. Examiners were appointed by the universities; and this movement was an effective counterpoise to the evil intentions of dishonest traders. If an imperfect or corrupt copy was detected, it was immediately confiscated, and no compensation allowed. The booksellers could neither buy books nor sell them without leave; and they were also compelled to expose a priced list of those in their possession. As if all these restrictions were light and unimportant, the bookseller was compelled, by a French law of 1342, to lend out books to the poor students, for which a merely nominal charge was fixed by the university.

Scarcely anything is known respecting the laws and regulations of bookselling in this country during the eleventh, twelfth, and the greater part of the thirteenth centuries, when literature experienced an utter stagnation. The manuscripts were especially inferior; but the cause of this is not far to seek. The

Bookselling before Printing.

tachygraphoi, or swift writers, not only employed a number of contractions, abbreviations, and symbols, but many of the commoner words were 'indicated by single turns of the pen.' Some of these were employed by the earlier printers.

The year 1276, when Henry III. was king, and when Roger Bacon was living, is generally regarded as synchronising with the revival of 'polite' literature. Among the notabilia of this period, the figure of Richard de Bury (1281-1345) stands forth in bold relief. An indefatigable book-collector, the personal friend of Petrarch, and one of the most powerful men in the kingdom, this man has an universal as well as a particular interest. Not content with amassing an immense collection, he employed numerous scribes, bookbinders, and illuminators, to increase the facilities for study. His 'Philobiblon,' written shortly before his death, is a delightful classic. 'We wished for books, not bags,' he exclaims; 'we delighted more in folios than florins.' And again: 'O blessed God of gods in Zion ! What a flood of pleasure rejoiced our hearts as we visited Paris, the Paradise of the world ;' for 'there are delightful libraries in cells redolent of aromatics ; there are flourishing greenhouses of all sorts of volumes ; there are academic meads trembling with the earthquakes of Athenian peripatetics pacing up and down; there are the Promontories of Parnassus and the Porticoes of the Stoics . . . there in very deed we scattered with an open treasury and untied purse-strings ; we scattered money with a light heart, and redeemed inestimable books with dirt and dust.' Edward III. enabled him to 'oppose or advance, to appoint or discharge; crazy quartos and tottering folios, precious, however, in our sight as well as in our affections, flowed in most rapidly from the great and the small, instead of new year's gifts and remunerations, and instead of presents and jewels. Then the cabinets of the most noble monasteries were unlocked, caskets were unclasped, and sleeping volumes which had slumbered for long ages were roused up; and those that lay hid in dark places were overwhelmed with the rays of a new light.' De Bury very properly denounces slovenliness in connection with book-usage, such as holding a volume with unwashed hands; handling with dirty nails; leaning upon them with greasy elbows, and munching cheese or fruit over them; all of which practices he holds up to especial abhorrence.

In 1373, the University of Oxford issued a decree forbidding any one selling books without a licence. The abuses of the university regulations relative to booksellers rendered this law necessary. The Rev. H. Anstey's 'Munimenta Academica' contains much valuable information concerning the early history of booksellers in Oxford, including 'a statute to prevent the removal of valuable books' from the city. The statute, in Latin, refers to the large number of booksellers in Oxford. These men, not being sworn to the university, carried off several valuable books and sold them, to the detriment of the 'sworn stationers.' The statute, therefore, 'enacted' that no bookseller, unless duly sworn, should sell any book, whether his own or not, exceeding half a mark in value, under

Bookselling before Printing. 15

pain of certain specified penalties. In another place we are informed that, as the duties of the university are laborious and anxious, 'every one on gradation shall give clothes to one of the stationers.' In a curious indenture, dated 1459, 'between the University of Oxford and the town, to determine what persons shall be held to be of the privilege of the university,' the list includes 'alle stacioners.'

It seems almost superfluous to state that transcribing was but one of the many items which the production of books involved. We quote a few examples from the wardrobe account (1480), of Edward III., edited by Sir N. H. Nicolas as illustrating the importance of binding, gilding and garnishing. 'For vj unces and iij quarters of silk to the laces and tasselsfor garnysshing of diverse Bookes, price the unce xiiij—*d.*,vij*s.* x*d.* ob. ; for the making of xvj laces and xvj. tassels made of the said vj unces and iij of silke price in grete ij*s.* vii*d.*' These monies were paid to Alice Claver, a 'sylkwoman.' And again, to Piers Bauduyn, stacioner for bynding, gilding and dressing of a booke called 'Titus Livius,' xx*s.*; for bynding, gilding and dressing of a booke of the Holy Trinitie, xvj*s.*; for bynding, gilding and dressing of a booke called 'Frossard,' xvj*s.*; for bynding, gilding and dressing of a booke called the Bible, xvj*s.*; for bynding, gilding and dressing of a booke called 'Le Gouvernement of Kinges and Princes,' xvj*s.*; for bynding and dressing of the three smalle bookes of Franche, price in grete vj*s.* viiij.; for the dressing of ij bookes whereof oon is called 'La Forteresse de Foy' and the other called the 'Book of Josephus,' iij*s.* iiij*d.*; and for bynding, gilding and dressing of a booke called the 'Bible Historial,' xxs.

The dissolution of the monasteries entailed a grievous loss to literature. Even Bale, who regarded the monks with anything but a favourable eye, lamented the destruction. He would not, he says, have been offended for the general wreck 'if the chiefe monuments and most notable works of our most excellent writers had been preserved.' If there had been in every county in England but one library for the preservation of noble works, he thinks it would have been something towards the preservation of learning for posterity. But to commit such a wholesale destruction is a 'most horrible infamy.' Many of those who purchased the monasteries reserved the books, but not because of any love which they bore towards learning—'some to serve theyr jakes, some to scoure theyr candlestyckes, and some to rubbe their boots.' Many books were sold to the grocers and soapsellers, whilst several cargoes were exported to foreign countries. Bale declared that he knew a 'merchant man, whyche shall at thys tyme be namelesse,' that bought the contents of two noble libraries for forty shillings, that the leaves and manuscripts thus obtained he used intead of grey paper, and that the material he secured lasted him for about twenty years. In another place the same writer remarked that he found several notable volumes of antiquity, the titles, dates and commencements of which he copied. Leland, also, was instrumental in rescuing a number of chronicles and other books from ruin.

Bookselling before Printing.

We need not, however, traverse the innumerable byepaths of literary enterprise, be it the persecution of the authorities, the trials and triumphs of authorship, or the subterfuges and anomalies of bookselling. In touching upon the subject of literary history, a vast and boundless area at once appears before the imagination. It is easy enough to begin, but most difficult to know where and when to leave off, for the ramifications are endless, and the interest intense. Indeed, there is no history like unto the history of books. The hopes, the aspirations, the achievements and the results of the master-minds of the world can in no wise be regarded as unimportant. And if bookselling plays only a subordinate part in any or all of these attributes, it is at all events a part which cannot be ignored or overlooked. The influence of the bookseller, since the time of Pomponius Atticus, has been great, and it will be our duty in the following pages to indicate in some small degree the part which he, as a tradesman, has played in the past three or four centuries of English History.

CHAPTER II.

THE DAWN OF ENGLISH BOOKSELLING.

THE new birth — the Genesis of modern history, thought and movement—the invention of printing, had no greater influence upon any phase of life than upon that of literary enterprise, with which, indeed, it was synchronous. So closely allied as is the art of printing with the practice of bookselling, our limits do not permit of even a cursory view of the initial stages of the former. It must suffice us, therefore, to state, as a sort of landmark, that the first press appears to have been erected at Mayence in 1445, and that one was not introduced into this country until about 1477, when Caxton set up at Westminster. Without entering on the debatable ground as to where or with whom Caxton learned the art with which his name is so closely identified, it will be enough to state that in or about the year above mentioned he commenced a 'vertuous ocupacion and besynese' in the Almonary opposite the gatehouse of Westminster.

Caxton was wise and discreet. He knew full well the pains and penalties to which his continental brethren had been subjected, and he saw through the thin veil of righteous hypocrisy. Then, as now, the men who were loudest in advocating charity were

The Dawn of English Bookselling.

the quickest to resent, and the severest to punish those who attempted to put that estimable quality into force. Religious *vade-mecums* were naturally the best 'selling' books, and Caxton printed many such, but he confined his attention principally to the production and sale of the old romances and tales of chivalry at that time so popular. The charm and fascination of mediæval England for students at the present day cannot by any justification be extended to the dreary stuff with which our forefathers satisfied their mental appetites. Although we know nearly everything connected with Caxton and his books,—thanks to the energy of Mr. William Blades—there is one particular phase of his bookselling career of which we know scarcely anything. We have no clear records relative to the charges made for the sixty or seventy books which he printed, published and sold; we have little means of arriving at an approximate calculation as to which sold best, although several of them ran into a second edition, and, in the instance of 'The Golden Legende' (1483) a third was called for. But the amount of Caxton's funeral expenses justify the conclusion that he was of some considerable importance and wealth, which again, might have been acquired through channels other than bookselling. The demand for books at this period was not so much due to the increased supply as to the great reduction in the prices. This reduction, soon after printing was introduced, amounted to about four-fifths. In the 'Privy Purse Expenses of Elizabeth of York,' 1503, we have the following entry :—

'Itm for a prymer and saulter, xx$d$.'

a sum which Mr. Charles Knight pointed out would then have bought half a load of barley, and was about equal to the six days' wage of a labourer. As time went on, and the people became more enlightened, the demand for books increased, than which there was no more effectual way of calling cheap books into existence.

The first printers not only printed a book, but finished it off in every respect, and then sold it. The mechanical production was naturally a very tedious process, and many specimens still in existence are monuments of patience and artistic skill. The peculiarities of early books were very numerous, and a few of these are thus pointed out :—All the ancient printers, or at least those of the fifteenth century, had only very small presses, and two folio pages, little larger than two pages of foolscap, was the largest surface they could print. It is probable, also, that the system of laying down pages, or 'imposing' them, that we now have, was not then known. Their mode of procedure was as follows. They took a certain number of sheets of paper—three, four, five, or more—and folded them in the middle, the quantity forming a section. Three sheets, thus folded or 'quired,' is called a ternion; four sheets a quaternion, and so on. Hence the first sheet would contain the first two pages of the ternion and the last two pages —that is, pages 1 and 2 and 11 and 12. The second sheet, lying inside the first, would contain pages 3 and 4 and 9 and 10; the third sheet having pages 5 and 6 and 7 and 8. If the reader will take three slips of paper, and fold them in the same manner, marking the number of the pages, the process will be easily understood. It is obvious that when a system of this kind was adopted, there was danger lest the loose sheets should become disarranged, and not follow in their proper order. To obviate such an accident, there was written at the bottom of the first page of each leaf a Roman numeral, as j, ij, iij, (1, 2, 3), and so on. This plan was originally adopted by the scribes, and the printers merely imitated it. But the book being made up of a number of quires, there was a danger lest the quires themselves should become disarranged. To prevent this there was at the foot of each page written a letter of the alphabet. The first sheet would bear the letter a, the second b, and so on. When these two indications were present, the binder could never be in doubt as to the order of the different sheets. The first page of the book was marked a j, the third page a ij, the fifth page a iij, and so forth. The next quire presented the letters b j, b ij, b iij, and so on. These indications at the feet of the pages are known as signatures. When the page bears one of them it is said to be 'signed,' and where there is no mark of the kind it is said to be 'unsigned.' In the earliest books the signatures were written with a pen, and the fact that many copies which have been preserved do not now bear signatures, is owing to the fact of their being written so close to the margin that they have since been cut off, while the book was being rebound. It was many years after the invention of typography that signatures were printed along with the matter of the pages. The earliest instance we have of the use of printed signatures is in the 'Preceptorium Divine Legis' of Johannes Nider, printed at Cologne, by Johann Koelhof, in 1472. It has, however, been pointed out that the inventor of signatures was Anthony Zarot, who introduced the art of printing into Milan, and that they were inserted in an edition of Terence printed by him in 1470. The point is purely typographical.

Speaking of early bookbinding, Mr. Charles Knight observes that 'the board between which the leaves were fastened, was as thick as the panel of a door. This was covered with leather, sometimes embossed with the most ingenious devices. There were large brass nails, with ornamental heads, on the outside of this cover, with magnificent corners to the lids. In addition, there were clasps. The back was rendered solid with paste and glue, so as to last for centuries. Erasmus says of such a book, as for Thomas Aquinas' *Secunda Secundæ*, no " man can carry it about, much less get it into his head." An ancient woodcut shews us the binder hammering at the leaves to make them flat, and a lad sewing the leaves in a frame, very much like that still in use.'

The number of copies printed of each impression could not have been large,—probably not more than a hundred or two at the outside of even very popular books. The market experienced no glut for a long period after Caxton. Caxton rarely undertook the publication of a work unless he had some sort of guarantee, or unless the persuasions of 'many noble and divers gentlemen' resolved themselves into some tangible proof. In 1483, the scarcity of books appears to have been so great that an Act of Parliament was passed to promote their importation from foreign countries.

In addition to printing and selling, Caxton almost invariably edited, rearranged, and sometimes wrote or translated the works which he published,—a practice common with the earlier printers. The 'Noble Hystoryes of Kynge Arthur' (1485), for example, was 'deuyded in to xxi bookes chapytred and emprynted and fynysshed, in thabbey westmestre.' To nearly every book which he printed Caxton added prefaces or prologues, explanatory or otherwise, which are exceedingly characteristic. In the case of 'the Boke Eneydos' (1490), he states that 'this present book is not for a rude uplandish man to labour therein, nor read it; but only for a clerke and a noble gentleman, that feeleth and understandeth in feats of arms, in love, and in noble chivalry.' It may be pointed out here that the first English book printed in England is generally considered to be 'The Dictes and notable wyse Sayenges of the Phylosophers' (1477), translated from the French by Caxton's patron Earl Rivers. The first book printed in English is 'The Recuyell of the Historyes of Troye,' which is a translation from a French *traduction* of a Latin work; it was 'begonne in Bruges in 1468 and ended in the holy cyte of Colen 19 Sept. 1471.' The second edition of 'The Game and Playe of the Chesse,' without date, but issued probably about 1481, was the first printed book in the English language which contained woodcuts, but it was not printed in England.

As a matter of fact, bookselling was in every way subordinate to printing with Caxton and his more immediate successors. His example was emulated by his apprentices, Wynkyn de Worde (*d.* 1534), and Richard Pynson (*d.* 1530). The former, with a singular reverence for his master, invariably gives Caxton's initials the precedence of his own name. He published over 400 books, whilst his fellow-labourer issued about half that number. De Worde carried on business 'in flete strete, at the sygne of the sonne agaynst the condyth.' A map of London of the date of Elizabeth shows the conduit to have been at the south end of Shoe Lane, Fleet Street. Pynson's was farther up, being situated outside Temple Bar. The two men printed, in several instances, editions of the same books, but the spirit of rivalry was at all times a friendly one. Pynson's books are, as a general rule, superior in merit and utility to those of Caxton and Wynkyn de Worde. It may be pointed out that before the end of the fifteenth century there were 71 printing presses in Italy, 50 in Germany, 36 in France, 26 in Spain, 14 in Holland, 7 in Switzerland, 4 each in Austria and Bohemia, and only 3 in England. But Ames and Herbert have recorded the names of 350 printers engaged in producing books in England and Scotland between 1471 and 1600; and it is computed that this number issued about 10,000 publications.

From the earliest times the publication of books has been a fearful bogey in the eyes both of court and of church authorities. Book-censorship was essentially an outcome of monarchism, whose chief aim was to terrify where it could not subdue. Probably the oldest mandate for appointing a book-censor was that issued by Berthold, Archbishop of Mentz, which was dated January 10th, 1486, and the contending parties had 'high jinks' of it for very many years. So early as 1515, an Act of Parliament was passed at Edinburgh, forbidding any one to print or publish any books, ballads, songs, 'blasphematious' rhymes or tragedies, in Latin or English, until such had been 'seen, viewed and examined by some wise and discreet persons' duly appointed. England appears to have enjoyed a certain amount of immunity from the obnoxious interference of the State until 1526, when anti-popery books were condemned, and those who sold them liable to the most severe penalties; this statute was repealed a few years after by another law, which sought to suppress Catholic publications with the same rigour as had just previously been evinced towards books propagating the Protestant innovation. Dr. Furnivall has published, in 'Political, Religious, and Love Poems,' a curious 'List of Books Proscribed in 1531,' dated the first Sunday in Advent. It runs thus: 'These bokes folowyng were opynly at poules crosse by the autorite of my lorde of london vnder his Autentycal seale, by the doctor that that day prechide, prohibite, and straytely commaunded of no maner of man to be vsed, bought, nor solde, nor to be red, vnder payne of suspencion, and a greter payne, as more large apperyth in for-sayde autoryte.' The list of thirty books, includes 'a prologe' to each of the five books of Moses, the 'Revelation of Antechriste,' the New

Testament, with an Introduction to the Epistle to the Romaynes, the Psalter and the Primer (the last three in English), two works of Tyndale, and a 'boke of thorpe or of John Oldecastelle.' In addition to those specially named, the prohibition applied to 'alle other suspect bokes, both in Englissh and in laten, as welle now printed or that here-after shall be printed, and not here afore namyd.'

The Act of 25 Henry VIII., c. 15, sought to prevent printers and booksellers from levying impositions. The fourth and last section of this statute runs to the effect that if any complaint be made either to the King, Lord Chancellor, Lord Treasurer, or any of the Chief Justices, it should be inquired into, and judgment meted out by the 'discretions' of 'twelve honest and discreet persons.' The same officials or functionaries had power also given them to 'reform and reduce such inhancing of the prices of printed books from time to time by their discretions, and to limit prices as well of the books as for the binding of them,' and where offenders are convicted, the punishment laid down is that they 'lose and forfeit for every book sold' at an unfair price, the sum of three shillings and fourpence, half of which was to be given to the king, and the other half to the aggrieved party. A similar Act was passed 8 Anne, c. 19, § 4, which enforced a penalty of five pounds for every book sold at a higher price than the 'discreet' persons should affix to it. The latter Act was repealed 12 George II., c. 36, § 3, but the former is actually still in force, for it has never been expressly repealed.

The Dawn of English Bookselling. 27

The Stationers' Company took up the hue and cry. Although this institution originated in 1403, its first charter was not received until May 4, 1557, during the reign of Mary. The number of 'seditious and heretical books, both in prose and verse,' that were daily issued for the propagation of 'very great and detestable heresies against the faith and sound Catholic doctrine of Holy Mother the Church,' became so numerous, that the Government were only too glad to 'recognise' the Company, and to entrust it with the most absolute power. The charter was to 'provide a proper remedy,' or, in other words, to check the fast-increasing number of publications so bitter in their opposition to the Court religion. But, stringent and emphatic as was this proclamation, its effect was almost *nil.* On June 6, 1558, another rigorous Act was published from 'our manor of St. James,' and will be found in Strype's ' Ecclesiastical Memorials ' (ed. 1822, iii., part 2, pp. 130, 131). It had specific reference to the illegality of seditious books imported, and others 'covertly printed within this realm,' whereby 'not only God is dishonoured, but also encouragement is given to disobey lawful princes and governors.' This proclamation declared that not only those who possessed such books, but also those who, on finding them, do not forthwith report the same, should be dealt with as rebels.

It will be seen, therefore, how easy it was, in the absence of any fine definition, for books of whatever character to be proscribed. There was no appeal against the decision of the Stationers' Hall representatives, who had the power entirely in their own hands.

A few months after Mary's desperate and futile attempt at checking the freedom of the press, a diametrically objective change occurred, and with Elizabeth's accession to the throne in November, 1558, the licensed stationers conveniently veered around and were as industrious in suppressing Catholic books as they had been a few weeks previously in endeavouring to stamp out those of the new religion. The irony of fate was indeed hard upon the poor stationers!

The Reformation contributed greatly to the demand for printed books, for upon the dissolution of the monasteries, the office of scribe was practically obsolete. The ecclesiastical authorities vainly hoped to see the trade in printed books die a natural death, and the revival of the old methods of diffusing knowledge. 'Under Henry VIII.,' observes D'Israeli, 'books became the organs of the passions of mankind, and were not only printed, but spread about; for if the presses of England dared not disclose the hazardous secrets of the writers, the people were surreptitiously furnished with English books from foreign presses.'

A few months after Elizabeth's accession an injunction was issued, in 1559, to the effect that no one might print any book or paper whatsoever, unless the same be first licensed. It was not long after she renewed the charter of the Stationers' Company, than with characteristic perverseness she, in or about 1577, upset it by making several grants quite upon her own responsibility. John Jugge, her Majesty's printer, secured the privilege of printing Bibles and Testaments; 'Richard Tothill the printinge of all kindes *Lawe bookes*, which was common to all printers, who

The Dawn of English Bookselling.

selleth the same bookes at excessiue prices, to the hindrance of a greate nomber of pore students.' John Day, ABC's, and catechisms, ' with the sole selling of them by the collour of a commission ;' James Roberts and Richard Watkyns, all almanacs and prognostications; Thomas Marshe, Latin books used in the grammar schools ; Thomas Vautrollier, of all Latin books other than latin school books ; 'one Bryde a singing man,' all music books ; William Seres, salters, primers and prayer books ; and 'Francis Flower a gentleman beinge none of our companye hath privilidg for printinge *the Gramer* and other thinges, and hathe farmed it oute to some of the Companie for one hundred poundes by the yere, which C li. is raised in the inhaunsinge of the prices above th' accustomed order.' The foregoing names occur in a list, probably drawn up by a stationer, and presented to the Queen, first as 'The griefs of the printers, glass-sellers and cutters susteined by reson of privilidges. granted to privatt persons,' but was ultimately modified into 'Complaint of diuerse of their hyndrance by graunts of privelidges.' The memorandum (which is reprinted in *Archæologia*, xxv. 101, and *Bibliographer*, vi), is followed by a list of ' the names of all such Stacyoners and Printers as are hindred by reson of the presaid Privilidges '— to the number of thirty-five. Besides these there were 140 'that han byne made free of the Stacyoners since the begynnynge of the quenes maiesties reign that now is, besides a great number of apprenticez ; ' in addition to these there were ten others 'as do lyve by bookselling being free of other companies, and also hindered by the said privilidges.'

The terrified stationers were much alarmed, and accordingly drew up a petition which met with nothing but a severe reprimand 'for daring to question the Queen's prerogative.' But, 'approaching her Majesty a second time much more humbly than before,' the company was at length granted the exclusive right of printing and selling psalters, primers, almanacks, ABC's, the 'little Catechism,' and Nowell's English and Latin catechism. Roger Ward, and John Wolf, a fishmonger, treated the Queen's ruling with the most supreme contempt, likewise the Stationers' Company. He 'printeth what he lysteth' was the company's complaint. The memorandum describing the officials' defeat is a choice piece of drollery; 'comminge to the house of one Roger Warde, a man who of late hathe shewed himselfe very contemptuous againste her Majesty's high prerogative, and offering to come into his pryntinge house to take notice of what he did, the saide Roger Warde faininge himselfe to be absente, hys wyfe and servants keepeth the dore shutt againste them, and saide that none shulde come there to search.' John Wolfe,—who was perhaps an unmarried man!— did not fare so well, for he paid the penalty of his daring by way of imprisonment. In spite of decrees, and a host of means to bring transgressors to the bar of judgment, the many so-called privileges of particular persons and bodies corporate were being constantly infringed. The Queen's prerogative was repeatedly questioned, and frequently set at nought. And with the dawn of the seventeenth century, the 'rights' of the monopolists existed only in name.

Another amusing episode in the early days of copyright may be related. Francis Reynault (or Reynold), a Frenchman who fell under the displeasure of the Inquisition for printing the Bible in English. He had, at the time of the row, a number of primers in English, which aroused the jealousy of the Stationers' Company during the reign of Henry VIII. He was frightened, and begged Coverdale and Grafton to intercede with Cromwell to grant him a licence to sell what he had already printed, and engaging to print no more in England unless he had an Englishman to correct the proofs for him.

The evolution of the bookseller from the typographer took place during the reign of Elizabeth, an interesting fact which is proved from contemporary evidence. In 1582, Christopher Baker,—then Upper Warden of the Stationers' Company—committed to paper a most interesting and valuable summary of the Printing Patents granted up to that time by Elizabeth. From this evidence we glean that in the reign of Henry VIII. there were but few printers, which were of 'good credit and component wealth, at whiche tyme before, there was another sort of men, that were writers, Lymners of bookes and dyverse thinges for the Church and other vses called Stacioners ; which have and partly to this daye do vse to buy their bookes in grosse of the saide printers, to bynde them vp, and sell them in their shops, whereby they well mayntayned their families.' In the reign of Edward VI., although printers greatly increased, it became so costly an art that 'printers were dryven throughe necessitie, to compound before [hand] with the booksellers at so lowe value, as the printers themselves were most tymes small gayners, and often loosers.'

From a sixteenth century document in the Lansdowne collection, we learn, 'that the booksellers being growen the greater and wealthier nomber, have nowe many of the best copies and keepe no printing house, neither beare any charge of letter, or other furniture, but onlie paye for the workmanship' (*Archæologia* xxv.). An early example of the co-operative method may be cited in 'The Four Sons of Aimon' (1554), which had been printed both by Caxton and Wynken de Worde, and was again reprinted in 1554 by William Copland; a certain number of copies were struck off for particular stationers, with their names on the imprint. Some copies have the name of John Waley, and others that of Thomas Petet.

In noticing Arber's 'Transcripts of the Stationers' Registers,' Mr. H. B. Wheatley has pointed out—in the *Bibliographer*—that 'the number of copies that went to make up an edition was fixed in the interest of the workmen. The utmost recognized limit, irrespective of the size, price or popularity of the book, was 1250, so that the master-printer was put to the cost of resetting his book in type, even in cases where he was certain of a larger sale ; and this circumstance accounts for the slight variety in different editions of popular books in those days. Double impressions of 2500 were allowed of primers, catechisms, proclamations, statutes, and almanacs. Of the grammar and accidence four double impressions, or 10,000 copies of each, were allowed to be printed annually ; but in 1587 it was decided that should further impressions of these be needed in any one year, they should consist of 1250 copies only.'

The war between the bookseller and the author almost synchronised with the introduction of printing; and it still goes merrily on! They appear to agree only in regarding their interests as antagonistic. Nearly every literary quarrel will be found to contain a greater or lesser element of bibliopolic vagary. And on the other hand, perhaps nothing can exceed the abuse and scurrilous invective which have been hurled at booksellers and publishers. For many years after the invention of printing, the press was chiefly employed in increasing the stock of literature provided by classic authors, and the producers were therefore trading on fairly safe ground. The selection was not so much a matter of discrimination as of taste or convenience. The supply almost regulated the demand. The unhappy guerilla warfare between the two parties commenced in real earnest so soon as authorship by profession became an established, if hopelessly miserable, fact. It should be remembered that the early printers, such as Gutenberg, Faust, Dolet, and Caxton were men emphatically of 'light and leading.' They were followed, in the seventeenth and eighteenth centuries, by others whose only remarkable trait was ignorance, and who stuck at nothing to advance their own ends, and fill their own pockets. They ridiculed the notion of any other than a common right in literary property, and cared nothing for an author's feelings, which, indeed, they appear to have persistently ignored.

The horror with which eminent men refused to be

classed as authors is almost proverbial, and only too clearly indicates the status of the then professional. The feeling is not even now obsolete. ' To say truth, ma'am, 'tis very vulgar to print,' observed Sheridan's Sir Benjamin Backbite, and there was a good deal of force in the remark. The effusions of the *dilettanti* were circulated among their friends in MS., in which condition they remained until they fell into the hands of some enterprising bookseller. The poems of the noble but ill-fated Surrey, although circulated in MS. during his lifetime, were not printed until 1557. Sidney's ' Astrophel and Stella ' was never written with the intention of being published, but two impressions of it issued from the press in 1591, with a notice from its bookseller, Thomas Newman. One of the most interesting examples of the 'horror' to which we have alluded offers itself in ' England's Helicon ' (1600), which is a collection of poems by various writers, and published by John Flasket. The curious address to the reader refers to stationers making free with each other's property, but Flasket was hoisted with his own petard. By helping himself pretty freely to other people's work he raised a perfect hornet's nest around his own ears, and was compelled to paste slips of paper over the names which he had cited.

A sort of 'half-and-half' arrangement appears to have obtained connection with Barnabe Googe's ' Eglogs, Epytaphes, and Sonettes ' (1563), which was 'imprinted at London, by Thomas Colwell, for Raffe Newbery, dwelyng in fleetstrete a little aboue the conduit in the late shop of Thomas Bartelet.'

The Dawn of English Bookselling.

But we will let Mr. Googe tell the story in his own way, but with the orthography modernized :—' A very friend of mine, bearing as it seemed better will to my doings than respecting the hazard of my name, committed them all together unpolished to the hands of the printer. In whose hands during his absence from the city till his return of late they remained. At which time he declared the matter unto me: shewing me, that being so far past, and paper provided for the impression thereof, it could not without great hinderance of the poore printer be now revoked. His sudden tale made me at the first utterly amazed, and doubting a great while what was best to be done, at length agreeing both with necessity and his council, I said with Martial "iam sed poteras tutior esse domi."' There was none of this reticence and modesty in M. François De La Mothe Le Vayer (1588-1672), who, upon being informed by his bookseller of the slow sale of one of his books, is reported to have said, 'I know a secret to quicken the sale.' He procured an order from the Government for its suppression, and as a consequence the whole impression rapidly sold!

Great movements are proverbially the outcome of small causes. And such was the case when the contumacious John Wolfe, upon 'being admonished that he being but one so meane a man should not presume to contrarie her Highnesse governmante,' unceremoniously retorted, 'Tush, Luther was but one man, and reformed all the world for religion, and I am that one man that must and will reforme the government in this trade.' In spite of the fact that the opposition was bought off, and that on July 1, 1583, Wolfe was admitted a freeman of the Stationers' Company by redemption, paying the usual fee of 3*s.* 4*d.*, a great concession was made to the unlicensed printers, by which any of them might, with the authority of the master and wardens, reprint such works as the owners did not care to reproduce, or such as had long been out of print. For this privilege the unlicensed individuals were to pay at the rate of 2½ per cent. on the cost of the book.

Book entries appear to have occupied a very minor place in the consideration of the Company, and were inserted in the Register only when the fee of 4*d.* or 8*d.* was charged. The first copy entered on the books is 'to William Pekerynge, a ballett called *a Rise and Wake*, 4*d.*' The motive for entering was perhaps more as an advertisement than anything else. The fines levied by the Company (observes Mr. Wheatley) in early days formed a very considerable item in their revenue, and the amount received from them was sometimes more than from all other sources put together. Men were heavily fined for not serving the office of warden, and on August 18, 1578, Oliver Wilkes was fined 20*s.* for refusing to serve on the livery, with the option of imprisonment if he did not pay the money. It is more than passing strange that the leading men of the fraternity were neither excused nor let off nominally. Richard Tottell, for example, was fined in July, 1588, for keeping an apprentice two years unrepresented; and in May, 1586, Christopher Barker, the Queen's printer and elder warden, was also fined for the same misdemeanour. William Norton, who lived at the King's Arms, St. Paul's Churchyard, and who died in 1593, an original member of the Company, and one of the first six who came on the livery after the renewal of their charter, was fined for keeping open shop, and selling books, on St. Luke's Day, and also on Sundays, a practice for which other minor lights had to pay penalties. Several got into trouble for using 'undecent language.' This entry, under date March 7, 1591, sufficiently explains itself:—' Thomas Gosson for his copie, "*A ballad of a yonge man that went a wooying,*" &c. Abel Jeffes to his printer hereof *provyded alwayes* that before the publishing hereof the undecentness be reformed.' This entry is struck through, and in the margin is written, 'Cancelled out of the book for the undecentness of it in diverse verses.' Four years later Jeffes was again in hot water for printing certain 'verye offensive' things.

The rapidity with which books and pamphlets multiplied during the sixteenth century caused each successive Parliament and sovereign great consternation and alarm at the problematical consequences. Laws, as we have seen, were passed, and indictments framed, but all to very little purpose. The printer disposed of his secretly-printed wares to the innumerable pedlers and chapmen, who, in their turn, disseminated the proscribed literary merchandise in various and remote parts of the country. Perforce, the poor printer was made the scape-goat—when caught: he it was who pandered to the party that paid him, irrespective of his own views. The bookseller was, by the very nature of his calling, an 'artful dodger,' who, so soon as he detected danger ahead, could gather up his goods and chattels, and, to use an Americanism, 'make a retrograde movement for a stratagetic purpose.' The printer was much more heavily handicapped; but where the supply fell short of the demand, the people were supplied through the medium of foreign presses and agencies against which red-tapeism was quite powerless. The authorities were baffled and befooled all along the line. Webbe, in his 'Discourse of English Poetrie'(1586), speaks of the 'innumerable sortes of Englysshe bookes, and infinite fardles of printed pamphlets, wherewith thys countrey is pestered, all shoppes stuffed, and eury study furnished.' Generally the authorship was a profound secret; sometimes it was an 'open' one, and at others more or less distinctly implied in the complimentary odes and sonnets of friends and admirers added by way of proem. It is to such practices that we may trace many of the existing doubts and uncertainties. But much of our bibliographical confusion is attributable to another cause, in which the luckless bookseller plays the leading part. Anything that would 'sell' he would have printed without any compunction. Acting as his own editor, he had only himself to blame for his inaccuracies, and his back was broad enough to bear any amount of curses that would in any case fall to his share. A man who indulged in poetical frivolity in his youth, and who in after years became famous, was fair game for the bookseller, who would forthwith not only collect and publish or republish those tentative efforts, but all others that could by any possible means, fair or foul, near or remote, be fastened to the same authorship. In some few instances this energy has proved positively beneficial to posterity.

The history of the old printer-booksellers is a very fascinating one: their quaint mannerisms, their squabbles, fraternal and otherwise, their escapades, and their triumphs over difficulties, all give colour to by-paths which are almost as charming as the very high road of literature itself. A knowledge of botany adds tenfold to the interest of a country walk; and to the 'grubber' among the black-letter quartos and folios of three and four centuries since an imprint is much more than an imprint, for it forms quite a little chapter of a component whole. There is a marvellous continuity, not individually, perhaps, but certainly collectively, in the annals of bookselling, from Caxton, Wynkyn de Worde, and Pynson, to Murray, Rivington, and Longman. Times have changed, and we with them, but the fundamental principle—the propagation of knowledge—remains the same. Where they printed in tens, we print in tens of thousands; where they sought the exclusive patronage of one or two great men, we appeal to a circle which has no limits, to a *clientèle* whose taste is universal, and to a constituency in which every person thinks and acts differently.

It is not necessary nor even desirable in such a work as this to give a chronological account of the vikings of literary enterprise; but it will not be out of place to indicate a few of the more important points in the history of this wide-spreading subject.

Pugnacity, as we have seen, was a well-developed element in the constitution of the early booksellers. Before the advent of authorship by profession, they relieved the monotony of every-day life by quarrelling among themselves. These trade differences have many points of interest and even value to us, for during their course some important evidence has been unconsciously disclosed. Regard for the sacred rights of property was not one of the articles in the bookseller's creed. In or about 1525, for example, Robert Redman assumed and altered one of the best devices of Pynson, and also infringed upon his rights to print law-books. The case is laid before the public on October 12, 1525, at the end of an edition of 'Lytyltons Tenures,' in a Latin letter. The Royal Printer—for such was Pynson—was by no means unpleasantly particular in his employment of adjectives. 'Behold, I now give to thee, candid reader, a Lyttleton corrected (not deceitfully) of the errors which occurred in him. I have been careful that not my printing only should be amended, but also that with a more elegant type it should go forth to the day: that which hath escaped from the hands of Robert Redman, but truly Rudeman, because he is the rudest out of a thousand men, is not easily understood. Truly I wonder now at last that he hath confessed it his own typography, unless it chanced that even as the Devil made a Cobbler a Mariner, he made him a Printer. Formerly this scoundrel did profess himself a Bookseller, as well skilled as if he had started forth from Utopia. He knows well that he is free who pretendeth to books, although it be nothing more.'

In April, 1527, Redman made matters worse by removing to the sign of the George, in St. Clement's parish, the very house which Pynson had vacated. In this year, also, Pynson made another onslaught upon his rival in an edition of the 'Magna Charta.' But the quarrel was probably 'made up' in 1532, when we find Redman occupying Pynson's residence next to St. Dunstan's Church, and when, according to Herbert's contention, Pynson retired from business, and made over his stock to Redman. Henry Pepwell, who died in 1539, was one of the most extensive of the earlier publishers and booksellers. Ames was of opinion that Pepwell acted as a sort of agent, at the Holy Trinity, St. Paul's Churchyard, for works printed abroad; he bequeathed to Bermondsey church in which parish he was born, 'a mass lbook, of five shillings value, for prayers to be made for his soul.'

Richard Grafton, whose operations extend from 1537 to 1571, is one of the most interesting persons who combined the threefold functions of printing, bookselling, and authorship, in the early days of typography. In addition to Hardyng's 'Chronicles,' which he reprinted, and to which he 'added a continuacion of the storie in prose to this our tyme, now first imprinted, gathered out of diuerse and sondery authours that haue writē of the affaires of Englande' (1543), he also reprinted and continued Hall's 'Chronicles' (1550). Next to Grafton in chronological sequence, but perhaps before him in importance, comes John Day, whose name is so linked with literary enterprise from 1546 to 1584. Bibles, sermons, and ABC's were all strong features with Day. But he is a notable personage in many respects; he published books during the reigns of Edward VI., Mary, and Elizabeth. In the first of the three reigns he established a reputation as a printer of Bibles, and in the last he had the distinction of being the only one in his trade who possessed Old English characters, and with these Foxe's edition of the Saxon Gospels was printed. John Foxe, of 'The Book of the Martyrs' fame, worked for Day as author, translator, and editor. Day's motto was, 'Arise, for it is Daye.' Day issued, in 1560, the first Church music-book in English, and a few months previously (*i.e.* October 2, 1559) he was fined by the Stationers' Company for printing without first having obtained a licence. He commenced business at the sign of the Resurrection, near the Holborn Conduit, and removed in 1549 to a house adjoining the City wall, Aldersgate. This latter place did not content the industrious John, and so several of his friends procured from the Dean and Chapter of St. Paul's a lease of a little shop at the north-west door of the church. This aroused the jealousy of rival tradesmen, who obtained from the Mayor and Aldermen an injunction to prevent the design being carried out. But the civic dignitaries had no right to interfere, and a petition from the Archbishop to the Lord Treasurer, it may be assumed, was effective; but the books in existence bearing the St. Paul's Churchyard imprint are confined to the year 1578, and limited to less than half-a-dozen works. William Seres was Day's partner from 1546 to 1550, when each acted independent of the other. Day died at Walden, Essex, July 23, 1584.

William Middleton, whose shop was at the sign of the George, next to St. Dunstan's Church, appears to have succeeded Redman as a printer, after the latter's wife married Ralph Cholmondley ; and among his thirty or forty books, perhaps the most notable is Heywood's 'Four P's ; a very merry Enterlude of a Palmer, a Pardoner, a Poticary, and a Pedlar,' a posthumous production, dated 1569. Herbert points out that there appear to have been three early (English) editions of Froissart's 'Chronicle,' one by Pynson, another with Pynson's name but pirated, and a third by Middleton. There is still another link between Redman and the booksellers of a later period ; for Henry Smyth, on the authority of Ames, was his son-in-law, and issued books at the sign of the Holy Trinity, the most notable being an edition of Littleton's 'Tenures' (1545). Richard Tottell was one of the best known and most popular of the sixteenth century booksellers, and his operations extend over nearly the whole of the last half of that period. His shop was at the sign of the Hand and Star, within Temple Bar ; and, in addition to the licence already referred to, it may be pointed out that in 1557 he published Tusser's 'A Hundreth good Pointes of Husbandrie ;' in 1562, Grafton's 'Abridgement of the Chronicles of England ;' and in 1579, in conjunction with Henry Binneman, Stowe's 'Summary.' He was Master of the Stationers' Company in 1578, and a few years afterwards he 'retired into the country, when his son carried on the business for him.'

And so we might go on, *ad infinitum*, giving the names, the signs, and quoting the titles of the books issued by the old printer-publishers; but the list would only have a very circumscribed interest, which, as in the other cases, almost solely depends upon the particular works for whose mechanical production they were responsible. 'The literature of Protestant England passed, about the time of James I., from the exuberant delicious fancifulness of youth into the sober deliberativeness of manhood. The age of romantic chivalry, of daring discovery, of surpassing danger was passing away. A time of wonderful thoughtfulness, of strong research, of national quiet had come. Learning had become common to most educated persons. The most recondite subjects in theology and among the Schoolmen, the highest problems in nature, the subtlest inquiries into the human spirit, the first principles of human society, every theory of national government daunted not, but fascinated thinkers. Selden owned, "All Confess there never was a more Learned Clergy, no Man taxes them with Ignorance;" and the writings of Bacon, Lord Herbert of Cherbury, Selden, Hobbes, Prynne and others, represent the attainments of many of the laity.'[1]

But this healthy revival in literature coincided with a curiously decisive retrograde movement in bookselling. The earlier members of the fraternity had been on the whole fairly honest and pretty well educated,—very much more so than the followers of

---

[1] Arber: Introduction to Earle's 'Micro-cosmographie.'

any other trade. The great new birth of the Reformation called an innumerable quantity of booksellers into existence, and the ranks of the trade were augmented by the riff-raff of nearly every walk of life, who not only had no characters to lose, but gloried in the fact. They starved the authors who had nothing but their wits to live on, and dragged to the very lowest depths of degradation the struggling movement of authorship by profession. They thieved from all quarters, and then flaunted their stolen wares in the very faces of the proprietors, who, as we have already shewn, had no means of retaliation other than those of a personally aggressive nature,—and these, perhaps for obvious reasons, do not appear to have been often put into requisition. The booksellers, therefore, had it all their own way.

CHAPTER III.

BOOKSELLING IN THE TIME OF SHAKESPEARE.

I.

FEW men suffered so much from the vagaries of the booksellers as Shakespeare, for they not only paid him nothing for his 'copy' which they stole, but edited and improved him in a manner and with a degree of effrontery which have no parallel in literary history. Tradition throws a little light upon a few of these methods, all of which, however, point to a clandestine or surreptitious publication. Apart from the historical importance of the subject, the publication of Shakespeare's plays and poems may be taken as a sort of index to the manner in which sundry other works crept into a printed form of existence. All the leading authors were subjected to very similar treatment.

To commence with Shakespeare's first published book, it may be pointed out that the plague of 1591-3 was not only instrumental in causing the London theatres to be closed, but it afforded the great dramatist a little leisure, which he utilized in the composition of 'Venus and Adonis.' This appeared in 1593, on April 18, of which year it was duly entered in the Registers of the Stationers' Company by R. Field. It was published probably by J. Harrison, of the White Greyhound, St. Paul's Churchyard, who certainly issued the editions dated 1594, 1596, and 1600. There is a very interesting fact in connection with the printing of this book. The printer, Richard Field, was a fellow-townsman of Shakespeare's, and, granting the assumption that he served his apprenticeship with T. Vautrollier, it is satisfactory to know that he married this man's daughter Jakin on January 13, 1588, and that, when Vautrollier died in 1599, Field succeeded to the business, occupied the same premises in Blackfriars, and adopted the same signs and marks of the Anchor. That 'one touch of nature' which, to use a quaint expression of Aubrey, 'this William' described as making 'the whole world kin,' had a practical outcome here in giving a fellow-townsman a 'turn,' and also again in 1594, when 'The Rape of Lucrece' appeared. The bookseller in this case, as in the former, was J. Harrison, who, however, employed another printer—P. Short —for the 1598 edition. There were two J. Harrisons, father and son, who were rather extensive booksellers in Shakespeare's time: the former commenced about 1573, and appears to have issued scarcely anything after 1606, whilst the latter published books between 1611 and 1638. The elder (Mr. Fleay points out) resigned his interest in the Shakespeare volumes, and appears to have altered his place of business about 1599. W. Leake whose operations extend from 1594 to far into the first half of the seventeenth century, was publishing at the Greyhound in St. Paul's Churchyard certain books which Harrison had hitherto owned ; and after 1599, the latter's imprints do not indicate his whereabouts in London. One of his books, Stowe's 'Summarie of the Chronicles of England' (1604), a little 16mo of over 500 pages, concludes with a list of errata laconically designated 'faults escaped'! In 1602, when he issued an edition of 'Venus and Adonis,' Leake had either removed to another part of the Churchyard, or had selected a new sign, which was that of the 'Holy Ghost.' So far back as June 25, 1596, Leake had entered this poem, and apparently retained all his rights thereto until February 16, 1616, when W. Barret entered it, and, in the following year, published an edition. No fewer than eleven quarto editions of 'Venus and Adonis' appeared from 1593 to 1630. The 'Passionate Pilgrim,' 1599, bore Leake's imprint; and at various periods of his career he either published or sold Beaumont and Fletcher's 'King and No King,' and ' Philaster,' Lilly's ' Euphues,' and, in 1637, Marlowe's ' Hero and Leander,' when his shop was in Chancery Lane, 'neere the Roules.' R. Jackson, who issued ' Lucrece' in 1616—the year of Shakespeare's death—had a shop in the Conduit, Fleet Street, and we meet with his name between 1590 and 1625 in connection with the works of Ariosto, Greene, Gervase Markham, and also Old Testament Proverbs and biblical Abridgments.

It is rather an interesting fact that, with one unimportant exception, neither of the printers nor booksellers who were concerned in the volumes of 'Venus and Adonis' and 'Lucrece' had anything to do with the plays of the same author. For some time Andrew Wise, of the Angel, St. Paul's Churchyard, appears to have monopolized the publication of the plays, but as they increased in number, and as the demand grew, this monopoly was soon broken through. During 1597 three plays were printed. The first was an imperfect and pirated version of 'Romeo and Juliet.' The other two were 'Richard II.' and Richard III.,' and both were printed by Valentine Simmes for Andrew Wise. The titles are masterpieces of windy rhodomontade, and the following is an example:—'The Tragedy of King Richard III., containing, His treacherous Plots against his brother Clarence; the pittieful murther of his innocent nephewes; his tyrannicall vsurpation; and the whole course of his detested life, and most deserued death.' Professor Dowden points out that of 'Richard II.' four quartos had appeared before the end of 1615, and of 'Richard III.' seven quartos had been issued prior to 1630. This would allow a period of eighteen months for each issue.

'Romeo and Juliet' was first published in quarto form in 1597, 'as it hath been often (with great applause) plaid publiquely by the right Honourable the L[ord] of Hunsdon his servants.' In 1596 it was entered for E. White; but the first quarto was made up partly from copies of portions of the original play, partly from recollection and from notes taken during the performance. And although Burby's edition of 1599 claims to be 'newly-corrected, augmented, and amended,' this was only approximately correct.

Following the three plays of 1597, there came, in the next year, two more. These were, the first part of 'Henry IV.' and, 'Loves Labour Lost.' The former was issued by Andrew Wise, and a second edition, dated 1599, claims to be 'newly corrected by W. Shakes-peare.' The latter, or 'Loves Labour Lost,' bore

E

the imprint of Cuthbert Burbie or Burby, whose shop was then situated near the Exchange. This particular edition of 'Loves Labour Lost' is very noteworthy, for it was the first play upon which Shakespeare's name occurs. Whether Mr. Burby was overburdened with a desire to give credit where it was due, or whether he considered the chances of sale enhanced by giving the author's name, we cannot undertake to say, but perhaps there was a modicum of the two causes at work. Burby, on the whole, was a fairly generous fellow, for in 1608 he gave 20*l*. to the poor of the Stationers' Company. Books bearing his imprint are to be found ranging between the years 1592 and 1607.

Wise published, also in 1598, editions of 'Richard II.,' and 'Richard III.,' the former being printed by Valentine Simmes, and the latter by T. Creede. In 1600 no fewer than six new plays of Shakespeare came out, and, with two exceptions, bore the author's name. At this period Wise appears to have taken William Aspley into partnership in his business, either entirely, or only so far as certain plays were concerned. They issued conjointly the second part of 'Henry IV.' and 'Much Ado About Nothing.' Professor Dowden points out that the two parts of the former were written before the entry of the first in the Stationers' Register, February 25, 1597-8. The second play was entered August 23, 1600, and a 'well-printed' edition appeared, as already pointed out, in the same year. Two rival editions of 'A Midsummer Night's Dream'—of which the second was unquestionably pirated—appeared in 1600, the first by J. Roberts, and the second by T. Fisher, whose shop was at the White Hart,

Fleet Street, and who issued a few books between 1600 and 1602. That this 'strange and beautiful web woven delicately by a youthful poet's fancy,' should have been extremely popular and subjected to piracy, is not to be wondered at. The 'Merchant of Venice, which was entered in 1598, makes the fourth play bearing the date 1600, and of this there were two rival quartos, one of which was published by Laurence Heyes, of the Green Dragon, St. Paul's Churchyard, and the other by J. Roberts. The 1637 edition of this play was published by Laurence 'Hayes.' 'Titus Andronicus' and 'Henry V.' complete the list of 1600, and these are the two exceptions on which Shakespeare's name does not occur. 'Henry V.' was a sort of red-rag to the booksellers, for at least three imperfect quartos appeared before the end of 1608. The first was printed for 'Tho. Millington and John Busby. And are to be sold at his [? their] house in Cauter Lane, next the Powle head.' Both these men, with E. White, T. Pavier, and H. Gosson, were the booksellers who industriously employed themselves in foisting upon the public as the work of Shakespeare, or in a garbled form, as the case may be, 'Pericles' the 'True Tragedy of the Duke of York,' and 'Titus Andronicus.'

The 'Richard III.' of 1602 was probably the last Shakesperian play which bore the imprint of Wise and Aspley. From this time forward their rights, or supposed rights, to the publishing of Shakespeare's plays were transferred to Matthew Law, of the Fox, St. Paul's Churchyard, near St. Augustine's Gate. Editions of several plays were issued by him up to

1615, but none other than those which had been previously published by Wise or Wise and Aspley. Law, however, remained in business until 1626; one of his earliest publications was Nash's 'Christ's Tears over Jerusalem,' 1594, which J. Roberts had issued the year before.

An imperfect report of the 'Merry Wives of Windsor, is dated 1602. The 'rights' of this play were transferred on January 18, 1601-2, from T. Busbie to Arthur Johnson, who accordingly and in due course published it; but his name does not occur again in connection with Shakespeare. The second, or 1619, quarto, Mr. Quaritch points out as being valuable to the scholar from the fact that it contains in a great measure a different text to that which appears in the folio of 1623. In June, 1602, J. Roberts entered 'The Revenge of Hamlett, Prince of Denmark, as yt latelie was acted by the Lord Chamberlain his servants,' and it duly came forth in 1603, printed for N. Ling, under St. Dunstan's Church, Fleet Street, and J. Trundell. It was perhaps an imperfect report of the first form of the play. In the year following, Roberts printed and Ling published the second quarto of this play, 'newly imprinted and enlarged to almost as much againe as it was,' and this later form Professor Dowden conjectures to be due to Shakespeare's revision of his own work. In both instances the author's name is given. Ling was a rather prolific tradesman from 1582 to 1607, and he published works of such well-known men as Hayward, Nash, Sutcliffe, and Whittaker. On January 22, 1606-7, he entered 'Romeo and Juliet,' 'Loves Labour Lost,' and the 'Taming of

Bookselling in the Time of Shakespeare. 53

the Shrew,' but he only produced the last-named. J. Smethwick, whose operations extend from 1600 to 1640, seems to have taken over Ling's business, and also his shop in Fleet Street; at all events he entered the three above-named plays (and also 'Hamlet'), which were the property of Ling. His list of books includes Burton's 'Censure of Simonie' (1624), Drayton's 'Poems,' Greene's 'Never too Late,' and also certain works of Middleton and Nash, besides an edition of 'Romeo and Juliet' in 1609, and one of 'Hamlet' in 1611.

To Nathaniel Butter, of the Pied Bull, St. Paul's Churchyard, near St. Augustine's Gate, belongs the honour of first issuing 'Lear.' It was probably published surreptitiously, but it bore Shakespeare's name. It was entered November 26, 1607, but it had been acted nearly a year previously. Two quartos came out in 1608, both by Butter, 'one in 44 leaves in which the publisher's address was not given on the title, and the other, 41 leaves, in which it was. The latter is usually considered the earlier of the two, but it is equally probable that the former was the first issued. The number of leaves would be an argument for this supposition; as reprints in ancient days were usually more compressed than the originals' (Quaritch). There are few names more distinct than that of Butter in the bookselling annals of the first forty years of the seventeenth century, but it is as the founder of the English newspaper press that he is best remembered. In addition to issuing works of Casaubon, Coke, Davies, Decker, Tarleton, and very many others, he broke fresh ground in August, 1622, when 'The Certain News of the Present Week' came forth It was a small quarto of eighteen pages, and was edited by the publisher, who, on June 7, 1622, made another venture with 'A Courant of News.' Butter's experiments were very numerous.

From the fact that nearly all the quartos posterior to 1600 are more or less surreptitious, it may be inferred that some means were afterwards taken to prevent publication, but unsuccessfully so up to and including 1609. No new play appeared from this date until the famous folio of 1623. In 1609, however, 'Pericles,' 'Troilus and Cressida' and the famous 'Sonnets' were published. The first-named was entered in 1608 by Edward Blunt or Blount, and, as Professor Dowden points out, it came out with a very ill-arranged text in the next year by another bookseller, Henry Gosson, who had, it is believed, surreptitiously obtained his copy. Although only in part the work of Shakespeare, he is credited with the entire performance; five quartos were issued before 1631, but the play was not included in either of the first two folios—nor in fact until the third one, the rarest of all, dated 1664. 'Troilus and Cressida' concludes the list of plays which appeared during Shakespeare's lifetime. Its sponsors were R. Bonian and H. Walley, 'at the Spred Eagle in Paules Churchyeard, ouer against the great North doore.' The very rare preface to this play is most quaint and interesting, the writer prophesying 'And beleeue this, that when hee is gone, and his Commedies out of sale, you will scramble for them, and set up a new English Inquisition.' Bonian and Walley, or Whalley, published several books in conjunction with each other, notably Fletcher's 'Gentle Shepherdess,' but the examples of their books only cover a span of four or five years,—*i.e.* from 1607 to 1611.

On May 20, 1609, 'a book called Shakespeare's Sonnettes' was entered in the Stationers' Register by Thomas Thorpe, and an edition was issued in the same year, printed by 'G. Eld for T. T. and to be sold by William Aspley' or Apsley. Some copies of this edition were 'sold by John Wright,' dwelling at Christ Churchgate,' a fact accounted for by the practice of selling books in sheets, which gave each bookseller the opportunity of printing his own title-page, which was sometimes done in a very erratic fashion. The book presumably 'fell flat,' at all events a second edition was not printed until 1640. The publication was quite unauthorized, and the book is only another example of bookseller's vagary, particularly when Thomas Thorpe assumed the privilege of dedicating the work 'to the onlie begetter, W. H.' It would be foreign to our purpose to discuss the personality of W. H. which is, in fact, as fast a secret as the identity of Junius or the Man in the Iron Mask. But Mr. Thorpe was by no means a man of *one* dedication : he performed this office for 'St. Augustine, of the citie of God, with the learned comments of Io. Lod. Vives. Englished by J. H.' (1610), and this time it bore a more definite address, viz. 'to the honourablest patron of the muses and good mindes,' the Earl of Pembroke. Another example worthy of record appeared with Marlow's 'First Book of Lucan' (1600), upon which occasion he addressed himself to Blount the Bookseller:— 'Blunt, I purpose to be blunt with you, and, out of my dulness, to encounter you with a dedication in memory of that pure elemental wit, Chr. Marlowe, whose ghost or genius is to be seen walk the church-yard in, at least, three or four sheets,' and so forth.

The most interesting bibliopolic phases of Shakespeare's career terminate with the year 1609, to be revived again to a certain extent, but in a totally different direction, in 1623, when the first folio appeared. The circumstances in relation to this publication have been so often retailed, that they are almost quite familiar to every one. For the sake of continuity we will just indicate the leading points. This, the first collected edition, was 'set forth,' or, in other words, edited, by his 'friends' and 'fellows,' John Heminge and Henry Condell, and it was published by the two leading booksellers, Isaac Jaggard and Edward Blount. It contains all the dramatic works usually found in modern editions except 'Pericles.' The editors allude to the earlier quartos as 'stolne and surreptitious,' and imply that their edition is printed from Shakespeare's manuscript, of which there is not a scrap in existence. But as a matter of fact several of the plays were printed from the quartos. The one great point of value attached to this folio is that it contains eighteen plays of which no quarto editions exist. The second folio, dated 1632, printed by Thos. Cotes for Robert Allot, is a reprint of the first 'conjecturally emended, to some extent, the emendations being more often wrong than right.' The third and rarest folio was 'printed for P. C.' in 1664, and contains seven plays absent from the two preceding collections, but which, with the exception of a portion of 'Pericles,' are not by Shakespeare. The fourth is notable to us from the fact that it is a sort of connecting link between two great men in English literary history. It came out in 1685, under the auspices of Henry Herringman, the publisher who issued a great number of Dryden's works, and who assisted the poet in time of need.

II.

The literary history of nearly all the sixteenth and seventeenth century authors, when it comes to deal with the manner in which their works crept into print, tells pretty much the same tale. No cause, in fact, has resulted in so much uncertainty and controversy as the tricks of the booksellers, who can scarcely be trusted even upon oath. Among many other bad qualities popularly supposed to be inherent to the bookseller is laziness. That trenchant satirist, Tom Nash, delivers himself to the following effect in 'Pierce Penilesse' (1592) :—' If I were to paint Sloth .... by St. John the Evangelist, I swear that. I would draw it like a stationer that I know, with his thumb under his girdle, who, if a man come to his stall to ask him for a book, never stirs his head, or looks upon him, but stands stone still, and speaks not a word, only with his little finger points backward to his boy, who must be his interpreter; and so all the day, gaping like a dumb image, he sits without motion, except at such times as he goes to dinner or supper, for then he is as quick as other three, eating six times every day.'

There is a story in connection with the publication of nearly every sixteenth century book, so that it becomes a difficult matter to decide what to include and what to omit. The wiser plan perhaps will be to confine ourselves to the better known writers. When, for example, the first three books of the 'Faerie Queene' (1590) made no inconsiderable stir, William Ponsonby, or Ponsonbie, upon his own sole authority and quite without the poet's knowledge, issued a collection of poems under the title of 'The Visions of Petrarch' (1591) as the work of Spenser. It contained, *inter alia*, several pieces, slightly altered, that appeared more than twenty years before as 'devised by S. John Vander Noodt,' and when no reference of any kind is made to Spenser. 'A Theatre,' &c. (1569), opens with six epigrammatic sonnets which are identical with the first six in the 'Visions,' and, moreover, eleven of the fifteen sonnets in 'A Theatre' are among 'The Visions of Bellay' published with 'The Visions of Petrarch.' Prof. Hales has pointed out that there is as little difference between the two sets of poems as is compatible with the fact that the old series is written in blank verse and the other in rhyme. Why the bookseller should have adopted such tactics we cannot even suggest, and perhaps it would be an idle task to hazard conjectures.

That industrious antiquary, Anthony à Wood, had

an especial dislike to booksellers, and he complains of its being the 'usual thing in those days to set a great name to a book, or books, by which the sharking booksellers or snivelling writers get bread.'

Most of the elder writers appear to have tried all the leading booksellers, deeming, perhaps, one transaction with one individual quite sufficient. Robert Greene, for example, had many, but Edward White and Thomas Cadman were the principal ones. The former, whose shop was 'at the little north door of St. Paul's, at the sign of the Gun,' issued 'Morando' in 1584, 'Euphues' in 1587, 'Perimedes, the Blacksmith,' in the following year, and 'Friar Bacon and Friar Bungay' in 1594. John Busbie published 'Ciceronis Amor' (1597), 'Never Too Late' (1590), and the second part of the latter, viz. 'Francesca's Fortunes.' Thomas Cadman, whose shop was 'at the great north door of St. Paul's, at the sign of the Bible,' issued 'Planetomachia' (1585), 'Pandosto' (1588), and 'The Spanish Masquerado' (1589). Greene's most valuable prose work, 'The Repentance of Robert Greene' (1592), was published by Cuthbert Burby or Burbie, whose shop was the 'middle' one in the Poultry, under St. Mildred's Church, in 1592; and who removed, in or about 1594, to near the Royal Exchange, where he was carrying on business in 1599. There is a reference in the address of the 'Printer to the Gentlemen Readers' to the death of Robert Greene, 'whose pen in his lifetime pleased you as well on the stage as in the stationers' shops.' But William Ponsonby, Thomas Woodcock, and Roger Warde, among others, published one or more works of this prolific writer, whom Anthony Wood charges with 'that high and loose course of living which poets generally follow.'

George Peele, who, according to Collier, was the son of Stephen Peele, a ballad-writing bookseller, was likewise a man of many publishers. William Barley, of Gratious Street, sold several of his works, including 'Edward I.' (1593). William Wright, whose shop was adjoining St. Mildred's Church, in the Poultry, issued Peele's 'Farewell to Norris and Sir Francis Drake' (1589). Peele's 'The Honour of the Garter' (1593 ?) bore the imprint of J. Busbie, 'King David' (1599) that of A. Islip, 'Merry Conceited Jests' (1627) that of F. Faulkner, and 'Alcazar' that of R. Bankworth. It will be seen, therefore, that Peele's knowledge of the London booksellers was extensive. The same may be said of Thomas Nash; but many of his pamphlets bear no imprint at all, or, what is just as bad, a bogus one: their tone and character rendered this amount of secrecy most essential. His 'Anatomie of Absurditie' (1590) was issued by Thomas Hackett; 'Christ's Teares' (1593), by J. Roberts; 'Have with you to Saffron-Walden' (1596), by J. Danter; 'Lenten Stuffe' (1599), by N. Ling; and 'Summer's Last Will and Testament' (1600), by Walter Burre. W. Jones, C. Burbie, and Richard Jones also published for Nash. The last-named, perhaps more than any other, will always be associated with the satirist's name. Indeed, he almost deserves to be reckoned among the smaller lights of literature. His dedications form quite a feature in literary by-paths. In 1590 he produced the first two

editions of Marlowe's 'Tamburlaine the Great,' but
the edition dated 1592 is more particularly interesting
to us from the address of Jones, or Jhones, or Johnes.
'I have,' he said, 'purposely omitted and left out
some fond and frivolous gestures, digressing, and, in
my poor opinion, far unmeet for the matter, which I
thought might seem more tedious unto the wise than
any way else to be regarded, though haply they have
been of some vain-conceited fondlings greatly gaped
at, what time they were shewed upon the stage in
their graced deformities: nevertheless, now to be
mixtured in print with such matter of worth, it would
prove a great disgrace to so honourable and stately a
history.' In the same year he exercised his talents
in connection with Nash's 'Pierce Penilesse: his
Supplication to the Devil.' And as this 'Address
to the Gentlemen Readers' is short, as well as characteristic, we cannot refrain from quoting it:—
'Gentlemen, In the Author's absence I haue been
bold to publish this pleasaunt and wittie discourse of
"Pierce Penilesse, his Supplication to the Diuell;"
which title, though it may seeme strange, and in
it selfe somewhat preposterous, yet if you vouchsafe
the reading, you shall finde reason, as well for the
Authour's vncouth nomination, as for his vnwonted
beginning without epistle, proeme, or dedication: al
which he hath inserted conceitedly in the matter;
but Ile be no blab to tell you in what place. Bestow
the looking, and I doubt not but you shall finde
dedication, epistle, and proeme to your liking.—
Yours bounden in affection, R. J.' In 1591 he
wrote an introduction to N. Breton's 'The Bower of

Delights.' There are nearly a hundred books in existence with Jones's imprint, embracing the last thirty years of the sixteenth century. He kept a shop at the south-west door of St. Paul's Church, and, according to Timperley, lived at the sign of the Rose and Crown, near Saffron Hill, in Holborn; and at the upper end of Fleet Lane, over against St. Sepulchre's Church, at the sign of the Spread Eagle.

In prosecuting an inquiry into the general state of bookselling just three hundred years ago, a frequent and not altogether explicable circumstance is that in relation to the different imprints which appear in some cases in the same year on one work. There was practically no such thing as copyright; and the moment a manuscript left the author's hand, and found its way into the printing-office, all claim on the part of the author ceased. If one bookseller had sufficient confidence to publish a poem or a play, and it proved successful, the chances were a thousand to one that rival tradesmen would offer rival copies. We may take, as a by no means extreme example, Marlowe's 'Hero and Leander,' of which Taylor, the Water Poet, repeated verses as he plied his boat on the Thames. The first and second editions were printed in 1598 for Edward Blount. John Flasket, of the Black Bear, in St. Paul's Churchyard, published an edition in 1600, and another six years afterwards. In 1609, Blount and W. Barret appear to have gone into partnership, and to have succeeded Flasket at the Black Bear; for at this address they issued two editions, one in 1609 and the other in

1613. In 1629, Richard Hawkins, of Chancery Lane, and eight years later William Leak, of the same quarter, were publishers of distinct editions of this work. In fact, it is most difficult to say to whom the copyright belonged, or if, indeed, one had more right to it than another.

George Chapman had almost a fresh bookseller for every new pamphlet or play. One of his earliest works—'Skia Nuktos' (1594)—was issued by William Ponsonby; and more than one bore the imprints of both William Aspley and the ingenious Thomas Thorpe. Walkley, Bonian and Walley, John Budge, Lisle, and George Norton are among the best-known members of the fraternity who published for Chapman. Thorpe, Ling, and Stansby published some of Ben Jonson's works.

The last few years of the sixteenth century were notorious for the publication of a vast quantity of scurrilous literature. In 1599 most of this was committed to the flames by order of Whitgift and Sancroft, but the effect of this was not perceptible upon the slippery sharp-shooters. As an example of the attacks upon private vices, we quote one of the introductory epigrams which occur in 'The Scourge of Folly' (*circa* 1611) of John Davies, of Hereford:—

> 'At stacioners shops are lyes oft vendible,
> Because such shops oft lye for gains untrue :
> But truth doth lye there oft contemptible ;
> Unsold, sith old ; but lyes are often new.
> Then should my booke sell well, sith full of lyes,
> Ah, would they were : Nay, sure they leazings bee
> In saying such and such do villanies ;
> When none so nam'd commit such villany.

> But I use namelesse names, because their shame
> Should light on nobody that beares the blame.'

We may be sure that Richard Redman, located at 'ye West Gate of Paules,' the vendor of Davies's book, declined the soft impeachment so far as he was personally concerned. Nash has a contemptuous reference in 'Pierce Penilesse' to the inferior writings of the time :—' Who can abide a scurvie pedling poet to plucke a man by the sleeue at eurie third step in Paules Churchyard, and when he comes in to survey his wares there's nothing but purgations and vomits wrapt vp in wast paper.' Barnaby Rich, in his preface to the courteous and friendly reader, in 'A New Description of Ireland' (1610), says,—'One of the diseases of this age is the multitude of books, that doth so overcharge the world that it is not able to digest the abundance of idle matter that is every day hatched and brought into the world, that are as divers in their forms as their authors be in their faces. It is but a thriftless and a thankless occupation, this writing of books : a man were better to sit singing in a cobbler's shop, for his pay is certain a penny a patch! but a book-writer, if he get sometimes a few commendations of the judicious, he shall be sure to reap a thousand reproaches of the malicious.'

Doubtless Michael Drayton was of Rich's opinion on the subject of authorship. Writing to the friend so well known to us through the medium of 'rare Ben Jonson,' Drayton exclaims,—' I thank you, my dear sweet Drummond, for your good opinion of Polyolbion. I have done twelve books more, that is, from the 18th book, which was Kent (if you note it), all the east parts and north to the river of Tweed; but it lieth by me, for the booksellers and I are in terms; they are a company of base knaves, whom I scorn and kick at.' Considering the elephantine ponderosity of Drayton's books, it was not at all surprising that he and the booksellers were 'in terms' and that they got no further. However, three years later the second part actually put in an appearance, but in the meantime his natural enemies had been dealing hardly by him. The preface is despairingly, and we might almost say savagely, inscribed 'To any that will read it.' From this source we learn that the stationers, who were concerned at the slow sale of the former part, had left out the epistle to the readers! But we will relate the incident in Drayton's own words. He complains of the cold reception which the first portion of his great work met, and that he not only failed to receive the encouragement which his friends predicted, but that he had been subjected to base detraction, and so forth. 'Such a cloud,' he laments, 'hath the devil drawn over the world's judgment. Some of the stationers that had the selling of the first part of this poem, because it went not so fast away in selling as some of their beastly and abominable trash (a shame both to our language and our nation), have despightfully left out the epistle to the readers, and so have cousened the buyers with imperfect books, which those that have undertaken the second part have been forced to amend in the first, for the small number that are yet remaining in their hands.' Even in 'the good old times' of slow travelling, slow eating, and slow reading, a poem which ran into about 30,000 lines was scarcely likely to be read by everybody. 'Where art thou, Michael?' was the cheery inquiry of John Davies of Hereford, and under the accumulation of miseries, Echo might well have answered, 'where indeed?'

If, however, precedent goes for anything, the bookseller might have justified himself by citing more than one instance. William Turner, in the dedication to Elizabeth of his 'New Herbal' (1568), complains of a crafty, covetous and Popish printer, not satisfied with suppressing the author's name and leaving out the preface, but furnishing his own preface and publishing as if it were the production of his own brain! Another example may be found in the case of an exceedingly rare little work, 'A Petite Palace of Petties his Pleasure' (1576). The printer-publisher, 'R. B.,' supplied the address 'to the gentle Gentlewomen,' and also that to 'all readers.' It is with a charming *naïveté* that he describes his manner of procedure. After the book had been in his 'custodie' for some time, he was 'eftsoones ernestly sollicited to publish' it, which he at length resolved to do. 'I have,' he goes on to say, 'put the same in printe, vsing my discretion in omitting sutch matter as in the Aucthores iudgement might seeme offenciue;' urging, as a plea, that the printer may sooner offend in printing too much than in publishing too little. But the old booksellers did not confine themselves to editing and prefatory or dedicatory writing. They had a strong partiality for title-pages, which after all are not unimportant in the by-ways of bookmaking. The great aim, of course, was to obtain an attractive 'nomination,' which more often than not was half the battle towards selling out an edition. Whether the title had an immediate or remote reference to the subject-matter does not appear to have been considered material,—or in fact whether it had reference to anything at all in particular. Who, for example, could divine the burthen of Yates' 'Castel of Courtesie, whereunto is adjoyned the Hold of Humilitie, with the Chariot of Chastitie thereunto annexed' (1582), or Gascoigne's 'The Droome of Doome's Day' (1576), or Breton's 'A Flourish upon Fancy' (1577), or many hundreds of others that might be named? Clearly the bookseller was in most cases solely responsible for the titles ; and if the first was not satisfactory a second or a third was brought into requisition. Decker, in the 'Strange Horse-race' (1613), observes that ' The titles of books are like painted chimnies in great country-houses, make a shew afar off, and catch travellers' eyes ; but coming near them, neither cast they smoke, nor hath the house the heart to make you drink.' John Houghton, when starting his ' Collection for the Improvement of Husbandry and Trade ' (1682), cautions the booksellers to send him no new titles to old books for they ' will be rejected.' But the worthy John, who was an F.R.S., must have been very ' green ' if he thought the trade would heed his warning !

The old booksellers employed metaphors in quite a distinct fashion, and so the expression a ' good book ' is not understood to necessarily indicate a ' high ' toned religious or otherwise intrinsically meritorious work ; it simply meant one that sold well.[1] The term, which is still employed, is a very old one, and is re-

[1] See *Connoisseur*, January 31, 1754.

ferred to by Ben Jonson in his poem to his bookseller :—

> 'Thou, that mak'st gaine thy end, and wisely well
> Call'st a book good, or bad, as it doth sell,
> Use mine so, too : I give thee leave. But crave
> For luck's sake, it thus much favours have,
> To lie upon thy stall, till it be sought ;
> Not offer'd, as it made suit to be bought :
> Nor have my title-leaf on post, or walls,
> Or in cleft-sticks, advanced to make calls
> For termers or some clerk-like serving-man,
> Who scarce can spell th' hard names : whose knight scarce can ;
> If, without these vile arts, it will not sell,
> Send it to Bucklersbury,[2] there 'twill well.'

The following, a preliminary sonnet, 'Ad Bibliopolam,' from Henry Parrot's 'The Mastive, or young-whelpe of the Olde Dogge,' (printed for R. Meighen and Thos. Jones, 1615), is sufficiently *àpropos* to be quoted here :—

> 'Printer, or stationer, or what ere thou proove,
> Shalt mee record to Time's posteritie,
> Ile not enjoine thee, but request in love
> Thou so much deigne my Book to dignifie,
> As first it bee not with your ballads mixt ;
> Next, not at Play-houses mongst Pippins solde ;
> Then that on posts, by th' eares it stand not fixt
> For every dull-mechanicke to beholde ;
> Last, that it come not brought in pedlars' packs
> To common fayres of countrey, towne or citie,
> Sold at a Booth mongst pinnes and Almanacks.
> Yet on thy hands to lye thou'lt say 't wer pittie :
>   Let it be rather for tobacco rent,
>   Or butchers' wares, next cleansing week in Lent.'

---

[2] A famous street in London, noted in Ben Jonson's time for chemists and herbalists. See 'Merry Wives of Windsor,' iii. 3.

Like so many other apparently modern institutions, the practice of selling books of words at the theatre before the play began is a very old one. In the preface to William Fennor's 'Descriptions' (1616), we learn that books other than those bearing directly upon the entertainment, were sold at the theatre. 'I suppose' 'this Pamphlet will hap into your hands before the play begin, with the importunate clamour, "*Buy a New Booke*" by some needy companion.'

It has been pointed out that in the time of Shakespeare, the price of the copy of a play to the booksellers was about twenty nobles, or 6*l*. 13*s*. 4*d*. The patron to whom the play was dedicated paid about forty shillings for such an honour. These figures are represented at the present day by about five times as much. Undoubtedly, the law of supply and demand operated, and the more popular the play, the greater the demand for copies, and small probability was there of the successful author being content to receive the ordinary honorarium.

One of the most important facts in connection with the trade during the time of Shakespeare is that in 1595 the first Catalogue of books was published. It was compiled by a bookseller named Andrew Maunsell, who commenced business in or about 1570, at the sign of the Parrot, St. Paul's Churchyard. Very few books were printed by him, but he had an extensive connection as a publisher. He 'undertook' at least two of Churchyard's books, dated 1578 and 1579, respectively. The catalogue is of great value, bibliographically speaking; and its title runs as follows:—'The first part of the Catalogue of English

Printed Books: which concerneth such matters of divinitie as have bin either written in our owne tongue, or translated out of anie other language: and which have bin published to the Glory of God, and edification of the Church of Christ in England. Gathered into alphabet, and such method as it is, by Andrew Maunsell, bookseller. *Unumquodque propter quid.* London: printed by John Windet for Andrew Maunsell, dwelling in Lothburie, 1595.' There were three dedications, the first to Queen Elizabeth, the second to the clergy, and the third to the Master, Wardens and Assistants of the Stationers' Company in particular, and all other printers and booksellers in general. This last dedication is of especial literary and bibliopolic interest. 'Seeing' (observes Maunsell) 'many singular books, not only of divinity, but of other excellent arts, after the first impression, so spent and gone, that they lie even as it were buried in some few studies :—I have thought good in my proper estate to undertake this most tiresome business, hoping the Lord will send a blessing upon my labours taken in my vocation ; thinking it as necessary for the bookseller (considering the number and nature of them) to have a catalogue of our English books, as the apothecary his Dispensatorium, or the schoolmaster his Dictionary. By means of which my poor travils, I shall draw to your memories books that you could not remember ; and shew to the learned such books as they would not think were in our own tongue ; which I have not slighted up the next way, but have to my great pains drawn the writers of any special argument together, not following the order of the learned men that have written Latin catalogues, Gesner, Simler, and our countryman, John Bale. They make their alphabet by the Christian name, I by the surname: they mingle divinity, law, physic, &c., together; I set divinity by itself; they set down printed and not printed, I only printed. Concerning the books which are without authors' names, called Anonymi, I have placed them either upon the titles they be entitled by, or else upon the matter they entreat of, and sometimes upon both, for the easier finding of them.' The second part of this catalogue, relating to books on mathematics, arithmetic, geometry, astronomy, astrology, music, war, navigation, physic and surgery, appeared shortly after the first, and it likewise had three dedications. The first was to the Earl of Essex, the second to the Professors of Mathematics, Physic and Surgery, and the third, as in the former part, was addressed to the Stationers' Company. The third and perhaps the most valuable part never appeared: it was to have dealt with books on grammar, logic, rhetoric, law, history, poetry, &c. The first part is composed of [viii.] 123 folio pages, and the second, which was printed by J. Roberts, of [vi.] 27 pages.

III.

The imprint of a book is almost invariably an important and frequently an accurate guarantee of merit, and not only is this the case at the present moment, but something very analogous existed in times which have long since become merged in the dim obscurity of the past. In writing the literary account of a particular person or epoch, historians, almost without an exception, pass over in silence the part which booksellers played, and apparently consider it not only as beneath notice but as altogether superfluous. The essentially interwoven connection between bookselling and authorship is so great that the influence of the author must be taken side by side with the operations of the bookseller. We are in the present day startled with an extraordinary theory in connection with certain plays ostensibly the work of Shakespeare. And without entering upon debatable ground, we may serve a useful purpose in giving a brief account of the works which Bacon issued during his lifetime, and as sort of balance to our somewhat exhaustive account of the first publication of the works of Shakespeare, who, indeed, might have echoed the sentiments of the author of 'The Ant and the Nightingale, or Father Hubbard's Tales,' which was sold by Jeffrey Charlton 'at his shop at the North Doore of Paules' (1604). 'I never' (observes the writer) 'wisht this book better fortune than to fall into the hands of a true spelling printer, and an honest stitching bookseller.'

In 1597, Humfrey Hooper, whose shop was at the 'blacke Beare in Chauncery Lane,' brought out the first edition of the famous 'Essays.' There were only ten subjects dealt with in this extremely quaint volume of 32 leaves (excepting the title-page and dedication). 'To labour the staie of them,' observes Bacon in the address to his brother, 'had bin troublesome, and subject to interpretation; to let them passe had beene to adueture the wrong they mought receiue by vntrue coppies, or by some garnishment, which it mought please any that should set them forth to bestow upon them.' The second edition appeared in the following year, and, like the first, it bore the imprint of Hooper, who, from the very few examples of his publications now existing, we may assume was a young publisher that Bacon wished to assist. In 1596 he had published Dr. John Wood's 'Practicæ Medicinæ.' Editions of the 'Essays' followed upon one another with comparative rapidity, at least one appearing in 1604 and another in 1606, and then again in 1612 and 1624. Spedding doubted whether Bacon had anything to do with either of the issues of 1598, 1604, and 1606, which are said to be merely reprints without additions or alterations, except some changes in the spelling and the substitution of an English translation of the 'Meditationes Sacræ' from the original Latin. Whether John Beale's issue of 1606 was authorized or not we have no means of determining, but it is quite certain that Isaac Jaggard published pirated editions in 1606, 1612, and 1624. Jaggard's shop was at the sign of the 'Hand and Starre, near Temple Bar, Fleet Street,' and for a quarter of a century there were few more prolific booksellers than he. His publications include Carew's 'Survey of Cornwall' (1602), Fairfax's translation of 'Godfrey of Bulloigne' (1600), the first volume of an English version of Boccaccio, and the famous first folio of Shakespeare (1623). In the last instance, as we have already seen, Blount, another bookseller, divided the undertaking, and in most other cases the pecuniary responsibilities were shared by friendly rivals. The first and only complete edition of the 'Essays' published in Bacon's lifetime was printed for Hanna Barret and John Whittaker (1625), whose shop was at the sign of the King's Head in St. Paul's Churchyard. Hanna Barret was probably the widow of William Barret, who published several works—notably the productions of Montaigne, Bishop Hall, Sandys, and Bacon —between the years 1608 and 1624. Hanna Barret either retired from business or died in 1625, for we do not after that date meet with any examples of her publications.

'A Briefe Discourse, touching the Happie Union of the Kingdoms of England and Scotland' (1603), was printed for Fœlix Norton, whose shop was 'at the signe of the Parot' in St. Paul's Churchyard, and were also to be sold by William Apsley. Apsley published books between 1599 and 1630, including the productions of Decker, Casaubon, Chapman, and Shakespeare. The year 1604 saw two more books of Bacon brought forth, each by a different bookseller. First, the 'Certain Considerations touching the better pacification and edification of the Church of England,' bore the *imprimatur* of Henrie Tomes —surely an appropriate surname for a bookseller! —and secondly, 'Sir Francis Bacon: his Apologie,' was entrusted to Matthew Lownes, whose shop was situated in that happy hunting-ground of booksellers, St. Paul's Churchyard. The first edition of the former book is described as excessively rare; and of Henry Tomes nothing more is known than that his shop was 'over against Graies Inne Gate, in Holburne,' and that he published some books between 1604 and 1607, the most interesting and curious of which is perhaps 'The Commendation of Cocks and Cockfighting, wherein is shewn that cock-fighting was before the coming of Christ' (black letter, 1607). Matthew Lownes sold many books, often in conjunction with Isaac Jaggard, from 1596 to 1625; he was the son of Hugh Lownes of Rode, in Astbury, Cheshire, and was born about 1568. He died probably in 1625, in which year his widow gave 10*l.* to the Stationers' Company as a remembrance of the departed Matthew.

The 'Advancement of Learning,' or as it was first called, 'The Twoo Bookes of Francis Bacon, of the proficiencie and advancement of Learning, divine and humane' (1605) was also printed for Tomes. The first part consists of 45 leaves, and the second of 118; as was then sometimes the custom, each leaf had only one number, instead of two, as at the present time. An edition of this book was printed in 1629 for W. Washington, and another in 1633 for T. Huggins, of Oxford, neither of whom was particularly noted as a bookseller.

'De Sapientia Veterum,' better known as the 'Wisdom of the Ancients' (1609), next calls for notice, and this very carefully and beautifully printed little duodecimo was produced by Robert Barker, who enjoyed the honour of being his Majesty's printer, was granted, on July 19, 1603, a special licence for printing all statutes, and who, moreover, was one of a large family of printers. A translation of 'De Sapientia Veterum,' was printed in 1619 for

John Bill, who, from 1604 to 1630, had something more or less to do with a great number of books, and whose assigns continued in business until 1642. In addition to this, John Bill was the 'sponsor' of Bacon's greatest work, viz., the 'Instauratio Magna,' which appeared, in folio, during 1620. This book embodied an attempt to build up a new philosophy, and, as the 'Novum Organum' is but one part of a stupendous whole, it is therefore only a fragment, but it is the most carefully written of all Bacon's philosophical works. In 1622, the 'Historia Ventorum' —the first published part of the 'Historia Naturalis,' which was to be the third division of the 'Instauratio' —was printed for Matthew Lownes and William Barret; and in the following year the 'Historia Vitæ et Mortis' was printed for Lownes solely, to both of whom reference has already been made. The 'History of the Reign of Henry VII.' was another of Bacon's works that came out in 1622, in folio, and this, like the 'Historia Ventorum,' was printed for Lownes and William Barret.

Bacon's 'Translation of certaine Psalmes into English Verse,' a quarto of 22 pages, or 11 leaves, dedicated to Herbert of 'The Temple' fame, appeared during the year 1625, under the auspices of Hanna Barret and Richard Whittaker, as did also, in the same year, the 'Apophthegmes, new and old.'

William Lee, of the Turk's Head, Fleet Street, appears to have obtained the right of publishing 'Sylva Sylvarum' in perpetuity, for not only does the first edition (1627) bear his name, but the fifth of 1639, and the seventh of 1658. In 1629 appeared the 'Advertisement Touching an Holy Warre,' which, although written seven years previously, came forth with the name of Humphrey Robinson; and the next year the 'Assigns of John More, Esq.,' published 'The Elements of Common Law.' The history, from our standpoint, of Bacon's posthumous publications is naturally unimportant when compared with that of the books which appeared during his lifetime.

CHAPTER IV.

BOOKSELLING IN THE SEVENTEENTH CENTURY.

THE history of mankind is said to be made up of continuous generations: each possessing, where it is really alive, its separate characteristics. The history of bookselling, strictly speaking, has also such a sequence, but the claim to homogeneity can only be admitted when the subject is viewed as a whole. From the earliest times, booksellers sprang up with mushroom uncertainty and irregularity, and, again like fungoid growth, they passed into nothingness. In many instances their very names are buried in the depths of obscurity, and no amount of delving amid the strata of literary rubbish will bring them to the surface. In other cases, again, their names and the parts they played stand out clear and distinct in the records, not merely of literary by-paths, but of the broader and greater literature whose importance is national in character and universal in scope. Here and there we shall find instances of a son—and occasionally of a grandson—carrying on the business without break, but as a general rule the connections formed by one man either died with him or were transferred to a stranger. Still, the primary chain, whose links commenced with Caxton, is unbroken, for the great stream of books, in spite of foreign complications and internal dissensions, knows of no stoppage.

Leaving the first dozen years or so out of the question, the Restoration must be regarded as a radiating point of literary enterprise. The contributions of the later dramatists, such as Massinger and Ford, were followed up by Milton's, and later on by Dryden's. These two men practically span the cycle of the seventeenth century, for Milton was born in 1608, and the prolific pen of Dryden ceased in 1701. They are the two most distinct portraits in the whole gallery of the period, and beside them all others fade into insignificance.

The accession of James I. marks the commencement of a new and very much inferior era in English literature, which is in striking contrast to that which immediately preceded it. The state of bookselling in the seventeenth century is necessarily analogous to its foster-parent, literature. It made but very little advancement, and contributed not one iota to the amelioration of authorship by profession, which, if anything, retrograded. The howl of the author may be reckoned in an inverse ratio to the comfort and opulence of the tradesman.

We get a little insight into the proceedings of certain booksellers from George Wither's 'The Schollers Purgatory discovered in the Stationers Commonwealth. Imprinted for the honest Stationers' (1625). It seems that the stationers opposed the publication of the 'Hymns and Songs of the Church' (which was issued for the 'Assignes of G. Wither' in 1623), in spite of the interesting fact that publication was commanded by the king. Wither likens some of the booksellers to the silent Smith of Ephesus, and in commenting on the 'large expense in this work,' he observes 'the bookseller hath not only made the printer, the binder, and the claspmaker a slave to him; but hath brought authors, yea, the whole commonwealth and all the liberal sciences into bondage.' If there is any truth at all in his charges, the Stationers' Company was a conglomeration of corruption, but the animadversions of an avowed satirist cannot always be accepted as gospel truth. From his shewing, however, the Company could settle upon any of its members a perpetual interest in books registered by them, even if the first copies were purloined from the author and printed without his leave. 'They annex additions to old books, and increase the price,' though the 'matter be altogether impertinent.' 'Good God,' exclaims the disgusted and somewhat profane author, 'how many dung-botes full of fruitless volumes doe they yearely foist upon his Majesty's subjects, by lying Titles, insinuations and disparaging of more profitable books! How many hundred reames of foolish prophane and senseless ballads do they quarterly disperse abroad? And how many 1000*l.*'s do they yearly pick out of the purses of ignorant people, who refer the choice of their books to the discretions and honesties of these men!' Wither, like so many other authors, rarely employed one publisher twice. F. Bnrton issued the first two editions of 'Abuses Stript and

Whipt,' 1613 and 1614, whilst T. Snodham, Geo. Norton, N. Okes and J. Budge, were publishers at one time or another for Wither.

John Lilburne, who was by trade a bookbinder, played the part of hero with quite a creditable dignity. He was found guilty of publishing numerous seditious books, notably one of Prynne's. Not content with having him whipped at a cart's tail from the Fleet Prison to Westminster, the authorities placed him in the pillory for two hours, and from this undignified position he was thrown into the Fleet Prison, where he was kept until he conformed to the rules of the court. Further, he had to pay 500*l.* to the king, and give security for his behaviour. But 'Freeborn John,' as his friends nicknamed him, was not to be put down, for he not only underwent the sentence 'with undismayed obstinacy,' but uttered many speeches against the bishops, circulated innumerable pamphlets, from the pillory, and, last of all, when the Star Chamber ordered him to be gagged, he defied them. Indeed, Judge Jenkins is reported to have declared, 'if there was none living but he, John would be against Lilburne, and Lilburne against John.' He died August 29, 1657. Prynne was not much more fortunate than Lilburne, for a contemporary writer alludes to Prynne being in the pillory at Cheapside, and that while he stood there 'they burnt his huge volume under his nose, which had almost suffocated him.' Michael Spark, in and about the year 1644, sold most of Prynne's books at 'the Blue Bible in Green Arbour.' Spark was fined 500*l.*, and for ever prevented from selling books

G

through his connection with Prynne's 'Histrio-mastix,'—a stupendous quarto of over 1000 pages.

The industrious operations of Mr. Nathaniel Butter, 'the great newspaper-monger' (to whom reference has already been made), and others of the trade who scrupled not at utilizing another man's idea, gave no inconsiderable impetus to the book-selling trade. Their trashy, stale, and almost invariably inaccurate news served a certain purpose, even if that purpose were antagonistic to enlightenment. It fostered and encouraged a taste for a higher class of literature, and so created, or rather extended, the desire for pamphlets and treatises on the burning topics of the day. The newspaper press, such as it was, was foully inferior. In reflecting upon the anomalies of the 'newspaper' news, Ben Jonson, in 'The Staple of News' (1625), makes an interesting reference to stationers.

'*P. jun.* See divers men's opinions! unto some
The very *printing* of them makes them News ;
That ha' not the heart to believe anything,
But what they see in *print*.
   Fitt. I, that's an error
Has abus'd many; but we shall reform it,
As many things beside (we have a hope)
Are crept among the popular abuses.
   Cymb. Nor shall the stationer cheat upon the time,
By buttering over again—
   Fitt. Once in seven years,
As the age doats—
   Cymb. And grows forgetful o' them—
His antiquated pamphlets, with new dates,
But all shall come from the mint.
   Fitt. Fresh and new-stamp'd—

Cymb. With the office-seal, staple commodity.
Fitt. And if a man will assure his News, he may ;
Twopence a sheet he shall be warranted,
And wave a policy for't.
 *   *   *   *
P. jun. What are your present clerk's habilities ?
How is he qualified ?
Cymb. A decay'd stationer
He was, but knows News well; can sort and rank 'em.
Fitt. And for a need can *make* 'em.
Cymb. True Paul's bred,
I' the churchyard.'

Much commotion was caused in England during 1629 by the want of large folio Bibles. To meet this the Cambridge printers printed an edition which they sold at ten shillings in quires. The king's printers at once set six printing-houses at work, and printed the folio Bible in the same manner, and sold it with 500 quarto Roman Bibles and 500 quarto English at five shillings each, so as to overthrow the Cambridge printers, and keep it entirely in their own hands. This, with a great quantity of other valuable information respecting the state of bookselling during the earlier half of the seventeenth century, we learn from a very remarkable and noteworthy pamphlet, 'Scintilla; or, A light broken into dark Warehouses of some Printers, sleeping Stationers, and combining Booksellers' (1641). It contains certain observations upon the monopolists of seven several patents and two charters. Their proceedings are declared to be 'anatomised and laid open in a breviat, in which is only a touch of their forestalling and ingrossing of books in patents and raising to excessive prices.' The imprint is not the least curious fact in connection with this book, which declares itself to be printed 'not for profit, but for the common weles good: and no where to be sold, but somewhere to be given.' The 'epistle to the reader' is emphatic and brief. 'Courteous Reader (or otherwise), if thou lookest for the reason of writing this book, here it is, and so Anonimous leaves thee. Non Nobis Solum, nati summ, sed partim patriæ.' The writer complains that the Church Bibles, which in former times were sold (in quires) for thirty or even twenty-five shillings, had been raised to forty, and that, from the impression of 3000, the booksellers netted an extra profit of 1500*l*. 'Those of a thinner sort have been sold at 1*l*. in quires; Partners have bought them cheaper buying a quantity, and those partners sold them severally at seventeen and six, not stocking or combining as they do now.' The Cambridge large folio, of the best paper, sold at 1*l*. 10*s*., was raised to 2*l*.; the medium folio from 1*l*. 2*s*. 6*d*., or even less, was surcharged with an extra 7*s*. 6*d*.; whilst the thin paper edition, usually sold at 16*s*., was raised to 1*l*. The London quarto Bible, in Roman type, with notes, had formerly been sold for 7*s*., 'but now with *no* notes 10*s*.' 'There hath been at least 12,000 of these Bibles with notes printed in Holland and sold very reasonably; and many brought from thence hither, and they have been seized by the King's printers, and the parties that imported them not only lost them, but were put in purgatory, and then glad to lose their Bibles and all cost to get off; and then the monopolists sold them again, and so kept all others in awe.' The London octavo edition was raised from

3*s*. 4*d*. (in quires) to 4*s*., whereas the cheaper issue had nine more sheets than the more expensive one. Of this edition 'there have been 10,000 printed in a year.' The duodecimo Holland Bible, sold at 2*s*. in quires, was better than the London one of 1639, sold at double the price.

But the monopolists did not stop at enhancing the prices of Bibles. They advanced Rclton's 'Statues' from 1*l*. 10*s*. to 1*l*. 18*s*. 6*d*. The Oxford and Cambridge 'Grammars' were raised from 5*d*. to 8*d*.,—the yearly impression being 20,000. Camden's 'Greek Accedence' 'by chance a year ago broke loose from the stake of the monopolist, and was sold at 6*s*. in the pound cheaper than they sell them, but they have by a combination tied him to the stake again.' The monopolists prevented the printing of the Concordance, and seized the imported copies, which, however, they sold again, and pocketed the profit. 'But a touch of this; for it is too tart, and I verily believe picks the subjects pockets, that eats brown bread to fill the sleeping stationers belly with venison and sacke, and robs the commonwealth.' The writer urged that the Statute of 25 Henry VIII., c. 15, concerning prices be put into force, and that there be at least 20 or 24 Assistants to the Company, and that none be twice Master. As things were then, some six or eight of the eldest members of the Company combined and carried everything their own way, aiming solely at furthering their own interests. A sort of sequel to this valuable pamphlet was published, but the earlier is that of most particular interest.

On September 30, 1647, it was enacted that no person

should make, print, or sell, publish or utter, or cause to be made, &c., any book, pamphlet, treatise, ballad, libel, or sheet of news whatever unless licensed. For infringement, the printer would be fined 20s., or in default as many days, and the bookseller just half that amount. Early in the following year a Scottish Act was passed which dared printers, under the penalty of death, to print unlicensed books. A new era, which had been formulating since 1640, began, and the War of Pamphlets had established itself in dead earnest. The battle raged loud and fierce, and nearly every one who could write at all joined in the fray. 'Diurnals' and 'Mercuries' came into existence, first occasionally, then weekly, and then bi- and tri-weekly. The law of which an abstract has just been given called into existence a new and formidable, if scurrilous and unscrupulous, army of scribblers, whose very *raison-d'être* was to controvert that which every one knew to be an infamous and tyrannical law. The following example is a scornful protest :—'The Kentish Fayre, or the Parliament sold to their best worth,' which was ostensibly 'printed at Rochester, and are to be sold to all those that dare to buy them.' The vital questions of the day engrossed the sole attention of the pamphleteers, and a great deal of that of the bookseller, who knew the class of literature most likely to go down, and who had very many means of getting rid of his stock. Then, as now, an author tried the experiment of publishing his own books, and the result was not a satisfactory one. The trouble, however, appears to have been not so much a matter of getting purchases as one of obtaining the money for those sold. No better example could be instanced than John Taylor's 'The Carrier's Cosmography' (1637), the full title of which is a matter of 146 words. Three reasons are given for publishing this book, the first of which is the benefit which it would confer upon the general public, the second to express gratitude to those who paid for his previous books, and the third because of those who could pay him, but would not: 'I am well pleased,' Taylor candidly admits, 'to leave them to the hangman's tuition, as being past any other man's mending, for I would have them to know, that I am sensible of the too much loss that I do suffer by their pride and cousenage; their not being so many and my charge so great, which I paid for paper and printing of those books, that the base dealing of those sharks is insupportable.' The famous N. Butter issued several of Taylor's books, and H. Gosson issued a few also.

The year 1648 is a landmark both in political and in literary history, for on December 23 of that year (according to tradition) Richard Royston, the royal bookseller, of the Angel, Ivy Lane, received the manuscript of 'Eikon Basilike; the Pourtraioture of his Sacred Majesty in his Solitude and Sufferings,' which was published before the 30th of the following month, when his Majesty was beheaded. Nearly 50 editions appeared by the end of 1649. Another book may be here mentioned, not only because it appeared a few years afterwards, but because of a similarly unbounded popularity and the impenetrable uncertainty surrounding its authorship. We refer to 'The Practice of Christian Graces, or the Whole Duty of Man,' which was printed by 'T. Garthwait at the little North door of S. Paul's, 1658.' In 1659 Garthwait issued another edition with a new engraved title, inscribed 'The Whole Duty of Man.'

The publication of London's Catalogue forms an important incident in the annals of bookselling. It is entitled 'A Catalogue of the most vendible Books in England, orderly and alphabetically digested' (1658). There are nearly 30 sections. It is dedicated 'to the gentry, ministers of the Gospel, and others of a peculiar choice, to the wise, learned and studious in the northern counties of Northumberland, bishopprick of Durham, Westmoreland and Cumberland.' There is a very interesting introduction relative to the use of books; and the 'Epistle to the Reader' concludes thus :—'And though the wise man saies, that of writing books there is no end (which I think is meant of such as are writ to no end), yet I hope this reducement of many into one, may prove of some good advantage, and to some good end, and that without prejudice to Solomon's text.' The entries are full, as may be seen from this example:— 'The Life of Tamerlane the Great, his Warres against the great Duke of Moso, King of China, Bajazet the great Turk, the Sultan of Ægypt, the King of Persia, &c., wherein are rare examples of Heathenish piety, mercy, justice, humility, temperance, &c. 8vo.' As a slight and to some extent approximate indication of the annual publications, we may point out that in London's Supplement, dating from August 1, 1657, to June 1, 1658, the number of books on divinity was 63, on history 26, on law 9, on physic and chirurgery 8, and on poetry 4.

Few books of the seventeenth century possess so much interest as the first edition of Walton's 'Complete Angler' (1653). An advertisement of the book runs as follows:—'There is published a Booke of Eighteen-pence, called the Compleat Angler, or the Contemplative Man's Recreation. Being a Discourse of Fish and Fishing, Not unworthy the perusal. Sold by Richard Marriot, in St. Dunstan's Churchyard, Flete-Street.' This very rare book is now valued at £52! Richard Marriot published several editions of this book up to and inclusive of the year 1671, and also the first collected edition of the 'Lives' (1670). The second part of the 'Complete Angler' was printed for R. Marriot and H. Brome, 1676. John Marriot, whose shop was in St. Dunstan's Churchyard, Fleet Street, sold various editions of Donne's poems, notably 'Poems by J. D., with Elegies on the Author's Death,' the first edition, dated 1633, that of 1635, and also the 'Poems,' 'to which is added divers copies under his own hand never before in print,' of 1650. All these were anonymous. Richard Marriot published Donne's 'Letters to Several Persons of Honour' (1651). The famous 'Temple' of George Herbert was printed and published at Cambridge.

The practice of one author having many publishers continued far into the seventeenth century, for on the title-pages of Thomas Heywood we find, to quote a few examples, H. Lownes, of the Star, Bread Street Hill, and close to Milton's father's house ('Edward IV.,' 1613); N. Butter ('Rape of Lucrece,' 1630, and 'If You Know Not Me,' 1639); R. Raworth, of Old Fish Street, near 'Saint Mary Maudlin's Church' ('The English Traveller,' 1633), and Adam Islip ('Hierarchie of the Blessed Angells,' 1635). Raworth and Islip were printers rather than booksellers; but N. Okes, and subsequently J. Okes, printed by far the greater number of Heywood's books. John Ford was no exception to the rule, for H. Seile, of the 'Tiger's Head,' Fleet Street, over against St. Dunstan's Church, issued 'The Lover's Melancholy' in 1629, and 'Fancies Chast and Noble' eight years afterwards; H. Shephard, of the Bible, Chancery Lane, 'The Ladies Triall,' 1639; Hugh Beeston, whose shop was near the Castle, Cornhill, 'Love's Sacrifice,' 1633; Richard Collins, of the Three Kings, St. Paul's Churchyard, ''Tis Pity,' &c., 1633; whilst 'J. B.' published that tragedy of tragedies, 'The Broken Heart,' 1633. T. Randolph's 'Hey for Honesty' (1650) may be noted here as furnishing another example of a bookseller writing a dedication. 'Reader, this is a pleasant comedy, though some may judge it satirical, 'tis the more like Aristophanes, the father; besides, if it be biting, 'tis a biting age we live; then biting for biting.' No doubt the readers were duly thankful for this rather superfluous information; but perhaps it was more to the point when the stationer declared 'Tom Randal, the adopted son of Ben Jonson, being the translator hereof, followed his father's steps. They both of them loved sack and harmless mirth, and here they shew it ; and I, that know myself, am not averse from it neither. This I thought good to acquaint thee with. Farewell. Thine, F. J.'   Some of Randolph's books were printed out of London, such as ' Poems, with the Muses Looking Glass' (1638), which was printed at the University Press of Oxford, and 'The Jealous Lovers'' (1634), which came from the kindred institution at Cambridge. 'Aristippus' (1630) was printed for John Marriot.

We have already made an incidental reference to the War of Pamphlets which commenced in 1640 ; and perhaps, so far as we are concerned, the most remarkable fact in connection with that episode is the untiring industry with which George Thomason, a bookseller, formed a collection of these 'books of an hour.' The period embraced is one of twenty years, and the aggregate result 'about 30,000 pieces, uniformly bound in 2000 volumes and accompanied by twenty folio volumes of catalogue.'   The collection was amassed with the utmost secrecy, and with the aid of a few faithful servants. At first, as the volumes were completed they were buried in boxes. As the number increased, this method became no longer feasible. After constant removals, giving the army of either party as wide a berth as possible, Thomason at last contrived a very ingenious dodge : he placed the volumes in his warehouse, in the form of tables round the room, covered with canvas. On one occasion, Thomason was dragged from his bed and imprisoned for seven weeks, but the one object and anxiety of his life remained undiscovered. When the Royalist cause was thoroughly broken up at the execution of Charles, a fictitious sale was made to the University of Oxford, where the collection would be in much less jeopardy than whilst it remained in the possession of a private individual. Thomason died in 1666, his collection still being at Oxford, in trust, to be sold for the benefit of his children. But a sale was not really effected until over a century afterwards, and not until several attempts had been made to dispose of the incubus. In 1762 the nation purchased of the Mearne family this very remarkable collection, which is now in the British Museum under the general title of the King's Pamphlets.

We can hardly realize the times when there were no literary papers for the twofold object of indicating the best books and of advertising all kinds of literary merchandise. Under such conditions the public had to find out for itself the best literary food, or to trust to the recommendation of friends. But he would not be a successful bookseller who had fewer than half-a-score methods of getting rid of his ware. An old advertising dodge was to place hand-bills of the titles and general scope of new publications close to the play-bills posted on the outside of the theatres, and in such positions publicity followed as a matter of course. Robert Heath, in his ' Epigrams ' (1650), refers to this custom in the address

> ' To my Bookseller.
> ' I have common made my book; 'tis very true;
> But I'd not have thee prostitute it too;
> Nor show it barefaced on the open stall
> To tempt the buyer; nor poast it on each wall
> And corner poast, close underneath the Play

That must be acted at *Black-Friers* to-day ;
Nor see some Herring-cryer for a groat
'To voice it up and down with tearing throat ;
Nor bid thy 'prentice read it and admire,
That all i' the shop may what he reads inquire ;
No : profer'd wares do smel : I'd have thee know
Pride scorns to beg : modestie fears to wooe.'

But selling books was not the only source of revenue to the bookseller. The circle of bookbuyers has always been much smaller than that of readers, and those who from force or choice came in the latter category simply paid a small subscription which entitled them to read at the booksellers' shops the most recent publication. If the perusal were not completed in one day, the reader noted the page at which he left off, and returned again and again until the book was finished. This curious practice, which was much in vogue during the seventeenth and eighteenth centuries, had its origin in ancient Rome. We are told that the celebrated French publisher, M. Ladvocat, always kept five or six copies of 'his Poets' upon the counter, and several chairs ready, so that any respectable person could come in and read without being at all obliged to buy. Another method, once very popular, of disposing of books was in the form of lotteries, especially during the middle of the seventeenth century. Ogilby, the author of 'Itinerarum Angliæ, or Book of Roads,' was a famous promoter of book-lotteries, as witness several advertisements in the *Gazette* during May 1668 ; he appears to have utilized Vere Street Theatre, where 'all persons concerned' were invited to 'repair on Monday, May 18, and see the volumes, and put in their money.' The 'first and greatest prize' included an Imperial Bible (valued at

25*l*.), illustrated editions of Virgil, Homer, and Æsop's Fables, besides other books, the aggregate value of the prize being 51*l*. The prizes gradually decreased in value down to the two last—Nos. 35 and 36—each of which was valued at 4*l*. The tickets were 5*s*. each. Raffles for books were very common in the earlier years of the eighteenth century; and Swift in his 'Journal to Stella,' under date April 27, 1711, speaks of having lost 4*l*. 7*s*. at play with a bookseller, and got but half-a-dozen books.

To return, however, to the more concrete phases of bookselling. The two booksellers who will for all time be associated with Milton are Humphry Moseley and Samuel Simmons. In the latter part of 1645, when Milton was nearly forty years of age, and when the Civil War was at its height, Moseley, who was then one of the leading booksellers and publishers of dramatic and poetical works in London, issued 'Poems, both English and Latin.' · This is noticeable from the fact that it is the first book bearing Milton's name, and also on account of its being the first collective edition of poems by him. It is an octavo of over 200 pages, and was 'sold at the Sign of the Princes Arms, in Paules Churchyard.' Moseley's preface, 'The Stationer to the Reader,' is of much interest, and if ever there was a piece of bibliopolic sophistry written, it is this. 'It is not,' observes the philanthropic Moseley, 'any private respect of gain, Gentle Reader (for the slightest Pamphlet is now-a-days more vendible than the works of learnedest men), but it is the love I have to our own language that hath made me diligent to collect and set forth such pieces, both in Prose and Verse, as may renew the wonted honour and esteem of our English tongue.' He speaks of 'these ever-green and not to be blasted laurels,' and thinks that 'I shall deserve of the age by bringing into the light as true a birth as the muses have brought forth since our famous SPENSER wrote.' The circumstances which attended the publication of 'Paradise Lost' are pretty well known, and so we need scarcely enter into the subject with any great degree of minuteness. Samuel Simmons, whose shop was next door to the Golden Lion in Aldersgate Street, purchased 'Paradise Lost' from Milton at the rate of 5*l.* per impression. Milton himself only received two payments, and in 1680, six years after the poet's death, Simmons acquired the copyright in perpetuity for 8*l.* from Milton's widow. In writing harrowing accounts of the hardships and under-payments of authors, fifth-rate journalists would do well to remember that these sums are represented by about four times the amount in our present currency. So that it is, in effect, inaccurate to state that 'Paradise Lost' was sold for 18*l.* Each of the three first impressions, it may be pointed out, was reckoned at 1300 copies, although Simmons had the option of going as high as 1500 in the actual printing. There are very many subjective points in connection with this famous book to which we must allude. 'Why,' asks Professor Masson, 'though Simmons had acquired the copyright in April 1667, and had entered the copyright as his in the Stationers' Books in August 1667, is his name kept out of sight in all the title-pages prior to that of 1668 . . . which is the first with preliminary matter—the preceding title-pages shewing no printer's name, but only the names of the three booksellers at whose shop copies might be had?' Mr. Masson suggests that Simmons was timid about publishing a book written by one 'whose attacks on the Church and defences of the execution of Charles I. were still fresh in the memory of all, and some of whose pamphlets had been publicly burnt by the hangman after the Restoration.' The first edition of 'Paradise Lost' is a very creditably printed work in small quarto, —of 342 pages where the Argument and other preliminary matter is absent, or 356 pages where this extraneous matter is present. The selling price of the volume was three shillings, which is now represented by at least half-a-guinea. One of the later impressions of 1668 contains a very interesting three-line advertisement: 'The Printer to the Reader. Courteous Reader, There was no Argument as first intended to the Book, but for the satisfaction of many that have desired it, is procured. *S. Simmons.*' When 'Paradise Regained' was finished, 'Paradise Lost' had been in circulation for four or five years, and a new edition was, for some cause or other, delayed by Simmons. This appears to have induced Milton to trust his sequel into other hands, and accordingly John Starkey, of the Mitre, Fleet Street, near Temple Bar, was entrusted with the new work. From the fact that the imprint declared it to be 'printed by J. M. for John Starkey,' &c. (1671), Professor Masson assumes that the book was printed on Milton's own account but this does not by any means follow. It was a very general rule for the printers to indicate their names by initials only on title-pages, and the two 'J. M.'s

Bookselling in the Seventeenth Century. 97

may therefore be merely a coincidence. Had it been 'printed *for* J. M.,' there would be more reason for concluding that Milton bore the whole cost of the mechanical part. With it was first issued 'Samson Agonistes.' A second edition did not appear until 1680, and this is in many respects inferior to the earlier, although issued by the same publisher. Eight years afterwards a third edition came out under the auspices of a new publisher—Randal Taylor. It will perhaps not be out of place to correct two very commonly accepted errors, perpetrated by De Quincey in his review of Schlosser's 'Literary History of the Eighteenth Century,' in reference to 'Paradise Lost.' He observes:—' Then came a fellow, whose name was either not on his title-page, or I have forgotten it [who put the 'Paradise Lost' in rhyme]. Him succeeded a droller fellow than any of the rest. A French bookseller had caused a prose French translation to be made of the 'Paradise Lost,' without particularly noticing its English origin, or at least not in the titlepage. Our friend, getting hold of this as an original French romance, translated it back into English prose as a satisfactory novel for the season.' The French version, 'The State of Innocence: and Fall of Man. Described in Milton's Paradise Lost. Render'd into Prose. With Historical, Philosophical and Explanatory Notes. From the French of the Learned Raymond De St. Maur. By a Gentleman of Oxford. London: Printed for T. Osborne, in Gray's-Inn, and J. Hilyard, at York. MDCC.XLV.,' was a paraphrase, evidently intended to assist French students of the original poem; and the translator gives St. Maur's preface, which precludes the supposition that he took it for 'an original French romance.'

The two Humphreys—Moseley and Robinson—published several things conjointly, and the following 'epigram' to these worthies from Sir Aston Cokain's 'Poems' (1658) will be read with interest:—

> 'In the large Book of Plays you late did print
> In Beaumont and in Fletcher's name, why in't
> Did you not justice? Give to each his due?
> For Beaumont of these many writ in few:
> And Massinger in other few: the main
> Being sole issues of sweet Fletcher's brain.
> But how came I, you ask, so much to know?
> Fletcher's chief bosom-friend inform'd me so,
> And print their old ones in one vol. too:
> For Beaumont's works and Fletcher should come forth
> With all the right belonging to their worth.'

In 1661, 'The Beggars' Bush' of Beaumont and Fletcher was issued by Humphrey Robinson and Anne Moseley at their respective shops, and ten years later 'young Mr. Robinson gave 10*l*. to the Company of Stationers to be bestowed upon a piece of plate in memory of his father.' In addition to his self-imposed task of editing Milton, Moseley, in 1650, published Robert Heath's 'Clarastella,' together with poems occasional, elegies, epigrams, satires, &c. The 'Stationer' in his address to 'the Reader' coolly apologizes for his presumption in publishing the book without the author's knowledge and consent, and urges as a plea of justification, 'the gallantness and ingenuity' of the author, whom he describes as a gentleman 'so eminent in everything, that I could not imagine but that the meanest of his recreation (for such is this) might carry much in it worthy of public view, besides, the approbation of some friends hath heightened my desire of publishing it; who, upon their revising it, do assure me it is a sweet piece of excellent fancie and worthy to be called the author's own issue.' Heath was abroad when this volume appeared. Moseley issued, *inter alia*, Sir Walter Raleigh's 'Apologie' (1650), which was, it seems, first published in the ill-fated author's 'Judicious and Select Essayes,' and this likewise was first published by Moseley, and contained a dedicatory epistle to Sir Walter's son, Carew, from the pen of the energetic bookseller.

The Great Fire of London, which commenced on September 2, 1666, destroyed buildings covering between four and five hundred acres, and extended from the Tower to the Temple Church, involving amongst the general wreckage the destruction of books and literary property to the value of about 150,000*l.*, according to Pepys' calculation, or nearly 200,000*l.* to Evelyn. Roughly speaking at our present valuation, the amount would be very close upon 1,000,000*l.* sterling. Most of the booksellers, whose stock fed the flames, were, as Pepys puts it, 'utterly undone,' and 'my poor Kirton,' from being a substantial tradesman with about 8000*l.* to fall back on, was made 2000*l.* or 3000*l.* worse than nothing. Writing on September 27 to Sir Samuel Tuke from 'Sayes Court,' Evelyn observes that, soon after the fire had subsided, the other trades went on as merrily as before, 'only the poor booksellers have been indeed ill-treated by Vulcan; so many noble impressions consumed, by their trusting them to ye churches,'—and he further speaks of this loss as 'an extraordinary detriment to the whole republic of learning.' Two months after the letter from which we have just quoted, Evelyn writes to the Lord High Chancellor, Sir Edward Hyde,—afterwards Lord Clarendon,—in this strain:—'I did the other day in Westminster Hall give my Lord Cornbury, your lordship's son, my thoughts briefly concerning a most needful reformation for the transmitting a clearer stream for the future from the press, by directing to immaculate copies of such books as being vended in great proportions do for want of good editions amongst us export extraordinary sums of money, to our no lesse detriment than shame: And I am so well satisfied of the honour which a redress in this kind will procure even to posterity (however small the present instance may appear to some in a superficial view) that I think myself obliged to wish that your Lordship may not conceive it unworthy of your patronage. The affair is this: Since the late deplorable conflagration, in which the Stationers have been exceedingly ruined, there is like to be an extraordinary penury and scarcity of classic authors, &c., used in grammar schools, so as of necessity they must suddenly be reprinted. My Ld. may please to understand, that our booksellers follow their own judgement in printing the ancient authors according to such text as they found extant when first they entered their copy.' Evelyn names certain authors who have been in this way reprinted in a corrupt form, and vouchsafes this explanation :—'The cause of this is, principally the Stationer driving as hard and cruel a bargain with the Printer as he can : and the Printer taking up any smatterer in the tongues, to be the less loser ; an exactness in this no ways importing the stipulation : by which means errors repeat and multiply in every edition, and that most notoriously in some most necessary school-books of value, which they obtrude upon the buyer, unless men will be at reasonable rates for foreign editions.' To prevent all this abuse, Evelyn suggested that, first, it should be decided which particular text be in future followed ; secondly, that a Censor be appointed ; and thirdly, that the expense of the two be borne by the Company.

At last the grievance became so serious, that on May 12, 1680, a Proclamation was issued for suppressing the printing and publishing of unlicensed news-books and pamphlets, which were characteristic for inaccuracy and wilful perversion of news. All persons whatsoever were thereby prohibited from printing or publishing any news-letters or pamphlets without his Majesty's authority. James II. had not succeeded to the throne more than three months when an order, dated May 21, 1685, was issued to the Stationers' Company by the Censor of the press, Sir Roger L'Estrange. This document referred to the intolerable freedom of the press, and authorized regulations by which law-books were to be licensed by the Lord Chancellor, the Lord Keeper, the Lord Chief Justice, or by some one appointed by them ; historical books by the Secretary of State, or deputy ; books of Heralds by the Earl Marshal ; divinity, physics, philosophy, arts and sciences, either by the Archbishop of Canterbury or Bishop of London. The Chancellors or Vice-Chancellors to have sole jurisdiction in this matter in their respective Universities. The Stationers' Company had strict orders to see that this law was enforced, and that no unlicensed book be entered or published at their Hall. Clarendon, writing from Dublin Castle to the Earl of Rochester, March 14, 1685-6, speaks of the trashy news-letters circulating throughout the kingdom, and that he has ordered the prohibition of all such until properly licensed.

We have already described the first two important book-catalogues, and the short reference to the Great Fire brings us to a third of these lists. It was entitled 'A General Catalogue of Books, printed in England since the dreadful fire, 1666, to the end of Trinity term, 1676;' and its publisher was Robert Clavel, who had, in 1658 and 1659, issued from the Stag's Head, near St. Gregory's Church, in St. Paul's Churchyard, William Chamberlayne's 'Love's Victory' and 'Pharomida.' The 'Catalogue,' which was continued every term till 1700, is a thin folio, and includes an abstract of the bills of mortality. The books are classified under their respective headings of divinity, history, physic and surgery, miscellanies, chemistry, poetry, and so forth, and the publisher's name of each book is given. From this valuable publication we learn that the number of books printed in England, from 1666 to 1680, was 3550: of which 947 were divinity, 420 law, and 135 physic, so that two-fifths of the whole were professional books, 397 were school-books, and 253 were on subjects of geography and navigation, including maps. On the average of the fourteen years, the total number of works produced annually was 253; but deducting reprints, pamphlets, single sermons, and maps, the average would be much under one hundred. This (points out one writer) will show an increase upon a former period, namely, from 1471 and 1660, when the average number of distinct works published each year in this country was seventy-five. But as a matter of fact very many more than are here indicated were published, but as the means even in Clavel's time of ascertaining an approximate estimate of the actual number printed were very slender, so it is now simply impossible to obtain anything nearer than the foregoing figures. Clavel has been very rightly described as 'an eminent bookseller,' and Dunton summarizes his virtues in the following manner:—' Mr. Robert Clavel is a great dealer, and has deservedly gained himself the reputation of a just man. Dr. Barlow, bishop of Lincoln, used to call him *the honest bookseller*.[1] He has been Master of the Company of Stationers [1698 and 1699], and perhaps the greatest unhappiness of his life was his being one of Alderman Cornish's jury. He printed Dr. Comber's works.' It seems, however, with reference to the last statement, that Henry Brome, of the Gun, St. Paul's Churchyard, shared the publication of certain of Dr. Comber's works: at all events the two booksellers are more often than not found sharing the expense of certain publications,

[1] *Ergo*, were all the others the reverse?

and old books bearing their imprint are even now commonly met with. The Brome family was connected with the printing and publishing trades from the early part of the sixteenth century; and in 1591, 'the Widdowe Broome' published one of Lilly's works. Henry Brome may be almost regarded as 'cheery Mr. Cotton's' bookseller, for in addition to publishing the second part of the 'Complete Angler' (1676), he issued Cotton's 'The Planter's Manual' (1675), and his 'Catalogue of some books printed for and sold by H. Brome since the dreadful fire of London, to 1675,' includes Cotton's 'Virgil's Travesty,' which was sold at 1s. 6d.; 'Lucian's Dialogues Burlesques' and 'The Fair One of Tunis,' each sold at 2s. 6d.; and 'Horace, with a song at every Act,' for which Mr. Brome asked the small sum of one shilling. Of a more ambitious nature was 'The Commentaries of M. Blaiz d'Montluck,' &c.,—a folio volume priced at 14s.; and 'The Life of the Great Duke of Espernon' was another of Cotton's books which occurs in a list which brings Brome's publications down to a more recent date by three years (*i.e.* 1568). He likewise 'undertook' books in conjunction with T. Bassett, to whom the great Jacob Tonson was apprenticed, and so, as we have already endeavoured to demonstrate, there is a strong and unmistakable continuity in the annals of bookselling, if not of a primary, then at least of a secondary nature.

Few books have attained so universal and permanent a fame as the first of all allegories, 'The Pilgrim's Progress.' To Nathaniel Ponder, of the Peacock, in the Poultry, near the church, belongs the honour of having acted as sponsor to this immortal book. It appears that Bunyan was released from prison in 1676, and came up to London with the MS. of his great work in 1677. Ponder's was a 'new name on Bunyan's title-pages, but it was destined frequently to reappear during the next ten years.' On December 22, 1677, Ponder 'entered then for his copy by virtue of a licence under the hand of Mr. Turner, and which is subscribed by Mr. Warden Vere, one book or copy intituled The Pilgrim's Progress from this world to that which is to come, delivered in ye Similitude of a Dream by John Bunyan, vj$d$.' Dr. John Brown, the latest and perhaps most exhaustive of Bunyan's biographers, states that the book was licensed February 18, 1678, and 'therefore early in the year was in the hands of that public which so quickly and for so long was to give it hearty welcome.' It was published at 1s. 6d., and printed in small octavo on yellowish-grey paper, and extended to 232 pages in addition to title, author's apology, and conclusion. 'A living artist,' observes Dr. Brown, 'has given us an ideal sketch of Nathaniel Ponder's shop at the time he first sent forth the book. A scholar is coming out from under the sign of the Peacock, and a peasant, whip in one hand and money in the other, going in; while near the shop door are a gay gallant and a fair lady, schoolboys, and grave men, all intently reading that story of the Pilgrim they have just purchased over the counter within. The picture is true to the time then, and true to the time now.' Ponder published eleven editions of 'Paradise Lost,' the twelfth (1689) being printed for Robert Ponder, and the fourteenth was 'printed for W. P., and sold by Nat. Ponder, in London House Yard, near the west end of St. Paul's Churchyard' (1695). On May 10, 1676, Ponder was committed by the Court at Whitehall—the king being present—to the gatehouse, for printing an unlicensed pamphlet, tending to the sedition and defamation of the Christian religion. He was discharged on the 26th; was ordered to pay due fees, and to enter into a bond of 500*l*. From one of Ponder's later lists, we glean the interesting information that both parts of 'Pilgrim's Progress,' and also 'Grace Abounding,' were sold at one shilling each; whilst for three other works, 'A Treatise of the Fear of God,' 'The Life and Death of Mr. Badman,' and 'The Doctrine of Law and Grace Unfolded,' the price of 1*s*. 6*d*. each was asked. But *Bunyan's second* part of 'The Pilgrim's Progress' was not the only one that appeared from the Poultry, inasmuch as Thomas Malthus, of the Sun, issued a 'second part' in 1683 by 'T. S.' Query, was this the 'T. S.' for whom Ponder published 'Divine Breathings' at or about the same time? Bunyan's second part did not appear until 1684, and only reached a new edition two years afterwards. Dunton has the following 'sugary' notice in his crack-brained memoirs:—'*Nathaniel* (alias *Bunyan*) *Ponder*. He has sweetness and enterprise in his air, which plead and anticipate in his favour.' Had Dunton not beslobbered nearly the whole of his fraternity in a like manner, it would have been an interesting question, How much was he paid for this puff?

Butler's booksellers, like those of Bunyan, were comparatively few, in spite of the enormous popularity of his one great book,—'Hudibras.' The first part was printed for Richard Marriot (already noticed), whose shop was under St. Dunstan's Church in Fleet Street, and it appeared in 1663; and about the same time the *Public Intelligence* contained the following warning to the public against a literary piracy:—'There is stolen abroad, a most false and imperfect copy of a poem called 'Hudibras,' without name either of printer or bookseller, as fitting so lame and spurious an impression. The true and perfect edition, printed by the author's original, is sold by Richard Marriot, under St. Dunstan's Church, in Fleet-street; that other nameless is a cheat, and will but abuse the buyer as well as the author, whose poem deserves to have fallen into better hands.' The second part appeared in 1664, under the auspices of John Martyn and James Allestry, at the Bell, St. Paul's Churchyard, and the title-page contains a very curious emblem of the house. Ten years later, the copyright appears to have been partly in the possession of Martyn and partly of Herringman, or at all events they issued editions conjointly. The third and last part was issued by Simon, of the Star, at the west end of St. Paul's Churchyard, in 1678.

Francis Kirkman and Richard Head were two of the few author-booksellers who 'adorned' the latter half of the seventeenth century, and perhaps it would be difficult to instance two greater scamps in the bookselling or any other trade. Kirkman (with Henry Marsh) published Nevill's comedy, 'The Poor Scholar,' in 1662, when he was living at the Prince's Arms, in Chancery Lane. He published 'Lust's Dominions' as a play of Marlowe's, which it was not, and ascribed 'The Countrie Girle' (1647) to Anthony [Tony] Brewer, solely from the initials 'T. B.' which appear on the title-page. In 1652 he translated 'the sixt part' of 'Amadis de Gaule' from the French, and also, nearly twenty years later, the second and third parts of 'Beliaris of Greece' (1671-2). In 1673 he brought out 'The Unlucky Citizen,' and a very curious and wretchedly printed little book called 'The Wits' about 1670. He entered into partnership with Head on two occasions, and was assisted by him in writing and publishing plays, farces, and drolls. The two were well-met, and both appear to have been intimately acquainted with the lowest type of men and women,—a result being seen in the scandalous character of their books. Head was drowned when crossing over to the Isle of Wight in 1678.

With a view, perhaps, of continuing the work of Maunsell, London, and Clavel, the *Mercurius Librarius* was published in 1680, the second number being dated April 22. It seems to have been the first periodical publication that anticipated the *Publishers' Circular* of the present day. 'All booksellers' (so ran the notice) 'that approve of the design of publishing this catalogue weekly, or once in fourteen days at least, are desired to send in to one of the undertakers any book, pamphlet, or sheet they would have in it, so soon as published, that they may be inserted in order as they come out : their books shall be delivered to them back again upon demand. To shew they design the public advantage of the trade, they will expect but 6*d.* for inserting any book; nor but 12*d.* for any other advertisement relating to the trade, unless it be excessive long.' This 'undertaking' had a very short life, and the next of its kind made its appearance on October 7, 1680, under the designation of *Weekly Advertisement of Books.* It was printed by R. Everingham, ' and annexed to the city mercury, from the office of the Royal Exchange, No. 250.' The sixth number, dated November 11th, contains the following caution :—' It is not unknown to booksellers, that there are two papers of this nature weekly published ; which, for general satisfaction, we shall distinguish. That printed by Thomas James is published by Mr. Vile, only for the lucre of 12*d.* per book. This printed by Robert Everingham is published by several booksellers, who do more eye the service of the trade, in making all books as public as may be, than the profit of insertions. All men are, therefore, left to judge who is most likely to prosecute these ends effectually ; whether a person that is no bookseller, nor hath any relation to that trade, or those who have equal ends with all others of the trade, in dispersing the said papers both in city and country. All titles to be inserted in this paper are either to be left with Robert Everingham, a printer, or to be delivered to Mr. Orchard, a porter.' Everingham printed numerous books and pamphlets during the last two decades of the seventeenth century, the most notable example being an edition (1690) of 3000 Bibles and 1000 New Testaments in 8vo, for the use of the Highlands of Scotland, and the Irish people generally. Dunton refers (in 1705) to this printer as being in partnership with one Whitledge, and observes :—' I employed them very much, and looked upon them to be honest and thriving men ; had they confined themselves a little sooner to household love, they might possibly have kept upon their own bottom ; however, so it happened that they loved themselves into journeymen printers again.'

Dryden was the central literary figure of the latter part of the seventeenth century ; and so in a somewhat similar manner may Henry Herringman be regarded in bibliopolic circles. It may therefore be not uninteresting to consider how and when these two men became connected. Dryden's unfortunate elegiac ode to Cromwell,—which was printed for William Wilson, and 'sold at Well-Yard, near Little Bartholomew's Hospital,' 1659,—was the incipient cause of his taking to hack-work. For, by endeavouring to obliterate the memory of these verses, he wrote 'Astræ Redux '—which was issued by Herringman in 1660,—which severed him for ever from the support of Cromwell's Lord Chancellor, Pickering, from whose rooms of state Dryden removed to lodge in the house of Herringman, which was in the New Exchange. From this spot he continued to correspond with several noblemen. Herringman was at this time one of the leading London publishers, and was, in addition to this, a personal friend of Davenant, and most of the wits of the day were not only his customers, but also his visitors. It was probably at this shop that Dryden became introduced to the leading literary men of the period. In 1668 Herringman issued three plays of Dryden, 'Indian Emperor,' 'Secret Love,' and 'Sir Martin Mar-all,' besides the essay on 'Dramatic Poetry'; and in the year following 'The Rival Ladies' and 'The Wild Gallant' came forth from the same house. These were succeeded in 1670 by 'Tyrannick Love' and 'The Tempest.' Pepys has an entry, under date of June 22, 1668, which is worth quoting:—' To the King's playhouse, and saw an act or two of the new play, 'Evening Love,' again, but like it not. Calling this day at Herringman's, he tells me Dryden do himself call it but a fifth-rate play.' This play does not appear to have been printed by Herringman until 1691. In the meantime he had issued, among others, 'Aurenge-Zebe,' 1676, 'All for Love,' 1678. In 1667 Herringman issued 'Annus Mirabilis,' and another edition in 1688, which was 'sold by J. Tonson.' With the flight of James II., and the downfall from the Poet-Laureateship, Dryden appears to have worked almost solely for Jacob Tonson, although for long after this period Herringman still published the plays of Dryden which he had previously issued, and Tonson's name occurs in many instances on these as one of the booksellers. One of Herringman's last publications appears to have been Etherege's 'She Would if She Could' (1693); not long afterwards he retired, and lived 'handsomely and hospitably' at Carshalton, where (according to Professor Morley) he and his wife Alice, after fifty-eight years of wedded life, died within six weeks and two days of each other in 1703,—two years after Dryden's decease.

Richard Bentley, who traded largely in plays, and

whose shop was for a long time at the Post House, in Russel Street, Covent Garden, was another of the few publishers who either employed, or was employed by, Dryden. The connection was short and unhappy. In 1675 Bentley issued 'The Mistaken Husband,' with the statement that it was revised by Dryden, who, however, denied having had anything to do with it. Although, as Mr. Saintsbury points out, Dryden spoke of Bentley with considerable bitterness afterwards, his name occurs frequently among the booksellers mentioned on the title-pages of Dryden's plays, —down, in fact, to 1693. Dryden and Lee's 'Œdipus' appears to have been solely 'undertaken' by him, and of which he issued editions in 1682 and 1692. A writer in *Notes and Queries* states that about 1682 Bentley issued a series of 'Modern Novels'—to which he gave his name—and that he was also the publisher of the first edition of Bishop Gibson's translation of Camden's 'Britannia.'[2] Dryden, in a letter of

[2] Gibson appears to have encountered great difficulties in bringing out his edition of Camden. He was greatly exercised to avoid 'a storm upon the booksellers' heads.' They were apparently a long time in arriving at a decision to undertake this new edition, and a further delay arose on account of paper: a large quantity was anticipated from Genoa, which they expected would 'fitt their business.' Gibson consoled himself with the reflection that 'the work is so generally known, and their reputation in order to any future undertakings does so much depend upon this, that I am confident the honour of the one of 'em, and their interest of the other will put it out of all danger of miscarrying.' In November, 1694, arose the difficulty, to whom should the new edition be dedicated? However, the edition duly appeared in 1695, but it did not 'go off' as was anticipated; and in 1723 a new title-page was printed for the remainder.

February 1695-6 speaks of 'Bentley, who cursed our Virgil so heartily.'

It was not a usual practice for an author to dedicate a play to his bookseller, and perhaps for very obvious reasons. In the prefatory epistle, 'To my friend the Stationer,' to 'The Innocent Usurper' (1694), Banks speaks in high terms of Bentley's generosity 'to a good poet,' which said generosity was, it appears, meted out 'suitable to the author and his book.' And it is not going out of the way to suppose, from some of his remarks, that Mr. Banks was fishing, not for compliments, but for something much more substantial. Evelyn, writing on January 20, 1696-7, to Dr. Bentley, in reference to the 'copy' of 'Silva,' alludes to it as being 'in the hands of Chiswell and your namesake, Mr. Bentley (Booksellers), who have sold off three impressions, and are now impatient for the fourth.' Bentley, also, seems to have been one of the earliest booksellers who advertised in the periodical press, as witness *The Present State of Europe* for January 1697, and possibly earlier. 'The New World of Words, or a Universal English Dictionary,' is the subject of one of these advertisements, but it was also sold by three other booksellers.

Booksellers, as we have already seen, did not confine themselves to selling books. Sir Robert Filmer's 'Patriarcha, or the Natural Power of Kings' (1680), was printed and sold by 'Walter Davis, bookbinder, in Amen Corner.' This work has a more than passing interest, inasmuch as it called forth Locke's 'Treatise on Civil Government' (1690). It is, however, a far cry from bookish matters to quack medicines, and yet the step was much more often than not taken by the old booksellers. Indeed, with many, books and pills are equally important items. It is not so common an incident to find booksellers offering not only a particular 'medical' work, but also the medicines which it recommended. Salmon's 'Select Physical and Chyrurgical Observations,'—'from my house at the Blew Balcony by the Ditch side, near Holborn Bridge, December 7, 1685,'—contains the following announcement :—' Whereas, Dr. William Salmon, the author of this treatise, being some time gone beyond sea, These are to give notice that all persons that have an occasion for any of his medicines mentioned in his catalogues or books, may be supplied by John Hollier, with whom the Dr. formerly lived.' Mr. Hollier, it seems, 'may be spoken' with at the shop of Thomas Passinger, the bookseller, at the Three Balls on London Bridge. Booksellers' shops, likewise, appear to have been general receptacles for letters : several of John Ray's letters to Hans Sloane were directed to be left at 'Mr. Wilkinson's, a Bookseller at the Black Boy over against St. Dunstan's Church, Fleet Street,' in 1689.

The literary *cause célèbre* of the dying years of the seventeenth century owes its origin to a bookseller. The contest between Bentley single-handed and Boyle backed by all the wit and learning of Oxford has been happily termed a splendid one. Thomas Bennett, of the Half-Moon, in St. Paul's Churchyard, was the bookseller who detained the MS. 'Phalaris' much longer than was at all necessary, and so set the scholars at loggerheads. Bennett secured more attention perhaps than he deserved, but Bentley's letters to him are unique of their kind. Dunton refers to his worthy as 'very much devoted to the Church, has a considerable trade in Oxford, and prints for Dr. South and the most eminent Conformists.' Atterbury was his friend and patron, and preached his funeral sermon in 1706, in which his religious and moral qualities were eloquently spoken of. Among the many interesting incidents which this quarrel occasioned, not the least was the bookseller's own vindication,—a tedious and somewhat incoherent defence, entitled 'A Short Account of Dr. Bentley's Humanity and Justice,' &c., 1699. Bennet makes an elaborate attempt to justify himself, but not successfully so.

CHAPTER V.

BOOKSELLING IN LITTLE BRITAIN.

THERE is scarcely anything in the annals of bookselling so remarkable as the comparatively narrow compass in which the trade has thrived. Until within the past few years, it was almost entirely confined to a radius of half-a-mile, taking St. Paul's Cathedral as the starting-point, and for over three hundred years there were very few migratory symptoms observable. Little Britain and London Bridge are the only two localities in which the trade has become entirely obliterated. The former is one of the very many quaint and old-world-like nooks that lie off the main thoroughfares of the Metropolis, where the antiquary may for a while ponder over the legends and stories of the place when in the zenith of its fame, and where everything is consecrated into Religion by the footprints of Time. Even within the past few years Little Britain has, however, undergone changes which are improvements only from a utilitarian point of view. The street is narrow, and the houses high, and if there is, here and there, a remnant or an architectural suggestion of an old-world time, with its wigs, its coaches, its three-corner hats and its sleepy complacency, there is, we regret to say, much too much of the nineteenth century element to permit the lover of the past to linger long in his day-dream. Even Washington Irving's charmingly fancical sketch of the locality—comparatively recent as it is—only serves to demonstrate the mutability of things, for, other than by caretakers, the street is uninhabited: Mr. Skryme, the undertaker with his quaint song, and the Lambs, they, or their prototypes, have long since passed into the inevitable unknown.

In the time of Edward II., the mansion of John, Duke of 'Bretagne' or Brittany, and Earl of Richmond, was the centre of attraction of the neighbourhood, around which the *élite* of the capital gathered with all its finery and its wit. But slowly and also surely the neighbourhood lost its aristocratic attractions, and so in due course the old family mansions of nobility became converted into dwelling-houses for well-to-do tradesmen; and the next step was in the direction of shops, mostly booksellers. The street itself is bounded on the west by Christ Church School and St. Bartholomew's Hospital, on the north by Smithfield and Long Lane, and on the east by Aldersgate Street, whilst Bull-and-Mouth Street separates it from the purlieus of Newgate.

It is, of course, impossible to determine when the locality became the habitat of booksellers. If not actually the first, then certainly the first *eminent* printer-bookseller who resided here was John Day, or Daye, to whom reference has already been made on page 42. We may, however, here quote a passage from Stowe's 'Survey,' in which, referring to the old city gate called Aldersgate, it is stated:— 'John Daye, stationer, a late famous printer of many good bookes, in our time dwelled in this gate, and built much upon the wall of the citie, towards the parish church of St. Anne.' But Day's new buildings did not preserve the old gate, which was rebuilt in 1617.

Alexander Lacy was living in Little Britain in 1566, when he printed 'The Poor Man's Benevolence to Afflicted Church.' Owen Rogers, who was made free of the Stationers' Company in 1555, lived in the immediate vicinity, his shop being at the Spread Eagle, 'neare vnto great saint Bartelmewes gate.' Owen Rogers is not only worthy of note from the fact that he printed and published 'The Vision of Pierce Plowman, newlye imprynted after the authours olde copy' (1561), but also because he appears to have been an obstreperous member of the Company, and was often fined for printing other men's copies without licence. Anthony Scoloker, who printed, about 1548, several books in conjunction with William Seres,—such as 'A brefe Chronycle concerning Sir Johan Oldcastell,'—resided in St. Botolph's parish, without Aldersgate. At about this time also, Richard Lant, who became one of the Stationers' Company in 1547, dwelt in the Old Bailey, and also in Aldersgate Street. Lant appears to have been another of those who had peculiar and convenient notions relative to the sacred rights of property. A contemporary speaks of him as setting his name to that notable work, 'The Rescuynge of the Romishe

Fox' (1545), 'not as the maker, but as the putter forth of it by hys prynt,' and adds, 'He is well contented to be under that vengence which hangeth over Babylon, to get a little money. And whereas he hath joyned his prynces auctoryte unto that, *ad imprimendum solum*, to bring hym also under the same curse of God, he hath playd no honest mannys part, no more than hath some other of his fellowes.' John Audeley lived in 'Little Britain-street without Aldersgate-street,' and in 1575 he issued 'A godly Sermon,' which he declares to have been made in 1338, 'and found out, being hyd in a wall, which sermon is here set forth from the old copy.' Nearly ten years before this, however,—*i.e.* June 29, 1566,— he printed certain ordinances decreed by the Court of the Star-chamber, for 'the reformation of divers disorders in printing and uttering of books.'

One of the most interesting figures in the annals of Little Britain is that of Richard Smith, the bookhunter. He was one of the 'Secondaries' of London from 1644 to 1655,—an office worth to him 700*l.* a year, which he resigned to devote himself entirely to book-collecting. Was there everanother such a man? Anthony à Wood describes him as 'infinitely curious and inquisitive after books,' and that 'he was constantly known every day to walk his rounds amongst the booksellers' shops (especially in Little Britain).' He left an interesting obituary list of certain of his bibliopolic friends, which is reprinted in *Willis' Current Notes*, February 1853; and of these Cornelius Bee—who, in 1660, issued 'Critici Sacri,' and who dwelt in Little Britain—is perhaps the only one of any importance: he died, according to Smith, on January 2, 1671, and was 'buried at St. Bartholomew's, without wine or wafers, only gloves and rosemary.'

Three years before the Great Fire of London,—in 1663,—Sorbière made the following observation: 'I am not to forget the vast number of booksellers' shops I have observed in London; for besides those who are set up here and there in the City, they have their particular quarters, such as St. Paul's Churchyard and Little Britain, where there is twice as many as in the Rue Saint Jacque in Paris, and who have each of them two or three warehouses.'[1] The bookselling zenith of Little Britain was attained in the seventeenth century; it may be said to have commenced with the reign of Charles I., and to have begun a sort of retrogression with the Hanoverian succession. Its importance may be inferred from a newspaper published in this district in 1664, which states that no less than 464 pamphlets were published here during four years. It was a sort of seventeenth century combination of the Paternoster Row and Fleet Street of the present day. It is the place where, according to a widely circulated tradition, an Earl of Dorset accidentally discovered, when on a bookhunt in 1667, a work hitherto unknown to him, entitled 'Paradise Lost.' He is said to have bought a copy, and the bookseller begged him to recommend it to his friends, as the copies lay on his hand like so much waste paper. The noble Earl (so runs this same tradition) showed his copy to Dryden,

[1] 'Journey to England,' p. 16.

who is reported to have exclaimed, 'This man cuts us all out, and the ancients too.' Though this anecdote, like a great many others, has been proved to be apocryphal, certain it is—as we have seen—the poem is in a way connected with the neighbourhood, inasmuch as Simmons' shop was in Aldersgate Street.

Roger North, in his 'Life of the Right Hon. Francis North,'[2] has an oft-quoted reference to Little Britain. From this interesting account we learn that during the latter part of the seventeenth century it was a plentiful and perpetual emporium of learned authors, and that men went thither as to a market. The trade of the place was, in consequence, an important one, the shops being large, and much resorted to by literary personages, wits, men-about-town, and fashionable notabilities generally. The booksellers then were men of intellect. But referring, by way of contrast, to the place during the earlier half of the eighteenth century, he laments that 'this emporium is vanished, and the trade contracted into the hands of two or three persons, who, to make good their monopoly, ransack, not only their neighbours of the trade that are scattered about the town, but all over England, ay, and beyond sea, too, and send abroad their circulators, and in this manner get into their hands all that is valuable. The rest of the trade are content to take their refuse, with which, and the fresh scum of the press, they furnish one side of the shop, which serves for the sign of a bookseller, rather than a real one; but instead of selling, deal as factors, and pro-

[2] Edit. 1826, iii. 293, *et seq.*

cure what the country divines and gentry send for; of whom each hath his bookfactor, and, when wanting anything, writes to his bookseller and pays his bill. And it is wretched to consider what pickpocket work, with the help of the press, these demi-booksellers make. They crack their brains to find out selling subjects, and keep hirelings in garrets, at hard meat, to write and correct by the groat; and so puff up an octavo to a sufficient thickness; and there is six shillings current for an hour and half's reading, and perhaps never to be read or looked upon after. One that would go higher, must take his fortune at blank walls, and corners of streets, or repair to the sign of Bateman, Kings, and one or two more, where are best choice, and better pennyworths. I might touch other abuses, as bad paper, incorrect printing, and false advertising; and all of which and worse are to be expected, if a careful author is not at the heels of them.'

The house of Bateman is worthy of an important chapter in the bookselling annals of Little Britain, and the best-known member (Christopher) of the family is described in the usual sugared style of John Dunton: 'There are few booksellers in England (if any) that understand books better than Mr. Bateman, nor does his diligence and industry come short of his knowledge. He is a man of great reputation and honesty.' Nichols states that Bateman would allow no person to look into books in his shop, and when asked a reason for this extraordinary rule, he answered, 'I suppose you may be a physician or an author, and want some recipe or quotation; and, if you buy it, I will engage it to be perfect before you leave me, but not after, as

I have suffered by leaves being torn out, and the books returned, to my very great loss and prejudice.' Bateman's shop was a favourite resort of Swift, who several times speaks of it in his *Journal to Stella*: 'I went to Bateman's, the bookseller, and laid out eight and forty shillings for books. I bought three little volumes of 'Lucian,' in French, for our Stella, and so, and so' (January 6, 1710-11); and again: 'I was at Bateman's, the bookseller, to see a fine old library he has bought, and my fingers itched as yours would do at a china-shop' (July 9, 1711). Saturday, when Parliament was not sitting during the winter, was the market-day with the booksellers of Little Britain; and at the time of Swift's writing the above, the frequenters of this locality included such worthies as the Duke of Devonshire, Edward Earl of Oxford, and the Earls of Pembroke, Sunderland, and Winchelsea. After the 'hunt' they often adjourned to the 'Mourning Bush' in Aldersgate, where they dined and spent the remainder of the day,—in bookish gossip, no doubt.

Another famous Little Britain bookseller was Robert Scott, whose sister was the Hon. and Rev. Dr. John North's 'grandmother's woman.' Scott was a man of 'good parts,' and was in his time, says Roger North, the 'greatest librarian in Europe; for besides his stock in England, he had warehouses at Frankfort, Paris, and other places, and dealt by factors.' When an old man, Scott 'contracted with one Mills, of St. Paul's Churchyard, near 10,000*l*. deep, and articled not to open his shop any more. But Mills, with his auctioneering, atlasses, and projects, failed, whereby poor Scott lost above half his means. ... He was not only an expert bookseller, but a very conscientious, good man, and when he threw up his trade, Europe had no small loss of him.'

The most celebrated family of booksellers, perhaps, who lived in Little Britain, was that of Balland, or Ballard, as the original name appears by the auction catalogues. The family was connected with the trade for over a century, and was noted, says Nichols, ' for the soundness of their principles in Church and State.' One Henry Ballard lived at the sign of the Bear without Temple-bar, over against St. Clement's Church, in 1597, but whether he was an ancestor of the family in question is not certain. Possibly he was. Thomas Ballard, the founder of the bookselling branch, was described by Dunton, in 1705, as ' a young bookseller in Little Britain, but grown man in body now, but more in mind :—

> "His looks are in his mother's beauty drest,
> And all the Father has inform'd the rest." '

Samuel Ballard, for many years Deputy of the Ward of Aldersgate Within, died August 27, 1761, and his only son, Edward, January 2, 1796, aged 88, in the same house in which he was born, having outlived his mental faculties. He was the last of the profession in Little Britain.

Dorman Newman was a well-known bookseller, whose shop was at ' The Chyrurgeons Armes,' near the Hospital gates, and in 1667 he issued the ' Life and Death of Thomas Woolsey.' Some years later —1690—he published the *Mercurius Reformatus*; and he is included in Dunton's 'picture gallery.' He was, observes John, 'a considerable dealer, but has been unfortunate,' and 'since his misfortunes is turned preacher.' Hugh Newman served his time with his relative Dorman, and his business relations with Dunton were both extensive and cordial.

Moses Pitt, who published a book, in Latin, on Logarithms in 1668; and John Williams, of the Cross Keys Court, who published a great number of funeral sermons in and about 1672, were two minor lights during the latter part of the seventeenth century. Few Little Britain booksellers and publishers shared a wider popularity than George Conyers, whose name is sometimes spelt 'Coniers,' and now and then seen abbreviated into 'G. C.' He appears to have removed from the Ring on Ludgate Hill, where he was from 1685 to 1689, and probably later, to the Gold Ring in Little Britain. His aim was to publish royal guides to nearly every subject under the sun, and, as a much less costly expedient, instead of engaging authors to write, he paid hacks to condense standard works into a small compass. We have now before us a quaint little 16mo, undated, which is composed of four distinct examples of these abridgements, three of which were sold at a shilling apiece, and the fourth at eighteen pence. Their titles sufficiently indicate their aim and scope:—' The Way to Save Wealth, showing how a Man may Live Plentifully for Twopence a Day' (72 pp.; Markham's 'The Compleat Husbandman' (38 pp.); 'The Husbandman's Jewell' (52 pp.); and 'Every Man his own Gauger' (68 pp.). The illustrations are few, and of course rude. Those whose notions are ultra-economic may be referred to the first-named of these books, in which will be found at all events directions how to make a hundred noble dishes of meat 'without either flesh, fish, or fowl,' how to make shoes and coals last long, how to save soap in washing, and cloth in cutting out a shirt, all of which must have been very valuable to the poor people of the period, but a perusal of the directions leads us to think that mystification rather than enlightenment would ensue. Another of Conyers' little books was ' 1000 Notable Things, directing how to read and write, and indite letters, to speak any language in a short time as fluent as a native.' Among other books which this publisher described—and sold—as 'so diverting and instructive that they will help the meanest capacity to be able to discuss on all subjects whatsoever,' may be named the 'History of Winds and Storms,' the 'Florist's Vade-Mecum, or Book for Gardeners,' 'Collins' Arithmetick,' and the 'Compleat Fisher, with cuts.' Conyers contributed a guinea to William Bowyer's relief fund in 1712, and for 33*l.* he sold his shares in certain books to Lintot (see p. 152, note). Dunton, of course, has a reference to him, but it is in a very off-hand fashion : he gives an eulogistic account of one Harrison, and then declares 'this is also the character of G. Conyers, in Little Britain.' Bowyer, it may be mentioned, commenced his long and useful career as a printer at the White Horse in Little Britain, his first work being 'A Defence of the Vindication of King Charles the Martyr,' 1699, but by the end of that year he had removed to White-friars.

John Nicholson, of the King's Arms, Little Britain, was another extensive bookseller whose name is frequently found in conjunction with that of Robert Knaplock, of St. Paul's Churchyard, and Samuel Ballard. Their lists included a large number of quaint and curious little books, such as Eachard's 'Gazetteer,' Rapin's critical works, Wiseman's 'Chirurgery,' 'all the novels of Mr. John Boccace,' with cuts, 'The Solitary Gardener,' and 'The Life of Gusman de Alfrache, done from a curious edition,' and so forth. Perhaps the most important book in the lists of Nicholson and Knaplock was Stebbing's edition of Sandford's 'Genealogical History of the Kings and Queens of England' (1707), a folio of nearly 900 pages. The book was issued by subscription, and there were large as well as small paper copies to be had. He was, also, one of the booksellers who, in 1704, contributed towards the production of John Harris' 'Lexicon Technicum.' Aaron Ward was publishing books at the King's Arms in 1737, and T. Ward at the same address in 1749. A. Ward and Daniel Midwinter issued Peter Bayle's 'Dictionary' in sixpenny parts. J. Ford, of the Angel, made a speciality, in a small way, of Isaac Watts' books; and Geo. Wilcocks, of the Green Dragon, J. Oswald, of the Rose and Crown, J. Newton, of the Rose Tree, Thos. Bickerton, and J. Sprint[3] were all eminent

---

[3] There were three Sprints who acted as booksellers: Benjamin, Samuel, and his son John. Samuel printed for Steele

Little Britain booksellers during the first quarter of the eighteenth century. Nearly all the lanes and alleys immediately contiguous to Little Britain had its bookseller. In Duck Lane there were several, one of the best known being J. Clarke, of the Golden Ball, who was agent for the *London Magazine*, and whose list appears in the *Grub Street Journal*, of June 1, 1732, and on other occasions.

It was from the Dolphin in Little Britain that Samuel Buckley, with another, published the first seven volumes of the original *Spectator*, from March 1, 1711, onwards. The circulation at the outset was 3000 daily, which increased as time went on, but by the close of its career had dwindled down to about 10,000 per week. A half-share of four volumes, and three more, was assigned to Buckley by Steele and Addison on November 10, 1712, for 575*l*.; two years later Buckley reassigned his share to Jacob Tonson, jun., for 500*l*. Buckley, who died September 8, 1741, likewise printed and published the *Daily Courant*, the *Monthly Register*, and Steele's *Englishman*. He appears to have removed from Little Britain about 1716 to Amen Corner, whilst W. Wilkins, the printer of the *Whitehall Evening Post*, the *London Journal*, and *The Englishman*, was living at Buckley's old address shortly after this.

Little Britain is not only famous as a spot of pilgrimage for all patriotic Americans—for here Benjamin Franklin obtained much of his technical

'and other eminent authors;' both are described by Dunton, the last as 'the handsomest man in the Stationers' Company.'

knowledge—but it has another sort of interest from the fact that in it once resided Tom Rawlinson, the 'Tom Folio' of the *Tatler*, No. 158, who stuffed four chambers in Gray's Inn so full of books, that his bed was removed into the passage.

Although a few years before Nichols published his 'Literary Anecdotes,' two booksellers, 'who used to sport their rubric posts close to each other,' resided in Little Britain, its glory as a bookselling locality has departed nearly a century and a half. The trade migrated to Paternoster Row—then inhabited in a great measure by mercers, haberdashers, and lacemen—and other quarters in the vicinity of St. Paul's. At the present moment the place maintains an air of eminent respectability and business-like sobriety, which is somewhat oppressive and irritating to those who have associated the sentimental side of human progress with its history.

CHAPTER VI.

BOOKSELLING ON LONDON BRIDGE.

LONDON BRIDGE, as it now stands, is not at all suggestive of bookselling, which has nothing in common with the busy and crowded thoroughfare. For convenience' sake, we may mention that the first stone structure was commenced in 1176, the architect being a priest of St. Mary Colechurch, in the Poultry, named Pious Peter, who died before its completion, and was buried in a fine chapel that stood thereon. The most singular features of the old bridge, observes Mr. Smiles, in his 'Lives of the Engineers,' were its upper platform, consisting of two rows of houses with a narrow roadway between, the chapel and drawbridge, and the turreted battlements at either end. The length of the roadway was 926 feet, and from end to end it was enclosed by the lofty timber houses, which were held together by arches crossing overhead from one range to the other, and thus keeping the whole in position. The streets were narrow, dark, and dangerous. There were only three openings along it on either side, provided with balustrades, from which a view of the river and its shipping might be obtained, as well as of the rear of

Bookselling on London Bridge. 131

the houses themselves, which overhung the parapets and completely hid the arches from sight.[1]

The books exposed for sale on the bridge were strictly special in form and size, but in point of subjects there was scarcely any limit. 'There appear to have been no tall folios, no heavy classics, ancient and modern' (writes a correspondent of *Notes and Queries*), 'no brain-racking metaphysical disquisitions, no political squibs. There was little that rose above the chap-book. The slender duodecimo mostly contained "things easy to understand," suited to the taste of light readers and male learners of all opinions; but, due allowance being made for the literary licence of those times, there does not appear to have been much in these catchpennies that was low or scandalous. . . . There were Cocker's Dictionary and Arithmetic, 'A Treatise on Thistles,' Gervase Markham's 'Horse Leech' and 'Accomplished Jockey,' Lambert's 'Countryman's Treasure,' and a handful of shabby abridgments of popular romances to be read aloud at night in chimney corners. For country girls in quest of service in 'Lunnon' there was 'The Compleat Servant Maid,' and for sailors about to embark at Pepper's-alley stairs there were the 'Seaman's Kalender' and the 'Mariner's Jewel.' For the humbler clergy there were an epitome of ecclesiastical history, a scrap or

[1] Peter Cunningham refers to some 'capital views' of London Bridge by Norden in the time of Charles I.; by Vertue, in 1747-8; by Boydell, in 1751; and by W. James (a picture at Hampton Court), *circa* 1756. Hogarth has introduced the ruinous old houses in his 'Marriage à la Mode' (the view from the window).

two of acrid religious controversy, and a few books on divinity, which, although of light and pocketable bulk, afforded a great amount of heavy reading. For visitors to town there were handbooks of London, and various disquisitions upon criminals and London cheating. Most of these publications must originally have been of very low price, and must have been published in large editions, as even now few of them are very rare or costly.'

It is impossible to ascertain the exact or even approximate date at which bookselling established itself on London Bridge. The church built in 1209, to which reference has already been made, was some years afterwards turned into a dwelling-house, occupied by tradespeople. In a patent roll of the ninth year of Edward I. (1280) mention is made of innumerable people dwelling on the bridge. We are justified, therefore, in assuming that so desirable a coign of vantage would not be neglected by the vendors of paternosters, and other religious paraphernalia calculated to smooth the road to heaven. The history of the bridge as a bookselling rendezvous may be safely said to date back to a time long before printing was introduced. But it is not until the middle of the sixteenth century that we have record of booksellers inhabiting this spot. Their numbers were of course few, and their names are almost entirely lost in oblivion. From the commencement of the seventeenth century their numbers and names assume a more definite, and their existence a more concrete, form. But in no single instance does the celebrity of a London-bridge bookseller in any sense compete with that of a Tonson or of a Lintot. The reason of this has been already indicated: they issued no works of any material importance; they had no poet in their 'employ;' they aspired to no 'original translations by the most eminent hands;' they sought not the influential patronage of the great, and they had no friends at the Court. If they published no original work, they at least had no occasion for subterfuge and lying to dispose of their wares. Most of their 'editing' and boiling down must have been done by themselves, assisted occasionally, perhaps, by a stray hack who knew a little Latin and less Greek, and whose time was spent either in the beer-shop, the sponging-house, or the jail. Deficient of literary merit as are these little 'bridge books,' they will always be worth collecting as literary curiosities, whilst to the student of the times, manners, and customs their value is very considerable.

The Looking Glass, the Three Bibles, and the Angel are the signs most frequently seen on the imprints of 'bridge books.' The first one appears to have been a particular favourite, for, whilst it was never unemployed, it was at one time used by two distinct booksellers. One of these, Thomas Norris, flourished on the bridge between 1690 and 1721, when probably he removed to Little Britain, where he—or at all events a namesake—was in 1724, as appears from Samuel Negus' list of printers and newspaper publishers,—Norris being included among those 'said to be High Flyers.' He subscribed to William Bowyer's relief fund. His business was an extensive and varied one, and his books were occasionally illustrated in a rough-and-ready sort of fashion. They are, of course, of the usual duodecimo form, and catchpenny titles. As an indication of the way in which Mr. Norris tempted his visitors to part with the coveted coin, we may as well quote a few of these ' nominations,' which are decidedly quaint and explanatory. His list included ' The Garden of Love's Craftiness,' for the elegant and sentimental young gentleman ; 'England's Witty and Ingenious Jester,' for the retailer of small talk and stale fun ; William Grismond's, the 'Fisherman's Daughter's Garland,' the 'Verteous Maiden's Garland,' the 'Politick Sailor's Garland,' the 'Ladies' Sorrowful Garland,' the 'Weeping Swain's Garland,' and probably a great many other 'garlands' for other and equally special purposes. No doubt Mr. Norris kept a stock of these sort of things on hand for anything in the way of a calamity or disaster that might occur. The 'garlands' run from one to four leaves each.

James Hodges, of the Looking Glass ' over against St. Magnus Church,' is the best known of all the bridge booksellers. He has a political as well as a trade history. He was constantly producing books between the years 1720 and 1757, and was perhaps the most active and enterprising of the fraternity in the locality. Another interesting feature about him is that he was the third bookseller who occupied the same premises in succession. J. Blare, who flourished *circa* 1688—1704, at the 'Looking Glass,' was succeeded by F. Hodges, who, we presume, was the father of the energetic James. J. Hodges was a member of the Common Council for Bridge Ward, and was one of the Court of Assistants of the Stationers' Company. He made a famous speech on April 15, 1757, in the City Senate, on moving the Freedom of the City to Pitt, and this oration is said to have commenced in this fashion :—' History, the key of knowledge, and experience, the touchstone of truth, have convinced us that the country owes the preservation of its most excellent constitution to the frequent fears, jealousies, and apprehensions of the people.' Hodges was a very popular man, and in the year following—1758—he was knighted on presenting an address to George II. He died at Bath in October, 1774. Hodges' books, for the most part, are of the usual bridge class, but he was probably the first bookseller who published novels on London Bridge. One of the best known, but perhaps not the earliest, was 'Matrimony' (1755) in two volumes, which, as with many others, B. Collins of Salisbury either printed or had a partnership interest. Sermons also were published or sold by Hodges, who likewise was one of the very few who advertised his wares in the newspapers. A list of some of his books appears in the *Grub Street Journal* ,February 15, 1732. The following is an example of Hodges' windy titles :—

> 'The Traveller's Pocket-Companion ; or, a Compleat Description of the Roads, in Tables of their Computed and Measured Distances, by an Actual Survey and Mensuration by the Wheel, from London to all the considerable Cities and Towns in England and Wales ; together with the Mail-Roads, and their several Stages, and the Cross-Roads from one City or eminent Town to another. With Directions what Turnings are to be

avoided in going or returning on Journeys, and Instructions for riding Post. To which is annexed, A New Survey-Map, which shews the Market-Days, and remarkable Things; the whole laid down in a Manner that Strangers may travel without any other Guide. Also an Account of the Expences of sending a Letter or Pacquet by Express from the General Post-Office, without Loss of Time, to any Part of Great Britain. By a Person who has belonged to the Publick Offices upwards of Twenty Years. London : Printed for the Author, and sold by J. Hodges, at the Looking-Glass over-against St. Magnus's Church, London Bridge. 1741. Price bound One Shilling and Sixpence.'

Arthur Bettesworth was another of the better known bridge booksellers, but he only resided in this locality during the earlier part of his career. His sign was the 'Red Lion' or 'Red Lyon.' He was publishing on the bridge in 1712. After a time he removed to Paternoster Row, still retaining his old sign. He was a prominent member of two bookselling 'congeries,' and was succeeded by Charles Hitch, his son-in-law and partner. Hitch was on the Commission of the Peace for the county of Essex, and was Master of the Stationers' Company in 1758, to which Company he bequeathed a sum of twenty guineas to purchase a pair of silver candlesticks. He died September 20, 1764.

William Pickering, who flourished on the bridge 'under St. Magnus Church' between 1556 and 1571, was, suggests Mr. Gray in *Notes and Queries*, probably succeeded by Hugh Astley, 1588—1608. Henry Gosson, the fourth (remarks the same writer), 'had a shop on London Bridge *circa* 1610—1628. Gosson's house must have been situated at the southern part of the bridge, and in 1635 we find him 'on London

Bridge, near to the gate.'² He is not noticed as being one of those who had their places burnt, according to Nehemiah Wallington's 'Records of the Mercies of God,' quoted by Thomson, nor, indeed, are any booksellers mentioned in that list. His still being on the bridge after the fire seems to confirm this. 'In 1608, a namesake—or possibly the same person—was carrying on business at the Tun, in Paternoster Row ; one of his publications, which was printed by Robert Raworth, being 'The Contention between the Brethren.' Most of his books were, of course, broadsides, ballads and the like, often printed in black-letter type, and occasionally 'adorned with cuts.' One of the most curious was perhaps 'The Old, Old, very Old Man,' i.e. Thomas Parr, who lived, it is stated, over 150 years, and who died November 15, 1635. This tract, the scope of which is set forth in 150 words, comprising its title-page, was written by John Taylor, and is reprinted in 'The Harleian Miscellany' (vol. vii.).

H. Tracy, of the Three Bibles, made a speciality not only of school-books, but also of a balsam 'lately brought from Chili, a Province of America.' Of him Dunton says, 'His religion is not confined to the church, any more than the shop. His behaviour in his family is grave and exemplary ; his devotion constant ; his care over his household is tender and impartial ; and to his servants he seems a father rather than a master.' He published, *inter alia*, Dyche's

---

² Stephen Powell had a shop 'on London Bridge neere to the gate,' in 1635, when he published 'An Essay of Drapery,' which had an engraved title-page.

'Youth's Guide to the Latin Tongue,' and Roger Rea's 'The Sector and Plain Scale compared;' the former at five shillings, and the latter at eighteenpence.

Stanley Crowder deserves some mention in connection with this chapter, as being probably the last, if not the only bookseller who remained on London Bridge prior to the final clearing out. Crowder, who died May 23, 1795, was an apprentice of Sir James Hodges, and for many years after quitting the bridge did a large wholesale trade at the Aldine Chambers, Paternoster Row. Proving at last unsuccessful, he applied for and obtained the office of Clerk of the Commissioners of the Commutation and Window Tax for the City of London.[3] Some of the better known bridge booksellers were:—John Tap, of St. Magnus Corner, 1610; Charles Tyus, of the Three Bibles, in the middle of the bridge, 1659, and probably succeeded by Thomas Passinger, who, at all events, had the same sign in use shortly afterwards and whose name is occasionally seen in company with that of Charles Passinger; John Williamson was at the 'Sun and Bible in the low buildings on London Bridge' in 1678; and in addition to those previously mentioned as having the Looking Glass as a sign, we may mention that it was also used by Ed. Midwinter, 1721, and T. Harris, 1741-4, the last-named of whom became a bankrupt in December, 1745. This list is, of course, very far from complete; and for lengthy catalogues of the bridge

[3] An interesting reference to Crowder occurs in the *Aldine Magazine*, December, 1838.

Bookselling on London Bridge. 139

booksellers the reader is referred to *Notes and Queries*, sixth series, fifth, sixth and seventh volumes.

The bridge, which had passed through so many storms, received in a manner of speaking a severe blow in 1633, when many of its houses were burnt. The great fire of 1666 also destroyed a number. Still more were burnt in 1727, and thenceforward its decay was rapid and its removal inevitable. In 1757 most of the houses and shops were reckoned among the things that were. In December, 1760, ' notice was given to the people on the west side of London Bridge to quit their premises by the 25th of March next,' with a view to the demolition of the buildings.' The toll was abolished on March 27, 1781; the gate at the Southwark end disappeared in 1766. The famous old bridge itself ceased to exist in 1832, and the stones of which it was constructed were, it is said, used to build or rebuild Ingress Hall, near Greenhithe, and the tough pieces of iron which held the stones together were converted into razors and pen-knives as mementos. *Sic transit gloria mundi!*

CHAPTER VII.

OTHER BOOKSELLING LOCALITIES.

THE history and associations of the immediate vicinity of St. Paul's Cathedral are indissolubly interwoven with the annals of bookselling. Literature and Paternoster Row are almost synonymous terms. The dull and narrow thoroughfare, with its nomenclature abbreviated into 'The Row,' is the most famous bookselling quarter in London,—we had almost said in the world. The derivation of the term is ascribed to various causes, one of which points to the fact that funereal processions on their way to St. Paul's began their *pater noster* at the commencement of the Row. The most probable theory, however, is that which connects the place with the rosary or paternoster makers, who resided and did a great business here until the Reformation. Dr. Brewer, quoting from an unstated source, alludes to 'one Robert Nikke, a paternoster maker and citizen, in the reign of Henry IV.' As a literary emporium the antiquity of 'the Row' is unquestionable.

From Stow's 'Survey of London' (edit. Strype), we learn that 'this street, before the fire of London (1666), was taken up by eminent mercers, silkmen

Other Bookselling Localities. 141

and lacemen; and their shops were so resorted to by the nobility and gentry, in their coaches, that oft-times the street was so stopped up that there was no room for foot-passengers.' After the great conflagration, most of the tradesmen removed to the vicinity of Covent Garden, whilst others again inhabited this place so soon as new buildings were erected. Near the east end there were 'stationers and large warehouses for booksellers, well situated for learned and studious men's access thither, being more retired and private.' 'After dinner,' on June 1, 1665, observes Pepys, 'I put on my new camelott suit, the best that I ever wore in my life, the suit costing me above 24*l*. In this I went with Creed to Goldsmiths' Hall, to the burial of Sir Thomas Viner, which Hall, and Haberdashers' also, was so full, that we were fain for coolness to go forth to Pater Noster Row, to choose a silk to make me a plain ordinary suit.' An 'extract from a periodical of 1705' has a reference to the 'semptresses of Paternoster Row' which points to the conclusion that collateral branches of the drapery trade lingered in the Row for a much longer period than is generally thought. At this present moment there is, we believe, but one existing representative of this trade in 'the Row.'

For a century or more the famous locality has been almost entirely inhabited by booksellers or stationers, such as the Longmans, Cookes, Harrisons, Hoggs, Rivingtons, Baldwins, and very many others, whose careers would each need a lengthy chapter. There are records, however, which prove that the Row was a regular bookselling locality in the middle of the sixteenth century. Henry Denham, for example, was living at the Star, in Paternoster Row, in 1564, and for several years afterwards; he adopted the Latin motto of 'Os homini sublime dedit.' In 1570 he published George Tuberville's 'Epitaphs, Epigrams, Songs and Sonnets.' It was not until the latter part of the last century, however, that 'the character of the trade in the Row became changed from old bookselling, or the issuing only of large and important new works by the principal houses, to general publishing, and particularly of periodicals. The issuing of works in weekly numbers was more particularly confined to Cooke, Hogg and Harrison. These all stood prominent as publishers of what have been called 'Paternoster row Numbers,' namely Family Bibles, with notes, editions of Foxe's 'Book of Martyrs,' and the works of Flavius Josephus; new and complete Histories of England, Histories of London, Life of Christ, and various other denominations of works, which, years back, more than now, were chiefly purchased by the more intelligent of the working classes, and were seen in the shape of handsomely bound folios in several of their houses. However it may be customary to kick the ladder down when we find we no longer want it, these sort of publications, it must be confessed, greatly contributed to lay the foundation of that literary taste and thirst for knowledge which now pervade all classes. To give such works as we have mentioned all the attraction possible, the title-pages were copious to an extreme; enumerating the whole contents of the book, the authors were generally called *esquires*, and had two

Other Bookselling Localities. 143

or three high-sounding Christian names.'[1] Among the booksellers of Paternoster Row, no one had a higher reputation or a more extensive business than William Taylor, who resided at the Ship, during the first quarter of the last century. And of all his undertakings, or part undertakings, none was more famous or more signally successful than 'Robinson Crusoe.' Taylor published the first part on April 25, 1719, and the second on August 20, in the same year. His catalogue is a matter of 16 pages, the subjects being divided into three sections—folio, quarto, and octavo and duodecimo—and including nearly every conceivable class of literature. Of the first part of Defoe's immortal book, four editions were sold in as many months.

When the bibliopolic glory of Little Britain and its immediately contiguous neighbourhood departed, some of its rays were transferred to St. Paul's Churchyard, which, in its turn, has been gradually deserted by booksellers during the past century, until, at the present moment, there is only one firm left. Its halcyon days, however, were previous to the Fire. The booksellers' shops were mostly on the north side. 'It was,' observes Mr. Treloar, 'at the 'White Greyhound' that John Harrison first published Shakespeare's poems ; at the 'Fleur de Luce and the Crown' appeared the first edition of the 'Merry Wives of Windsor,' and the 'Green Dragon,' the 'Fox,' the 'Angel,' the 'Spread Eagle,' the 'Gun,' and the 'Red Bull' are all associated

[1] Timperley's 'Dictionary of Printers' (1839), p. 838.

with the publications of the great dramatist."[2] 'Who,' exclaims Tom Nash in Pierce Penilesse,' 'can abide a scurvy pedling poet to plucke a man by the sleeve at evrie third step in Paules Churchyard, and when he comes in to survey his wares, there's nothing but purgations and vomits wrapt vp in wast paper?"

The following list includes most of the principal 'churchyard' booksellers, with signs and approximate dates, who lived in the seventeenth century:— M. Atkins, the 'Half Moon,' 1674; Robert Allot, the 'Black Bear,' 1629; William Apsley, the 'Parrot,' 1622; John Bartlett, 'The Golden Cup' in the Goldsmith's Row in Cheapside; 1610-40; Walter Burne, the 'Crane,' 1614; William Birch, the 'Peacock,' 'at the lower end of Cheapside,' 1678; John Budge, 'at the great South doore of Paul's,' 1609; Henry Brome, the 'Gun,'—who first published Milton's 'Character of the Long Parliament and Assembly of Divines' (1681); Robert Bostock, the 'King's Head,' 1645; Walter Kettilby, the 'Bishop's Head,' 1678; and Joshua Kirton, of the 'King's Arms,' who possesses the distinction of having been Mr. Pepys' bookseller, and who is thus referred to in the 'Diary,' under date November 2, 1660: 'In Paul's Churchyard I called at Kirton's, and there they had got a masse book for me, which I bought, and cost me 12s., and, when I come home, sat up late, and read in it with great pleasure to my wife, to hear that she was long ago acquainted with it.' And we have already seen to what extent

[2] 'Ludgate Hill, Past and Present.'

poor Kirton was the loser by the great Fire. Henry Kyrkham was living 'at the little North-dore of Paul's Church, at the sign of the 'Black Boy' in 1593; Richard Moore's shop was at the 'Seven Stars;' Giles Calvert's at the 'Black Spread Eagle,' from 1547; and John Wolfe's in 'Paules Chayne,' whence appeared 'Quip for an Upstart Courtier,' in 1592. Jefferie Chorlton, who did a large trade in sensational executions, arraignments, and the like, had a shop 'adjoining the great North door of Paules,' *circa* 1607. And so we might go on *ad infinitum* enumerating the various booksellers, all distinguished in some way or another for being associated with a particular book or author, whilst many of those named in the foregoing list have already been referred to in previous chapters.

Among bookselling localities, none was more unique than Westminster Hall. This historical place is a vast parallelogram, standing north and south, 290 feet long and 68 feet broad. The place is redolent with associations, what with Parliaments, coronation revelries, and impeachments. And of the last-named none was more famous than that of Warren Hastings (February, 1788—April, 1795). 'The place,' says Macaulay in his brilliant essay, 'was worthy of such a trial. It was the great hall of William Rufus, the hall which had resounded with acclamations at the inauguration of thirty kings, the hall which had witnessed the just sentence of Bacon, and the just absolution of Somers,[3] the hall

[3] This is more poetical than true. The proceedings against Bacon and Somers took place, not in Westminster Hall, but in

L.

where the eloquence of Strafford had for a moment awed and melted a victorious party inflamed with just resentment, the hall where Charles had confronted the High Court of Justice with the placid courage which has half redeemed his fame.'

The Hall was occupied by shops, stationers and otherwise, for a period of at least 200 years. A very early instance, which would place the term at a much longer span, is referred to in the *Gentleman's Magazine* of 1853, the object being a copy of the 'Legenda Aurea,' which was either bequeathed to the parish of St. Margaret's, Westminster, by Caxton himself, or given by his executors. Machyn's 'Diary' records the fact that in 1556 a 'boye that sold papers and printed books' was killed in Westminster Hall by being hit under the ear with a stone thrown by 'a hosier's boy above London Stone,' the said bookseller being a poor scholar of Westminster School. Nearly forty years after, Nash exclaimed, 'Looke to it, you booksellers and stationers, and let not your shop be infested with any such goose gyblets, or stinking garbadge as the jygs of newsmongers; and especially such of you as frequent Westminster Hall, let them be circumspect what dunghill papers they bring thether: for one bad pamphlet is inough to raise a dampe that may poysen a whole towne, or at the least a number, of poore clyents, that have no money to prevent il aire by breaking their fasts ere they come thether."

Referring to this place, Tom Browne, in his

the old House of Lords (Jesse's 'Literary and Historical Memoirs of London,' i. 394).

'Amusements' (1700) says, 'on your left hand you have a nimble-tongued, painted sempstress, with her charming treble, invite you to buy some of her knick-knacks, and on your right a deep-mouthed cryer, commanding impossibilities, viz., silence to be kept among women and lawyers.' This describes (says a writer in the *Gentleman's Magazine* for November, 1853) the situation of the shops or stalls, as ranged along the blank wall on the southern side of the Hall. Some years later, they occupied not only the whole of that side, but such portion of the other as was not occupied by the Court of Common Pleas, but which then sat within the Hall itself, as did the Chancery and King's Bench at its further end. Gravelot's print of the Hall during term-time shows this arrangement to have been followed,—a print, by-the-way, which had, in the original engraving, some verses appended at foot, in which the legal proclivities of 'fools' who ' fall out' are hardly hit. Another interesting point may be here noted: the stationers and booksellers in the Hall were emphatically a privileged class, inasmuch as they were exempt from the pains and penalties in the statutes in force relative to licences and regulation of the press. Here, as elsewhere, there were plenty of inferior books obtainable; Mr. Pepys, writing on October 26, 1660, and referring to some purchases made in the Hall, remarks, 'among other books, one of the life of our Queen, which I read at home to my wife, but it was so sillily writ that we did nothing but laugh over it.'

For convenience, the stalls were distinguished

by certain signs. One of the very early issues of 'Paradise Lost' (1668) contains the name, among others, of H. Mortlock, of the 'White Hart' in Westminster Hall, who also had a shop at the Phœnix, St. Paul's Churchyard. Raleigh's 'Remains' (1675) was one of the books printed for Mortlock, who was in all probability succeeded by Benjamin Barker, whose name occurs on Raleigh's 'Three Discourses' (1702) as being at the 'White Hart.' Mortlock probably acquired interest in some of the books sold previously by William Shears, Jun., who, like Mortlock, and several others, had a shop in addition to the stall in the Hall.

Few of the Hall booksellers were more prolific than he who bore the horticultural cognomen of Matthew Gilliflower. His sign was the Spread Eagle and the Crown, and perhaps one of his earliest part-ventures was the 'Refined Courtier' (1679). 'Both his eyes,' remarks Mr. Dunton, 'were never at once from home; for one kept house, and observed the actions of men, while the other roamed abroad for intelligence. He loved his bottle and his friend with an equal affection. He was very tetchy upon some occasions : yet thriving was part of his character. He printed L'Estrange's 'Æsop,' Lord Halifax's 'Advice to his Daughters,' and many excellent copies.' C. King and Stagg were two of the leading booksellers in the Hall during the earlier years of the last century, for nearly every 'proposal' had their names, whilst they are included among the 'unprejudic'd booksellers' who acted as agents for the *Gentleman's Magazine* during the first year of its existence. The former published that grimly humorous piece of satire, 'Neck or Nothing. A Consolatory Letter from Mr. D—nt—n to Mr. C—rll upon his being Tost in a Blanket' (1716). Fox, of the 'Half Moon and Seven Stars,' is described by Dunton as 'a refined politician . . . to his knowledge in trade, he has joined no vulgar crudition, which all his modesty is not able to conceal.' B. Toovey, whose name occurs, with seven others, in the imprint of 'The Life of Henry VIII.,' by Mr. W. Sh——, dedicated to Colley Cibber, Esq., 1758; James Collins and J. Renn were other tradesmen who sold books in this place.

Early in the reign of George III. the traders were ousted from Westminster Hall, but perhaps it was not until 1834 that the last traces of their existence here were swept away. 'The interior of Westminster Hall,' says the *Gentleman's Magazine* (September, 1834), 'which has so long remained in a dirty and mutilated state, is to be cleaned and repaired.'

CHAPTER VIII.

JACOB TONSON.

JACOB TONSON is a clear and distinct figure in the annals of English literature. There is, perhaps, no name recorded in literary history of one who contributed so little directly, and yet is so inseparably connected with certain and important parts of that history, than the subject of the present chapter. Appearing on the scene at a time when the fast developing business of publishing needed men with more judgment and discretion than the then drunken and ignorant printer, Tonson has, by sheer industry and good common sense, left a name and fame far greater and perhaps more honourable than any of his bookselling contemporaries. Basil Kennett wrote in September, 1696, "'Twill be as impossible to think of Virgil without Mr. Dryden, as of either without Mr. Tonson,' and that prognostication has to a great extent been fulfilled. It is a common thing to refer in disparaging terms to Tonson, who is described, in particular, in Mr. Hamilton's 'Poets Laureate,' as 'of a coarse and vulgar disposition, and treated authors with but little courtsey ' (p. 98). This is but one instance of a large number that could be quoted in support of a proposition which is not only absurd, but is absolutely a mis-statement of facts, as will be shewn in the course of this biography. One of the commonest of 'literary anecdotes' is concerning Dryden's quarrel with Tonson, but there are no records to justify such a term. That there were bickerings it is not denied, but what of them? Johnson ('Lives of the Poets:' Dryden) said, referring to the earlier part of Tonson's career, 'the general conduct of traders was much less liberal in those times than in our own; their views were narrower, and their manners grosser. To the mercantile ruggedness of that race, the delicacy [sic] of the poet was sometimes exposed.' In regard to the statement with reference to delicacy: had Dryden possessed much of this most useful element in a general way, it is passing strange that it should only have manifested itself when transacting business with Tonson. Delicacy was anything but a characteristic failing among literary men of Dryden's time. The relative charge of grossness may be circumstantially true, but as Jacob was in such constant association with many of the highest men of the period, he could not have been much more gross in his manners than his 'betters.' Count Cavours were indeed few then, while purity and extreme delicacy were charges never preferred against the members of the boisterous, devil-may-care Kit Cat Club. In spite of their occasional bickerings, Dryden seems to have had very considerable confidence in his bookseller, with whom his rents are to be left, and through whom messages are sent to his wife when the poet is absent.

Jacob Tonson was the son of a barber-surgeon of

that name who resided and carried on business in Holborn, and who died in 1668. Jacob was born probably in the year 1656, being fourteen years of age when he was apprenticed, on June 5, 1670, to Thomas Bassett,[1] a bookseller. The Great Fire of London, which was really an ill wind that subsequently blew a great deal of good to printing and bookselling, probably influenced the elder Jacob in apprenticing his two sons, Richard and Jacob, to the latter trade. Beside these two, it may be mentioned, there were three sisters, and to each of these five children their father bequeathed a legacy of a hundred pounds when the age of twenty-one was attained, Jacob Tonson was admitted a freeman of the Company of Stationers, December, 20, 1677, and, according to John Nichols, commenced business, 'as his brother Richard had done the year before.'

Scarcely anything is known of Richard. The brothers seem to have had as little business connection with each other as possible, and it is rare to find their names in juxtaposition. One exception is Dryden's 'The Spanish Friar,' 1681, which was 'printed for Richard and Jacob Tonson, at Gray's Inn Gate, in Grays Inn Lane, and at the 'Judge's Head' in Chancery Lane.' One of Richard's first publications must

[1] Bassett's shop probably was in Little Britain. In 1718-19 'it appears from Lintot's Account Book ('Lit. Anec.' viii. 293-5) that the latter purchased of Thomas Ballard 'a fourth of a half of the several shares of all the copies formerly belonging to Mr. Thos. Bassett, deceased (except his Law copies), 'in all 133 books.' According to another entry, Lintot bought of George Conyers 'a fourth share of the several Law copies and trials belonging to Mr. T. Bassett, deceased,' &c., in all 109 books.

have been Charles D'Avenant's 'Circe,' which was published in 1667, a second edition of this tragedy was issued in 1685, also by Richard; but the third edition was printed for Jacob Tonson in 1703. In 1677, Richard entered into a contract with another bookseller, Benjamin Shirley, to bear a portion of the expense in publishing 'The Life of the Valiant and Learned Sir Walter Raleigh,' an octavo of 243 pages; and what seems to have been an abridgment of this appeared ten years later, purporting to be 'the third edition,' in which his name still figures on the titlepage. Richard also sold in 1678 Rymer's 'Tragedies of the Last Age,' a work which received so much attention at the hands of Dryden; and Sedley's 'Antony and Cleopatra' (1677), Otway's 'Cleopatra,' S. Pordage's 'Siege of Babylon' (1678),' The Art of Making Love,' &c., were issued with Richard Tonson's name as bookseller. Although he published several other books, he took but a subordinate part in his calling. We do not know the date of his death; and in the absence of absolute proof it is fair to conjecture that his shop in Gray's Inn Gate was taken about 1698 or 1699 by his brother Jacob.

Jacob's *début* in trade circles seems to have been characteristically careful; and for the first year or two he contented himself with being simply the retailer of plays, books, and the like, issued by his more opulent and more experienced *confrères*. With a hundred pounds as capital, and a shop under the sign of The Judge's Head, in Chancery Lane, close to the corner of Fleet Street, Jacob could not afford to make great speculations. He cultivated the habits of prudence and patience, and was at length rewarded by securing the copy of Dryden's 'Troilus and Cressida,' one of the many attempts at adapting or improving Shakespeare, of which Dryden himself never thought much, and which was probably played at Dorset Gardens about April, 1679. The play itself was preceded by a discourse on the grounds of criticism in tragedy, to which, Dr. Johnson suspects, Rymer's book had given occasion. Dryden demanded twenty pounds for the copyright, but prudent Jacob hesitated to give this sum for even a play of the great Mr. Dryden, and consequently shared expenses and profits with Swalle, the play coming out probably late in 1679. The importance of this transaction was great, and the connection between Dryden and Tonson was only broken by the poet's death. Dryden's previous connection with Herringman has already been referred to.

Charles Knight states that in 1681 there was an indefatigable collector of the fugitive poetry, especially political, which formed the chief staple of many booksellers' shops, and the most vendible commodity of the noisy hawkers. Mr. Narcissus Luttrell recorded —according to his custom of marking on each sheet and half-sheet of the 'Sibylline Leaves' the day he received it—that on the 17th of November he received a copy of the first part of 'Absalom and Achitophel,' 'from his friend Jacob Tonson.' The bookseller must have made a large sum out of this poem, for, being issued at 2*d.*, its popularity and sale were immense.

Perhaps nothing so important had as yet transpired to bring Tonson into notoriety as the first volume of the *Miscellany*, which was issued in 1684. For some time previous the poet and the bookseller had been on excellent terms; for the former, in acknowledging a present of two melons from the latter, and speaking of the new project for issuing the famous *Miscellany*, observes: 'Since we are to have nothing but new, I am resolved we will have nothing but good, whomever we displease.' This is an excerpt from a letter dated September, 1684, and the first volume came out shortly afterwards. The project was so entirely successful that imitators were soon in the field, and, among these one of the earliest was Herringman's, or was, at least, issued in his name. Dryden refers to this publication in one of his letters, and states that most of the pieces therein given have been printed before. Nothing of the kind had, as Malone points out, been attempted for many years. The work was purported to be the production of the 'most eminent hands.'

The most celebrated imitation was, of course, the Pope-Lintot one. Writing to Wycherley, May 20, 1709, Pope observes: 'This modern custom of appearing in miscellanies is very useful to the poets, who, like other thieves, escape by getting into a crowd, and herd together like other banditti, safe only in their multitude.' He further quotes 'a good description of these kind of collections' from Strada. In the same letter he remarks: 'I can be content with a bare saving game, without being thought an eminent hand (with which title [2] Jacob has graciously dignified

[2] Some editions read, 'which *little* Jacob,' but we are inclined to think the word in this context to be the correct one. Pope, in this case, was speaking of the 6th vol. of Tonson's *Miscellany*.

his adventurers and volunteers in poetry). Jacob creates poets, as kings sometimes do knights, not for their honour, but for their money.' 'You will make Jacob's Ladder raise you to immortality,' observes Wycherley, in his reply to Pope.

The second volume of the *Miscellany* was issued in 1685, and the third in 1693. Tonson had now, as Knight remarks, 'become a sharp tradesman.' So far as we know, only one of Tonson's letters has been preserved, and as this is valuable and curious in many respects, it is here given. As will be seen, it was written prior to the publication of the third *Miscellany*, and probably late in 1692. It is exceedingly characteristic :—

'You may please, sir, to remember that upon my first proposal about the third *Miscellany*, I offered fifty pounds, and talked of several authors, without naming Ovid. You asked if it should not be guineas, and said I should not repent it; upon which I immediately complied, and left it wholly to you what, and for the quantity too: and I declare it was the farthest in the world from my thoughts that by leaving it to you I should have the loss. Thus the case stood, when you went into Essex. After I came out of Northamptonshire I wrote to you, and received a letter dated Monday, Oct. 3, '92, from which letter I now write word for word what follows : " I am translating about 600 lines, or somewhat less, of the first book of the Metamorphoses. If I cannot get my price, which shall be twenty guineas, I will translate the whole book, which coming out before the whole translation will spoil Tate's undertakings. 'Tis one of the best I have ever made, and very pleasant. This, with Hero and Leander, and the piece of Homer (or, if it be not enough, I will add more), will make a good part of a Miscellany."

'Those, sir, are your very words, and the only ones in that letter relating to that affair; and the Monday following you came to town.—After your arrival you showed Mr. Motteaux what you had done (which he told me was to the end of the story of Daphnis) and demanded, as you mentioned in your letter, twenty guineas, which that bookseller refused. Now, sir, I the rather believe there was just so much done, by reason the number of lines you mention in your letter agrees with the quantity of lines that so much of the first book makes; which upon counting the Ovid I find to be in the Latin 566, in the English 759; and the bookseller told me there was no more demanded of him for it.—Now, sir, what I entreat you would please to consider of is this: that it is reasonable for me to expect at least as much favour from you as a strange bookseller, and I will never believe that it can be in your nature to use me the worse for leaving it to you; and if the matter of fact as I state it be true (and upon my word what I mention I can show you in your letters) then pray, sir, consider how much dearer I pay than you offered it to the other bookseller; for he might have had to the end of the story of Daphnis for twenty guineas, which is in your translation, 759 lines; and then suppose twenty guineas more for the same number, 759 lines; that makes for forty guineas 1518 lines; and all that I have for fifty guineas are but 1446, so that, if I have no more, I pay ten guineas above forty, and have seventy-two lines less for fifty, in proportion, than the other bookseller should have had for forty, at the rate you offered him the first part. This is, sir, what I shall take as a great favour if you please to think of. I had intentions of letting you know this before; but till I had paid the money, I would not ask to see the book [which he acknowledges to have received from Dryden in an earlier part of this same letter, with which it is returned] nor count the lines, lest it should look like a design of not keeping my word. When you have looked over the rest of what you have already translated, I desire you would send it; and I own that if you don't think fit to add something more, I must submit: 'tis wholly at your choice, and I left it entirely to you; but I believe you can't imagine I expected so little; for you were pleased to use me much kindlier in Juvenal, which is not reckoned so easy to translate as Ovid. Sir, I humbly beg your pardon for this long letter, and upon my word I had rather have your good-will than any man's alive; and whatever you are pleased to do, will always acknowledge myself, Sir, your most humble obedient Servant, Jacob Tonson.'

A few extracts from this letter are common to every 'general reader,' and are often levelled against Tonson himself, as proving his mercenary qualities. It is simply a business letter, one that any shrewd man, with an eye to 'No. 1' might write. It would have been

---

[3] In the 'Sullen Lovers' (1668) of Shadwell one of the characters complains that his bookseller has refused him twelve-pence a line, when the intrinsic worth of some verses is at least worth ten shillings, and all can be proved to be worth three shillings 'to the veriest Jew in Christendom.'

surprising indeed if Tonson had allowed a rival tradesman to out-distance himself in a bargain without uttering a word of protest; especially when that bargain was one spontaneously offered by the poet himself. Dryden admits Tonson's soft impeachment, when he wrote, on August 30, 1693 : 'I am much ashamed for myself, that I am so much behind-hand with you in kindness. Above all things I am sensible of your good-nature, in bearing me company to this place [somewhere in Northamptonshire], wherein, besides the cost, you must needs neglect your own business; but I will endeavour to make you some amends, and therefore I desire you to command me something for your service.' In 1689 all Dryden's emoluments from the Government were taken away, so that he could hardly afford to be very independent.

The publication of Dryden's translation of Virgil was perhaps the most important incident in Tonson's career. This arduous task was commenced in 1694, or late in 1693, and was actually finished by the close of 1696, although, upon his own admission to Tonson, he considered the task as one which would require seven years to translate 'exactly.' Tonson issued the translation of Virgil in July, 1697. It was of course published by subscription, although its success was from the first almost a foregone conclusion. A hundred and two five-guinea subscribers' had each his arms printed at the foot of the 102 plates; whilst the two-guinea subscribers figured in the list of names only. The proportion in which the subscriptions were divided between Dryden and Tonson are not now known; Malone thinks the poet had 50*l.* for each book of the Æneid, a sum which some biographers conjecture to have been paid for every two books. Pope has stated that 'Dryden cleared every way about 1200*l.* by his Virgil' (Spence: Singer's Ed., p. 198). 'Virgil was one of the first books that had anything of a subscription, (and even that was a good deal on account of the prints, which were from Ogilby's plates touched up ')[4] (*ibid.*). There are several most interesting letters to Tonson from the poet during the progress of his great work. Arranging for a Coffee-house or tavern—the almost invariable rendezvous for such transactions—Dryden writes: ' Be ready with the price of paper, and of the books. No matter for any dinner; for that is a charge to you, and I care not for it. Mr. Congreve may be with us, as a common friend.' Much of the translating is done in the country,—hence, the necessity for epistolary communication. ' Some kind of intercourse,' writes Dryden, October 29, 1695, ' must be carried on betwixt us, while I am translating Virgil. Therefore I give you notice, that I have done the seventh Eneid in the country [i.e. at Burleigh, the seat of the fifth Earl of Exeter], and intend some few days hence to go upon the eighth: when that is finished, I expect fifty pounds in good silver; not such as I had formerly. I am not obliged to take gold, neither will I; nor stay for it beyond four-and-twenty hours after it is due. I thank you for the civility of your last letter in the country; but the thirty shillings upon every book remains with me, you always in-

[4] This refers to Virgilii Opera, per |Joh. Ogilvium edita et adornata. Lond., 1658. This work was issued in royal folio, with plates after Lombart, Faithorne, Hollar, &c.

tended I should get nothing by the second subscriptions, as I found from first to last.' Not long after this letter, Dryden writes thanking Tonson for his kindnesses, 'being very sensible that I have not hitherto deserved them.' A passage from the letter to Tonson, dated February, 1695-6, further illustrates the debased character of the coinage at that period, and the general mistrust which it occasioned. ' I shall lose enough by your bill upon Mr. Knight,[5] for after having taken it all in silver, and not in half-crowns neither, but shillings and sixpences, none of the money will go; for which reason I have sent it all back again, and as the less lost will receive it in guineas at twenty-nine shillings each. 'Tis troublesome to be a loser, but it was my own fault to accept it this way.'[6]

In this same letter the writer expresses regret that Tonson 'will not allow anything towards the notes,' and, apparently growing petulant towards the end of the epistle, exclaims, ' Upon trial I find all of your

[5] 'Probably a goldsmith, and well known afterwards as the cashier of the Southsea Company.'—Malone.

[6] Dryden's complaint about bad money is frequent in his letters to Tonson, and the incident has afforded Macaulay material for some comment on the coinage of that time. There is absolutely no foundation for the legend that Tonson wanted to cheat Dryden by paying him in debased coin. In 1695, probably in April, Dryden writes : ' You know money is now very scrupulously received ; in the last which you did me the favour to change for my wife, besides the clipped money, there were at least forty shillings brass.' It has been observed by one writer that the gold and silver coinage remained in a depreciated state until the new coinage took place under the care of Charles Montague, Chancellor of the Exchequer. The value of a guinea was fluctuating and uncertain.

M

trade are sharpers, and you not more than the others; therefore I have not wholly left you. Mr. Aston does not blame you for getting as good a bargain as you could, though I could have got a hundred pounds more.'

All men of light and leading subscribed to the Virgil. It was a known secret that its dedication to King William would be a good stroke of business, and Jacob Tonson, ardent Whig as he was, was exceedingly anxious to bring about this consummation. But Dryden had had enough of political and religious somersaulting. Writing to his two sons at Rome, where they were employed in the Pope's household, under date Sept. 3, 1697, Dryden observes: 'He [Tonson] has missed of his design in the dedication, though he had prepared the book for it, for in every figure of Eneas he has caused him to be drawn like King William, with a hooked nose.' Malone transcribed from the Harleian MSS. two verses occasioned by this circumstance :—

' TO BE PUBLISHED IN THE NEXT EDITION OF DRYDEN'S
VIRGIL.

'Old Jacob by deep judgment sway'd,
  To please the wise beholders,
Has placed old Nassau's hook-nosed head
  On poor Æneas' shoulders.

'To make the parallel hold tack,
  Methinks there's little lacking;
One took his father pick-a-pack,
  And t'other sent his packing.'

The principal plays and poems which Tonson published for Dryden are : 'Troilus and Cressida' (1679),

'Spanish Fryer' (1681, with R. Taylor), 'Threnodia' (1685), 'King Arthur' (1691), 'Alexander's Feast' (1697). On January 12, 1686-7, 'Mr. Jacob Tonson enters this caveat—that no person enter the poem called The Hind and ye Panther.' Tonson also published that unhappy attempt, 'Britannia Rediviva" (1688). During the last ten or dozen years of the seventeenth century, Tonson acted as 'sponsor' for a large number of publications, and partly shared, in addition, the responsibility of much other literature than that on the imprint of which his name alone appeared. He had become a great figure in the publishing line, and few poets—except, perhaps, the ultra-Tories—were there whose productions were not issued more or less under the direction of Jacob. In 1696 we find Dryden negotiating with Tonson for the publication of his son's play; and at about the same period Tonson issued Ch. Hopkins' 'Boadicea' (1697) and 'Friendship Improved' (1700). He had for several years partly published Congreve's and Otway's plays. Mr. John Dennis, 'the renowned critick,' and Sir Richard Steele (the latter at that time plain Mr.) had each entrusted some work to Jacob, who, in addition to sundry poetical effusions, could also supply his customers with Jeremy Collier's translation of Tully's 'Five Books of Morals; or, the Final End of Man;' with 'The Art of Making Love,' which went through two or three editions; and with Dr. Lister's account of his 'Journey to Paris in 1658.' Tate's[7] 'Monumental Poem,' in memory of Sir

[7] Swift, with exquisite irony, says, 'Nahum Tate, who is ready to take oath that he has caused many reams of verse to be

G. Treby, once Chief Justice of H.M.'s Court of Common Pleas, also bore Jacob's name, as did the 'Reports' of Sir Peyton Ventris; the opera 'Arsinoe,' by Clayton; and a great many others. Mr. Robert Bell, in his excellent edition of Dryden's poems, points out that, according to an entry in the Stationers' books, made by Tonson, in April, 1686, Dryden had completed, by James the Second's command, a translation of Varilla's 'History of Heresies;' but its publication was suppressed, in consequence of the credit of its author being destroyed by the appearance of Burnet's 'Reflections.' Witty Mr. Prior, too, was reckoned among Jacob's authors;[8] and in September, 1695, Prior, writing from Hague, sends the bookseller the 'Ode sur la Prise de Namur, par les armes du Roy, l'année 1692. Par Monsieur Boileau Despreaux,' which, with the English version, 'An English Ballad, on the Taking of Namur by the King of Great Britain, 1695,' appears in most collections of Prior's poems. Basil Kennett, brother of the more famous White Kennett, Bishop of Peterboro', writes Tonson, some time during 1696, in this strain: 'I

published, whereof both himself and his bookseller (if lawfully required) can still produce authentic copies, and therefore wonders why the world is pleased to make such a secret of it.'

[8] Dryden was 'Jacob's poet' just as much as Pope was 'Lintot's poet,' and Byron, Murray's. Byron relates that Murray was congratulated by a brother publisher upon having such a poet as himself. 'As if,' says the noble writer, 'one were a packhorse, or ass, or anything that was his,' or, as Mr. Packwood, who replied to some inquiry after 'Odes and Razors,' exclaimed, 'Lord, sir, we keeps a poet.' '"Childe Harold" and "Cookeries" is much wanted,' an Edinburgh bookseller wrote Murray.

wish I could contribute anything to fill up an odd page; but have no copy that would deserve the meanest place in a collection of your making. However, if you continue your commands, rather than disobey them, I will venture on some little attempt or other, not to serve you, but to show my unfitness for your service.'

Either in 1697 or 1698 Jacob Tonson removed his sphere of operations from the Judge's Head[9] to Gray's Inn Gate. The reason of this removal may or may not have been from the most common of causes —'more commodious premises.' We have already intimated the possibility that Jacob succeeded to the business his brother Richard had carried on at Gray's Inn Gate. So far, we have not been able to trace Richard's name as bookseller later than about 1690; and even at this date his publications are very few, and include nothing of any importance. Jacob remained at Gray's Inn Gate for twelve or thirteen years.

Tonson's name will for ever be associated with the production of Milton's 'Paradise Lost,' and also with Shakespeare's works, as well as Dryden's. Sir Godfrey Kneller's portrait of Tonson, with a folio copy of 'Paradise Lost' in his hands, is probably well known. Dryden, with the author's permission, it is said, turned Milton's story into an opera, entitled 'The State of Innocence,' which was published in 1674, the year in which Milton died. Simmons did not long retain the sole ownership of Milton's poem,

[9] John Bayley was living at this address in 1708, when he issued C. Goring's 'Irene,' and S. Billingsley in or about 1730.

but transferred his entire interest to Brabazon Aylmer, another bookseller, for 25*l*. Aylmer had not long enjoyed this copyright before he offered it to Tonson. Jacob hesitated much before closing any agreement, even after Dryden had told him that 'Paradise Lost' was one of the greatest poems ever produced in this or any other country. The times 'were not propitious to blank verse upon a sacred subject,' and Jacob was not at all certain about the proposed speculation turning up trumps. However, on August 17, 1683, he purchased half of the copyright, and the remaining half on March 24, 1690, Aylmer making a fairly good bargain out of the transaction. But four or five years passed before Tonson took steps to realize this outlay, and, after issuing proposals for bringing out the poem by subscription, the fourth edition of 'Paradise Lost' appeared in 1688, in folio, with a portrait by White, illustrations, and a list of more than 500 subscribers, including most of the eminent men of the day. Dryden was among them, and wrote the following lines, which were printed by way of motto under the portrait of the poet:—

> 'Three poets in three distant ages born,
> Greece, Italy, England did adorn,
> The first in loftiness of mind surpassed;
> The next in majesty; in both the last.
> The force of nature could no further go;
> To make a third she joined the former two.'

Tonson soon discovered the great value of the literary property which he had acquired. The fifth, or Tonson's second, edition appeared also in a large folio in 1692, and a sixth in 1695. The last is remarkable from the fact that it contains the first, and also one of the best, commentary on the poem, which was made by a Scotch schoolmaster, then resident in London, named Patrick Hume. The famous essays of Addison's, in the *Spectator*, also acted as a considerable impetus in the sale of this work, although its greatness was an acknowledged fact long before their appearance. Tonson himself had published at least six editions—making nine in all—before Addison called the attention of his readers to this remarkable poem. Tonson probably made many thousands of pounds out of 'Paradise Lost,' which, indeed, according to Spence (Singer's Ed., p. 261), Jacob verbally admitted having made more out of than any other poem. For more than half a century the Tonsons held undisputed and exclusive right in Milton's poems; and although the tacit acknowledgment held good until 1750, when other publishers also issued editions of Milton's poems, it was not until 1767 that the connection between Milton and the Tonsons finally ceased. In that year, Jacob Tonson, *tertius*, the grandnephew of the first bookselling Jacob, and the last bookseller of the name, died.

The last work of any note which Tonson published for Dryden was 'The Fables,' which the poet finished in December, 1699. Dr. Johnson gives the following agreement made respecting this last work :—

'I do hereby promise to pay John Dryden, Esq., on order, on the 25th of March, 1699, the sum of two hundred and fifty guineas, in consideration of ten thousand verses, which the said John Dryden, Esq., is to deliver to me, Jacob Tonson, when finished, whereof seven thousand five hundred verses, more or less, are already in the said Jacob Tonson's possession. And I do hereby promise, and engage myself, to make up the said sum of two hundred and fifty guineas, three hundred pounds sterling, to the said John Dryden, Esq., his executors, administrators, or assigns, at the beginning of the second impression of the said ten thousand verses.

'In witness whereof I have hereunto set my hand and seal, this 20th day of March, 169⅞.

'JACOB TONSON.

'Sealed and delivered, being first duly stampt, pursuant to the Act of Parliament for that purpose, in the presence of
'BEN. PORTLOCK,
'WILL. CONGREVE.'

Dr. Johnson also gives Dryden's receipt, dated March 24, 1698, the witness to which was Charles Dryden. The doctor also points out that the contract manifestly relates to the volume of 'Fables,' 'which contains above twelve thousand verses, and for which, therefore, the payment must have been afterwards enlarged.' The work was issued in folio, and contains Dryden's remarkable song, the second St. Cecilia Ode, commonly known as 'Alexander's Feast.'

Dryden died in May, 1700. The *Post-boy* of April 30, announced that 'John Dryden, Esq., the famous poet, lies a-dying,' and according to Mr. Saintsbury, 'at three o'clock the next morning he died very quietly and peacefully.' Tonson's first and only great patron had been connected with him for a period of over twenty years.

But apart from his close association with the works of Dryden, Milton, and Shakespeare, Jacob Tonson's immortality is assured through his connection with the famous Kit-Cat Club. This club was formed about 1688 by the leading Whigs of the day, and was held in Shire Lane, now Lower Serle's Place, the chief object of the members being to ensure the Protestant succession to William the Third. The title was derived from the cognomen of Christopher Cat, a pastry-cook, whose mutton pies were considered very excellent, and in which commodity, it seems the Kit-Cats largely indulged. The toasts, however, were said to be in honour of old cats and young kits. Ward, the scurrilous author of a 'Secret History of Clubs' (1709), states that the club was founded by 'an amphibious mortal, chief merchant to the Muses,' by which he refers of course, to Jacob Tonson, whom he also describes as waiting hopefully in his shop for the coming of some more of 'his new profitable chaps, who, having more wit than experience, put but a slender value as yet upon their maiden performances.' Tonson, it seems, not satisfied with standing the usual 'whet' to his authors, willingly provides pastry to eat therewith; still not being contented, he proposes a weekly meeting, where not only the feast could be discussed, but prospective poems, and other literary merchandise also. This 'generous proposal was very readily agreed to by the whole poetic class, and the cook's name being Christopher, for brevity called Kit, and his sign the 'Cat and Fiddle,' they very merrily derived a quaint denomination from puss and her master, and from thence called themselves the Kit-Cat Club. Tonson was secretary to the club, which migrated from Shire Lane to the 'Fountain Tavern,' in the Strand, and from thence, at the beginning of the eighteenth century, to a small house adjoining the mansion of Barnes Elms, near Barnes; Count Heidegger, the founder of Italian Operas, resided in the mansion. Charles Knight states that 'George the Second was here entertained with displays of fireworks and illuminated lamps, but the 'boets and bainters,' who were not in good odour with the Hanoverian dynasty, conferred a lustre upon Barnes Elms which did not go out so quickly as Heidegger's fireworks.' Sir Richard Phillips, in 'A Morning's Walk from London to Kew' (1817) describes the appearance at that time of the famous house in which the Kit-Cats formerly revelled. Phillips says, 'I found the Kit-Cat club-room nearly as it existed in the days of its glory. It is eighteen feet high, and forty feet long by twenty feet wide. The mouldings and ornaments were in the most superb fashion of its age, but the whole was falling to pieces, from the effects of the dry-rot. My attention was chiefly attracted by the faded cloth-hanging of the room, whose red colour once set off the famous portraits of the club that hung around it. Their marks and sizes were still visible, and their numbers and names remained as written in chalk, for the guidance of the hangers. Thus was I, as it were, by these still legible names, brought into personal contact with Addison, Steele and Congreve and Garth and Dryden,[1] and with many *hereditary* nobles, remembered only because they were patrons of those *natural* nobles.' The portraits of the members of the Kit-Cat were painted by Kneller, and are still in the possesssion of the descendant of the Tonson family, residing at Bayfordbury, Hertfordshire. In addition to those mentioned by Phillips, the others of the more famous painted by Kneller, and known by name at least, even to the present generation, are, Robert Walpole, William Pulteney, Vanbrugh, Congreve, Arthur Mainwaring, Francis Lord Godolphin, &c. The number of portraits is forty-two or forty-three. They are on canvas somewhat smaller than a three-quarters, but more than a half-length; a size which, according to Nichols, has ever since been denominated as Kit-Cat from this circumstance. The canvas is sufficiently long enough to admit a hand— the size being 36 in. long by 28 in. wide. A splendid volume under the title 'Kit-Cat Club,' done from the original paintings of Sir Godfrey Kneller, by Mr. Faber, sold by J. Tonson in the Strand, and F. Faber at the 'Golden Head, in Bloomsbury Square,' was published in 1735; containing an engraved title-page and dedication, and 43 portraits, beginning with Sir Godfrey Kneller, and ending with Mr. Tonson, who is represented in a gown and cap, holding in his right hand a volume lettered

---

[1] It is to be very much doubted whether Dryden ever fraternized with the Kit-Cats, Tory as he was. His portrait, moreover, does not appear among the engraved series.

'Paradise Lost.' The portraits were re-engraved in 1821, and were issued with illustrative text under the title of ' Memoirs of the Celebrated Persons composing the Kit-Cat Club,' a production which the *Quarterly Review* stigmatizes as 'one of the most blundering pieces of patchwork that the scissors of a hackney editor ever produced.'

The Kit-Cats came in for the usual share of abuse from the Tories, and Tonson in particular was singled out as the chief object of attack. One of these, 'Faction Displayed,'[2] 1704, is remarkable in embodying a triplet which had been written by Dryden to Tonson, when the former had sent to the latter for some money, which was refused. Dryden, it is said by Malone, wrote the following and sent them to Tonson with the message : ' Tell the dog that he who wrote these lines can write more :'—

> 'With leering look, bull-fac'd and freckled fair,
> With two left-legs, and Judas-coloured hair,
> With frowzy pores that taint the ambient air.'

The lines were not, of course, intended by Dryden to appear in print. In 'Faction Displayed,' the author of which is not known for certain, but was presumably William Shippen, further allusion to Tonson is made under the thin disguise of Bibliopolo, and following Dryden's triplet come these lines (Tonson appears on the scene just as the assembly of faction's 'darling votaries' is about to adjourn) :—

> 'Sweating and puffing for awhile he stood,
> And then broke forth in this insulting mood ;

---

[2] See Malone's Dryden, i. pt. i. iii.; *Notes and Queries*, 6th, S. X., 514, and XI. 37.

" I am the touchstone of all modern wit ;
Without my stamp in vain your poets write ;
Those only purchase ever-living fame,
That in my Miscellany plant their name.
Nor therefore think that I can bring no aid,
Because I follow a mechanic trade :—
I'll print your pamphlets, and your humours spread.
I am the founder of your lov'd Kit-Cat,
A club that gave direction to your state ;
'Twas there we first instructed all our youth,
To talk profane, and laugh at sacred truth :
We taught them how to toast, and rhyme and bite,
To sleep away the day, and drink away the night."
Some this fantastic speech approv'd, some sneer'd,
The wight grew choleric, and disappear'd.'

Another satire on the society, entitled 'The Kit-Cats : a poem,' is attributed to Sir Richard Blackmore. In this poem Tonson is frequently referred to as *Bocai*, a transposition of his Christian name. It is a lengthy, tedious piece, from which a couple of lines might be fairly applied to the poet himself,—

'More had he said, but strove in vain to keep
His falling eyelids ope, and fell down fast asleep,'

had we not known that Blackmore wrote half a dozen epics, and was not, consequently, of a very sleepy disposition. Under the circumstances, Jacob was naturally open to all sorts of attacks, insinuations and libels, even when the charges had no foundation in fact. Be that as it may, Jacob was an indispensable member of the society. When in Paris in 1703, the 'proud' Duke of Somerset writes him, 'Our club is dissolved till you revive it again, which we are impatient of.' Vanbrugh, also, is anxious for Tonson's

return, and on June 15, 1703, writes in this strain:
'The Kitt-Catt wants you, much more than you ever
can do them. Those who are in town are in great
desire of waiting on you at Barnes-elms; not that they
have finished their pictures neither; tho', to excuse
them (as well as myself), Sir Godfrey has been most
in fault. The fool has got a country house near Hampton Court, and is so busy about fitting it up (to receive
nobody), that there's no getting him to work.' Singer
in his edition of 'Spence's Anecdotes,' quotes a characteristic anecdote from 'Richardsoniana' (1776), said to
have been derived from Pope. Old Jacob Tonson got
a great many fine pictures, and two of himself, from
Kneller, by a judicious use of 'soft soap.' Sir
Godfrey was very covetous, but then he was very vain,
and a great glutton ; so he played these passions
against the other ; besides telling him he was the
greatest master that ever was, sending him every now
and then, a haunch of venison, and dozens of excellent
claret. 'O my G——, man' (said he once to Vander
Gutcht), 'this old Jacob loves me, he sends me good
things; the venison was fat! Old Geekie, the
surgeon, got several fine pictures of him too, and an
excellent one of himself ; but then his praises were as
fat as Jacob's venison ; neither could be too fat for
Sir Godfrey.'

Jacob's rise in the world, among the big-wigs, was
not without its drawbacks, if we may believe Nicholas
Rowe's[3] inscription, published in 1714, in the form of
a dialogue between Congreve and Tonson :—

[3] Tonson had published Rowe's 'Fair Penitent' in 1703, and
his 'Ulysses' in 1706.

'While, in your days of reputation,
You for blue garters had not such a passion,
While yet you did not live, as now your trade is,
To drink with noble lords, and toast their ladies,
Thou, Jacob Tonson, were to my conceiving
The cheerfullest, best, honest fellow living.'

In the arrangement of the Kit-Cat portraits Tonson and Vanbrugh appear side by side, a circumstance which probably causes Rowe to put the following words into the mouth of the bookseller:—

'I'm in with Captain Vanbrugh at the present,
A most sweet-natured gentleman and pleasant ;
He writes you comedies, draws schemes, and models,
And builds duke's houses upon very odd hills.'

In 1703 Jacob Tonson made a journey to Holland for the purpose of purchasing suitable paper and getting engravings made for his noble edition of Cæsar's 'Commentaries,' which appeared in royal folio with 87 plates, in 1712, and under the editorial care of Dr. Samuel Clarke. This edition, which John Nichols describes as 'perhaps the most magnificent work that has been issued from the English press,' is still commercially valuable. When at Amsterdam, Jacob's letters were sometimes addressed to him at 'Mr. Morris', the English house near the Fishmarket,' and sometimes to him at 'Mr. Valcks, on the Dam, near the Stadhouse.' The stay seems to have lasted two or three months. The ostensible object of his journey was much doubted by the opposite political party, as will be seen by the letter addressed to Jacob by Vanbrugh, dated June 15, 1703, from which an extract has already been quoted: 'The Tory's (even the wisest of them) have been very grave upon your going to Holland ; they often say (with a nod) that Cæsar's 'Commentaries' might have been carried through without a voyage to Holland ; there were meanings in that subscription, and list of names may serve for farther engagements than paying three guineas a piece for a book ; in short I could win a hundred pounds if I were sure you had not made a trip to Holland, which you may possibly hear sworn when you arrive home again ; so I'd advise you to bring a very exact journal, well attested.' Jacob Tonson, therefore, was obviously a man of considerable note in the political as well as the literary world.

Tonson is said to have removed from Gray's Inn Gate to 'Shakespeare's Head,' over against Catherine Street, in the Strand, about the year 1712. The third great epoch in Tonson's career was undoubtedly the projecting of an edition of Shakespeare, edited by N. Rowe in 1709-10, with Charles Gildon's critical remarks. The edition was in 7 vols. octavo, and was the first of the great dramatist issued with illustrations, which, as Dibdin truly remarks, were sufficiently characteristic: *e.g.*, that to Hamlet in the closet scene with the Queen, who is dressed like Queen Anne. In 1714 a 12mo edition in 9 vols. was issued, 'and then 'expired without a struggle,' says Dibdin in his 'Library Companion.'

The following sums, 'taken from the books of the late Mr. Tonson,' were paid for Shakespearian editorial work at various times:—To Rowe, 36*l*. 10*s*.; Hughes (for correcting the press and making an index to Mr. Rowe's 12mo edition), 28*l*. 7*s*.; Pope,

217*l*. 12*s*.; Fenton (for assisting Pope, and correcting for the press), 30*l*. 14*s*.; Gay (also for similar assistance), 35*l*. 17*s*. 6*d*.; Whalley (for correcting proofs of Pope's 12mo edition), 12*l*.; Theobald, 652*l*. 10*s*.; Warburton, 500*l*.; Johnson, for two editions, 475*l*.; Capell, 300*l*. Nearly a quarter of a century had passed since the fourth folio appeared, and a popular edition was a safe speculation. We have scarcely any facts concerning the number of copies printed. Of Pope's in six volumes only 750 copies were worked off, the subscription price being six guineas. Theobald's was larger; the number of volumes issued is stated to be 12,860, or rather less than 2000 copies.

Naturally, Addison's 'Cato' bore Jacob Tonson's imprint; for the copyright of which 107*l*. 10*s*. was paid, April 7, 1713. Spence records a statement of Pope's that Tonson did not like Addison. ' He had a quarrel with him, and after quitting the Secretaryship, used frequently to say of him, ' One day or other, you'll see that man a bishop! I'm sure he looks that way; and indeed, I ever thought him a priest in his heart.'

Two or three very interesting letters from Addison to Tonson were first printed in the *Gents. Mag.* for 1834, concerning an edition of a translation of Ovid's ' Metamorphoses,' which was produced in 1717, and held the field until the appearance of Beloe's edition in 1791. As an instance of the esteem in which Tonson was held, it is only necessary to point out that Addison, in endeavouring to secure the help of Dr. Haines in the Ovid, was informed by the doctor ' that he did not know how to deny Mr. Tonson any request that he made.' The Tonsons, also, must have made a very large sum out of the octavo editions of the *Tatler*,. the *Spectator*, and the *Guardian*, of each of which periodicals they issued numerous and large editions.

In 1719 Tonson spent some months in Paris,[4] where he gained a considerable sum by adventuring in the Mississippi Scheme. Good-fortune, like ill-luck, rarely comes singly, for, as some recompense for his attachment to the Whigs, and probably through the influence of the Duke of Newcastle and Secretary Craggs, Tonson secured a grant to himself, and his nephew and namesake, a son of his elder brother Richard, of the office of Stationer, Bookbinder, Bookseller, and Printer, to some of the principal public boards and great offices, for the term of forty years. In 1720 old Jacob seems to have left the entire business in the charge of his nephew, who, in 1733, obtained from Sir Robert Walpole a further grant of the employment just specified for forty years more, to commence at the expiration of the former term. This lucrative appointment was enjoyed by the Tonson family or their assigns till the month of January, 1800. But, according to Nichols ('Lit. Anec.' viii. 453), this appointment could not have been actually in the possession of the

---

[4] This fact give us an opportunity of quoting, not only two interesting examples of the 'Society news' of our forefathers, but also of illustrating the extraordinary inconsistency of statements that appeared simultaneously. 'We hear Jacob Tonson, senior, bookseller, is dead at Paris,' was a statement that appeared in *Read's Weekly Journal*, of Saturday, October 17, 1719. 'Mr. Jacob Tonson, sen., is so well recovered of his illness at Paris, that his nephew, Mr. Jacob Tonson, jr., will return with the next pacquet,' was one of the items which was published in *The Orphan Revived* of the same date as the previous extract !

Tonson family for very long after it was first acquired. Because we are told, at the reference just given, that John Mount and Thomas Sage 'purchased the remaining term in old Jacob Tonson's Patent for supplying many of the public offices (the Stamp-office among the rest), with stationery, &c., upon the death of the younger Jacob Tonson, the other brother Richard not choosing to continue the business.'

The fall of the Whig ministry in the latter part of 1710 was necessarily the occasion for much 'shuffling' of cards with respect to Governmental appointments, and its effect upon Tonson, though not quite serious, may be gathered from Swift's 'Journal to Stella,' of July 2, 1711: "Mr. Addison and I have at last met again. I dined with him and Steele to-day, at young Jacob Tonson's. The two Jacobs think it is I who have made the Secretary take from them the printing of the *Gazette*, which they are going to lose, and Ben Tooke and another are to have it. Jacob came to me t'other day to make his court; but I told him it was too late, and that it was not my doing. I reckon they will lose it in a week or two.' Steele was the *Gazette* writer, and purposely kept it 'very weak and very insipid.' Jacob's connection with the *Gazette* was as (nominally) the printer, he being, as appears from his Will, in partnership with John Watts.

Tonson's name was taken as a guarantee by the book-buying public. He seems to have done best, however, with his republications. In 1702, a couple of years after the poet's death, he issued the 'Works of the late famous Mr. Dryden,' in 4 vols. folio, the sale of which was considerable. The 'new editions' which he published in the subsequent twenty years were numerous. In 1702, also, he had issued Cowley's 'Works.' One of the latest editions of Dryden was the six-volumed one in 12mo, that came out in 1725. This contained the Dramatic works only; the illustrations are after Gravelot, and the dedication to the then Lord Chamberlain, the Duke of Newcastle, is from Congreve's pen. This particular edition is curious, inasmuch as, although bearing Tonson's general imprint, several of the plays have on their title-pages the names of the booksellers in whom the copyright was at that time vested. M. Poulson occurs on the 'Kind Keeper,' and on 'Œdipus;' G. Strahan and B. Motte on 'Don Sebastian;' and a small dialogue at the end of the last volume bears Motte's name. Speaking of Denham, Dibdin says, 'The neatest edition of his works, with which I am acquainted, is that of Tonson, of 1719; and there be those who love to possess the edition of Donne's poems, of the same date, and by the same printer.' Tonson issued the poems of Waller in 1711, with illustrations, and of this edition, Dibdin—no partial judge—speaks in high praise. Among other important works that came from the Tonsons, was Tasso's 'Jerusalem Delivered' (1724), in two quarto volumes, and an edition of Beaumont and Fletcher in ten volumes, which is still held in high esteem. In 1734-5, 'J. Tonson, and the rest of the proprietors,' published an edition of the plays—six in number—attributed to Shakespeare. 'The History of Sir John Oldcastle' contains the following curious 'advertisement: '—' J. Tonson, and the other proprietors of the copies of Shakespeare's plays, designing to finish their edition now publishing, with all speed give notice, that with the last play they will deliver *gratis* general titles to each volume of the whole work, so that each play may be bound in its proper place,' &c., &c. 'N.B. Whereas one R. Walker has proposed to pirate all Shakespear's plays, but through ignorance of what plays are Shakespear's, did in several advertisements propose to print 'Œdipus King of Thebes' as one of Shakespear's plays; and has since printed Tate's 'King Lear' instead of Shakespear's, and in that and Hamlet has omitted one half of the genuine edition printed by J. Tonson and the other proprietors; the world will therefore judge how likely they are to have a complete collection of Shakespear's plays from the said R. Walker.' With reference to Shakespeare; it is exceedingly probable that the very last speculation into which the Tonsons' firm entered was the edition of Capell, in ' ten sprucely printed crown octavo volumes.' Indeed, it is almost a certainty that the last bookselling Tonson died before the work was actually out of the printers' hands. Capell's dedication was dated November 9, 1767, whilst Jacob Tonson the third died in March of the same year. It may be assumed, however, that his younger brother took a little interest in the business for a short time after his decease.

After a life of unwearied exertion, honest trading, and unflagging zeal, old Jacob Tonson died in 1736, having principally resided on his estate in Herefordshire since about 1720. His nephew, Jacob Tonson *secundus*, predeceased him by four months only, dying at Barnes, November 15, 1735. Nichols gives currency to the anecdote, which he strongly doubts, relating to the death-bed scene of Jacob Tonson. Jacob is reported to have said, 'I wish I had the world to begin again,' and having been asked why he expressed such a wish, replied, 'Because then I should have died worth a hundred thousand pounds, whereas now I die worth only eighty thousand pounds.' This anecdote was probably manufactured by some libellous person who, perhaps, had a grudge against the bookseller. But the same anecdote is also related of the younger Jacob Tonson, in which case, however, it is still less authentic, for he died worth at least the hundred thousand pounds which was to have consummated his earthly bliss. The Will of the younger Jacob was written by himself, and fills 27 pages. 'After having devised his estates in Herefordshire, Gloucestershire, and Worcestershire, and bequeathed no less a sum than 34,000*l.* to his three daughters and his younger son Samuel, and disposed of his patent, he mentions his uncle, old Jacob Tonson, to whom he leaves fifty guineas for mourning; but knowing his love of quiet and retirement, he says he would not burthen him with the office of executor of his Will. He, however, recommends his family to his uncle's care, and exhorts all his children to remember their duty to their superiors and inferiors, tenderly adding, " and so God bless you all ! " '

 Lingering for a moment or two over the character of old Jacob Tonson, the barber-surgeon's son, we find it to be indubitably that of a thorough tradesman, not perhaps of a hero, but certainly of a generous, hearty, and good man with a plentiful sprinkling of the worldly in his composition. From his very earliest associations, excepting the occasional bickerings of Dryden, the correspondence which have been preserved prove beyond the shadow of a doubt that Jacob was esteemed by all the great men with whom he came in contact. Congreve's letters to the old bookseller are all couched in the most friendly and amiable terms. When in France in 1719, Vanbrugh, speaking of a visit to Cleremont, writes; November 5, in this strain:—' There was much talk about you ; and I do assure you, with no small regard and affection from everybody. Mr. Spence was there, who gave us a very agreeable and friendly account of you, and joined heartily with us, in drinking round your health, and your return.' Surely this is not the language of a sycophant, whose officiousness was to be substantially rewarded ! When at Hazle, near Ledbury, in Herefordshire, in 1722, Vanbrugh writes (June 18):—' You have regaled me with the best sider I ever drank since I was born ; but if you had sent me a bit of a letter along with it, I should have thought it better still.' Indeed, nearly all letters to him contain acknowledgment of some kindness received or good office performed by Jacob. Pope himself, who ran amuck nearly every one, seems to have been on friendly if not very intimate terms with him. In 1706 Tonson endeavoured to secure the right of publishing Pope's works, and wrote :—' I remember I have formerly seen you in my shop, and am sorry I

did not improve my acquaintance with you. If you
design your poem [5] for the press, no one can be more
careful in printing it, nor no one can give greater
encouragement to it than, Sir,' &c. Pope's pastorals
were published in Tonson's *Miscellany*, 1709. Notwithstanding the fact that Pope finally went over to
Lintot, Spence records several anecdotes which cannot but lead us to conclude that the two were on
excellent terms. For example: 'Ay, Mr. Tonson,
he was *ultimus Romanorum*' (with a sigh): speaking of poor Mr. Congreve, who died a year or
two before. (Section 1728-30.) On March 20,
1730-1, Gay writes to Swift, ' Lord Oxford, Lord
Bathurst, he [Pope] and I dined together at Barnes
with old Jacob Tonson.' And yet Jacob does not
quite escape from Pope's immortal satire, which was
published only about three years previous to the
dinner of which Gay speaks. In the Dunciad, as it
now stands Lintot is charged with emulating 'left-
legged Jacob,' but before Jacob's death the reading
was either 'with steps unequal' or 'with legs expanded.' We have already seen the origin of the
epithet 'left-legged,' and it may be taken for granted
that old Tonson's gait was an awkward one. He is
also described as short and stout. *Apropos* of
Tonson's legs the following anecdote is related:—
' The figure of Charles the First by Vandyke in the
Walpole collection has a singular defect; both the
gauntlets being drawn for the right hand. When
this picture was in the Wharton collection, old
Jacob Tonson, who had remarkably ugly legs, was

[5] Tonson saw a Pastoral of Pope's in MS.

finding fault with the two gauntlets, when Lady Wharton, said; 'Mr. Tonson, why might not one man have two right hands as well as another two left legs?' This particular incident is said to have given rise to Pope's remark.

John Dunton delivers himself concerning Jacob in this manner:—' He was bookseller to the famous Dryden, and is himself a very good judge of persons and authors ; and, as there is nobody more competently qualified to give their opinion upon another, so there is none who does it with a more severe exactness, or with less partiality ; for, to do Mr. Tonson justice, he speaks his mind upon all occasions, and will flatter nobody.'

But little now remains to be said of the Tonson family. After the deaths of the uncle and his nephew, the title of 'J. and R. Tonson' was still used until up to and including the year 1767. Old Jacob died either unmarried or issueless. Seventeen days after the decease of his nephew he made his will, in which he confirmed a settlement that he had made on him, and appointed his great nephew, Jacob Tonson, the eldest son of the second Jacob, his executor and residuary legatee. This, remarks Nichols, must have been an immense accession to what he already had derived from his father, who devised all his estates in Herefordshire, Gloucestershire, and Worcestershire, in what is called strict settlement, to his sons, Jacob, Richard, and Samuel, successively ; and the whole benefit of his patent between the two elder, whom he also made his residuary legatee.

The third Jacob Tonson, to whom Johnson applies the epithet of 'amiable,' served as High Sheriff for the county of Surrey in 1750; and in 1759 paid the customary fine for being excused serving in a similar capacity for the city of London and the county of Middlesex, his father and great-uncle both having paid the same fine in 1734. 'He carried on his trade, in the same shop which had been possessed by his father and great-uncle, opposite Catherine Street⁶ in the Strand, but, some years before his death, removed to a new house on the other side of the way, near Catherine Street, where he died without issue, March 31, 1767.' ('Lit. Anec.' i. 297.) He is the subject of a very eulogistic and deserved reference by Stevens in his edition of Shakespeare, published in 1778,—a notice which concludes in these words :—' He was the last commercial name of a family which will be long remembered, and if Horace thought it not improper from Quintilian's dedication to Trypho, let it not be

---

⁶ Speaking of 'Shakespeare's Head,' Charles Knight remarks: ' That house, No. 141, was remarkable as the shop of three of the most eminent amongst the old booksellers. Here the elder Jacob might have looked out upon the 'furies of the football war,' which Gay so well describes in his ' Trivia.' Here, Andrew Millar concluded, over many a hospitable entertainment in his upper rooms (for the old days of booksellers' bargains at taverns were over), his treaties with Fielding and Thomson, with Hume and Robertson. Here Thomas Cadell smiled with honest exultation as he wrote to Gibbon to tell him how wonderful was the success of ' The Decline and Fall of the Roman Empire.' Illustrious shadows flitted about that house, which, long since rebuilt, is now (1865) an insurance office.'

thought that we disgrace Shakespeare by appending to his works the name of Tonson.'

The younger brother Richard survived Jacob only a few years, dying in 1772. ' By his father's Will, the estate at Water-Oakley, in the parish of Bray, near Windsor, was directed to be sold, and the produce to be considered as a part of his personal property ; but, either by agreement with his family or by purchase,' it came solely into his possession. He was M.P. for Windsor at the time of his decease. The eldest daughter of the second Jacob was married to Alderman Baker, father to Sir William Baker, M.P. for Hertfordshire, and the lineal descendant of Tonson still resides at Bayfordbury, Hertfordshire.

CHAPTER IX.

BERNARD LINTOT.

ACCORDING to an entry in his Bible, published in *Notes and Queries*, 6th S. ii. 293, it appears that Barnaby Bernard Lintott, the son of John Lintott, a Horsham yeoman, was born at Southwater, Horsham, Sussex, on December 1, 1675. There were seven children, besides the famous bookseller, their names and dates of birth being duly registered in the Bible in question, which was in the possession of a descendant, Mr. J. P. Fletcher. Lintot, as he afterwards spelt his surname, was bound apprentice at Stationers' Hall, to Thomas Lingard, December 4, 1690, and was subsequently 'turned over' to John Harding, whom John Dunton graphically describes as 'of a lovely proportion, extremely well made, as handsome a mien,' &c., as any of his neighbours. He was 'made free' March 18, 1699.[1] Lintot dispensed with the less elegant Christian name of Barnaby at the commencement of his apprenticeship.

[1] 'He was Renter-Warden in 1715; elected into the Court of Assistants 1722-3, and served the office of Under Warden in 1729 and again in 1730; but died before the Upper Wardenship came to his turn.'—(' Lit. Anec.' viii. 161).

Nichols states that, soon after the date given, Lintot commenced business as a bookseller at the sign of the 'Cross Keys,' between the Temple Gates, and instances the 'Examen Miscellaneum,' 1702, a collection of prose and verse, in 189 pp., as the earliest publication that was issued bearing Lintot's name. Some of his earlier work is dated from 'The Cross Keys,' in St. Martin's Lane, near Long Acre, and at least four years before the date given by Nichols appears as a bookseller. This will be seen by consulting the 1698 editions of Settle's 'Empress of Morocco,' and also Crowne's 'Caligula.' With regard to the situation of Lintot's shop, Cuningham, in his 'Handbook of London,' describes Nando's as a 'Coffee house in Fleet Street, east corner of Inner Temple Lane, and next door to the shop of Bernard Lintot, bookseller.' Mr. E. F. Rimbault points out (*N. & Q.* 1st S. vi. 326) that 'if Lintot's shop was *between* the Temple Gates, as he himself tells us, it could not have been next door to Nando's.' But, rightly or wrongly, Cuningham was justified in stating that the 'Cross Keys' was next to Nando's, as will appear from the title-page of Farquhar's 'Beaux Stratagem,' Cibber's 'Perolla and Izadora' (1706) and several other plays.

Lintot's first bookselling decade was unmarked by anything approaching notoriety, and he seems to have made a steady but slow and perhaps sure progress in his trade. In 1703 he published Lady Chudleigh's 'Poems on Several Occasions,' and Thomas Baker's comedy, 'Tunbridge Wells.' Law-books and the drama formed the staple of his stock, and but few of either section were issued on his own responsibility. Mrs. Centlivre and Colley Cibber each had some plays brought out with Lintot's name attached, either as part proprietor or bookseller. Lintot's shop has been described as the 'constant morning lounge of literary men.' He published 'The Lawyer's Fortune,' by Lord Grimstone (1705), E. Smith's 'Phædra and Hippolitus' (1708), a tragedy which had quite an ephemeral success, and also work from the pens of such as Gay, Farquhar, William King, Fenton, Parnell, &c. Mr. John Dennis, also, gave Lintot 'a turn,' or, perhaps, according to the custom of those days, the case was the other way about, and in 1704 'Liberty Asserted' is printed for George Strahan, of the 'Golden Bull,' against the Royal Exchange, and Bernard Lintot, at the Middle Temple Gate. But in this particular case, perhaps, Strahan purchased the whole of the copyright from Dennis, and afterwards sold half of it to Lintot for the modest sum of 7*l.* 3*s.* From Lintot's account-book ('Lit. Anec.' viii. 293—304), we find that Dennis was paid 21*l.* 10*s.* for 'Appius and Virginia,' whilst his two essays—the one on Public Spirit and the 'Remarks on Pope's Essay,' combined, only fetched 3*l.* 4*s.* 6*d.*

Toland was the most learned and perhaps also the most unfortunate of all Lintot's hack writers. He was at once a political, polemical, and miscellaneous writer and antiquary, and not very distinguished at either. An Irishman by birth and a Roman Catholic by persuasion, he gravitated towards freethinking, and in 1696 published a work entitled 'Christianity not Mysterious,' which contains nothing of any note, but the title-page, which so frightened the Church magnates that it was ordered to be burnt by the hangman. One of Toland's works was among Lintot's first venture, viz. 'The Art of Governing by Parties' (June 12, 1701), for which he paid 20*l.* Toland, whom D'Israeli describes as 'a great artificer of title-pages, covering them with a promising luxuriance, and in this way recommended his works to the booksellers,' had no fewer than thirteen different works issued through Lintot in as many years. (Nichol's 'Literary Anecdotes,' viii. p. 302, 303). Toland received 10*l.* 15*s.* for his pamphlet on 'Naturalizing the Jews' (1714), and was to receive a similar sum when Lintot sold 2000 copies. The agreement, published by D'Israeli, runs thus :—' Whenever Mr. Toland calls for ten guineas, after the first of February next, I promise to pay them, if I *cannot show* that 200 copies remain unsold.'

In the account-book already mentioned there are several entries made of agreements entered into between Tonson and Lintot, ranging from the year 1717 to 1725, including, notably, three or four of Steele's plays. One entry may be here given as exemplifying the mutability of literary fame :—' 1722, Oct. 24. A copy of an agreement for purchasing 250 of the Duke of Buckingham's works—*afterwards jockeyed by Alderman Barber and Tonson together.*' Lintot, says D'Israeli, ' utters a groan over the Duke of Buckingham's works. Who can ensure literary celebrity? No bookseller would *now* regret being *jockeyed* out of his Grace's works!'

Gay, as already mentioned, was one of 'Lintot's authors,' and it is highly interesting to learn that within about four years he received 43*l.* for 'Trivia,' 43*l.* 2*s.* 6*d.* for 'Three Hours after Marriage,' and 75*l.* for the 'Revival of the Wife of Bath' (1717), for which, in 1713, a first sum of 25*l.* had been paid. Theobald, also had some transactions with Lintot, and under date April 21, 1714, we have the following entry :—'Articles signed by Mr. Theobald to translate for B. Lintot the twenty-four books of Homer's 'Odyssey' into English blank verse. Also the four tragedies of Sophocles, called 'Œdipus Tyrannus,' 'Œdipus Coloneus,' 'Trachiniæ,' and 'Philoctetes,' into English blank verse, with explanatory notes to the twenty-four books of the 'Odyssey,' and to the four tragedies. To receive for translating every 450 Greek verses, with explanatory notes thereon, the sum of 2*l.* 10*s.* To translate likewise the satires and epistles of Horace into English rhyme. For every 120 Latin lines so translated, the sum of 1*l.* 1*s.* 6*d.* These articles to be performed, according to the time specified, under the penalty of 50*l.*, payable by either party's default in performance.—Paid in hand 2*l.* 10*s.*' In the original book, the foregoing entry has a line drawn through it, and D'Israeli suggests that perhaps Lintot submitted to pay Theobald for *not doing* the 'Odyssey' when Pope undertook it.

We have not space to give all the entries, interesting as they are, in full here. But those relating to William King are too important to be passed over ' Here, too,' says D'Israeli, 'we find that the facetious

Dr. King threw away all his sterling wit for five miserable pounds.' The account-book enumerates eight, of which the following are the more important, their respective values being in parenthesis: —'Art of Cookery,' 1708-9 (32*l.* 5*s.*); 'Useful Transactions,'[2] pt. i. 1708-9 (5*l.*); 'Art of Love,' 1708-9 (32*l.* 5*s.*); 'Transactions,' pt. ii. 1709 (5*l.*); and the 'History of Cajamai,' 1709-10 (5*l.*). The following is a list of the most noteworthy works which Lintot acquired at various times, and the prices he paid for them:—Centlivre's 'Busybody,' 1709 (10*l.*); Cibber's 'Love's Last Shift,' a third interest, 1701 (3*l.* 4*s.* 6*d.*); 'Perolla and Izadora,' 1705 (36*l.* 11*s.*); 'Double Gallant,' 1707 (16*l.* 2*s.* 6*d.*); 'Lady's Last Stake,' 1707 (32*l.* 5*s.*); 'Venus and Adonis,' 1707 (5*l.* 7*s.* 6*d.*; 'Comical Lover,' 1708 (10*l.* 15*s.*); 'Cinna's Conspiracy,' 1712 (13*l.*); 'Nonjuror,' 1718 (105*l.*); D'Urfey's 'Modern Prophets,' 1709 (6*l.* 9*s.*); Farquhar's 'Beaux Stratagem,' 1706 (30*l.*); 'Recruiting Officer,' 1705 (16*l.* 2*s.* 6*d*). Fenton was paid in all 34*l.* 14*s.* 3*d*. The 'Accomplished Conveyancer,' in three vols., was bought for 105*l.* from Jacob, and Lintot seems to have secured a number of other legal works from the same source. N. Rowe's 'Jane Shore,' 1713 (50*l.* 15*s.*); and 'Jane Grey,' 1715 (75*l.* 5*s.*); and Settle's 'The City Ramble,' 1711 (3*l.* 10*s.*); Smith's 'Phædra and Hippolytus,' 1705-6 (50*l.*); J. Moore Smyth's 'The Rival Modes,' 1726 (105*l.*); Steele's 'Lying Lover,' 1703-4 (21*l.* 10*s.*).

One of Lintot's earlier publications was Tom

[2] Dr. King's famous banter on the Royal Society.

D'Urfey's 'Tales, Magical and Comical,' 1704, which was dedicated to the then Duke of Argyle in the usual fulsome strain. This publication is rather notable from the fact that it is alluded to in Dunton's 'character' of Lintot, whom John describes thus:—'He lately published a collection of Tragic Tales, by which I perceive he is angry with the world, and scorns it into the bargain; and I cannot blame him: for D'Urfey (his author) both treats and esteems it as it deserves: too hard a task for those whom it *flatters*; or perhaps for Bernard himself should the world ever change its humour, and *grin* upon him. However, to do Mr. Lintot justice, he is a man of very good principles, and I dare engage will never want an author of *Sol-Fa*[3] so long as the playhouse will encourage his comedies.'

Although Lintot had to some extent emulated Jacob Tonson's successful *Miscellany* publication in 1709, when the 'Oxford and Cambridge Miscellany Poems' came out under the general editorship of Fenton, it was not until three years after (1712), that Lintot actually and obviously imitated his more famous rival. The contributors to Fenton's, or the Oxford and Cambridge, collection of poems included Prior, Philips, Sir John Denham, 'Mr. Milton,' Otway, etc., so that from this fact it may be safely inferred that Lintot's name as a publisher was pretty well known.

The year 1712 witnessed the publication of 'The Miscellaneous Poems and Translations, by Several Hands. This volume contains two poems addressed to Lintot, apparently congratulating him on the appearance of his *Miscellany*. One, entitled 'Verses designed to be

[3] D'Urfey was a music-master.

prefixed before Bernard Lintot's New Miscellany, 1712,' is attributed to Swift, and is here given with the exception of the last line :—

> 'Some Colinæus praise, some Bleau ;
> Others account them so so ;
> Some Plantin to the rest prefer,
> And some esteem old Elzevir;
> Others with Aldus would besot us :
> I, for my part, admire Lintottus.
> His character's beyond compare,
> Like his own person, large and fair.
> They print their names in letters small,
> But LINTOT stands in capital :
> Author and he with equal grace
> Appear, and stare you in the face.
> Stephens prints Heathen Greek, 'tis said,
> Which some can't construe, some can't read.
> But all that comes from Lintot's hand
> Ev'n Rawlinson might understand.
> Oft in an Aldus or a Plantin
> A page is blotted, or leaf wanting:
> Of Lintot's books this can't be said,
> All fair, and not so much as read.
> Their copy cost them not a penny
> To Homer, Virgil, or to any ;
> They ne'er gave sixpence for two lines
> To them, their heirs, or their assigns.
> But Lintot is at vast expense,
> And pays prodigious dear for—sense.
> Their books are useful but to few,
> A scholar, or a wit or two :
> Lintot's for general use are fit,' &c.

This poem was reprinted in the last volume of the *Miscellanies* (1732), issued by B. Motte. The second and longer congratulatory poem is entitled ' On a Miscellany of Poems.—To Bernard Lintot,' and is described by Nichols as being 'by a nameless but not inelegant bard, perhaps Dr. William King, of the Commons.' It was, however, by Gay, and appears as 'Epistle XIII.,' in his volume of poems. After describing the way in which a skilful cook would so manipulate his materials as to please every guest, to 'feast at once the taste, the smell, and sight,' Gay goes on to say :—

> 'So, Bernard must a Miscellany be—
> Compounder of all kinds of poetry ;
> The Muses' Olio, which all tastes may fit,
> And treat each reader with his darling wit.
> Would'st thou for Miscellanies raise thy fame,
> And bravely rival Jacob's mighty name.
> Let all the Muses in the piece conspire,'

and so on, concluding with the following couplet:

> ' So long shall live thy praise in books of fame,
> And Tonson yield to Lintot's lofty name.'

In 1714 the *Miscellanies* were reprinted. This work is remarkable from the number of Pope's earlier poems which it contains, such as 'The Rape of the Lock,'[4] 'Windsor Forest,' 'An Essay on Criticism,' a translation of book I, of Statius' 'Thebais,' verses to the author of the poem entitled 'Successio,' 'St. Cecilia's Ode,' and two or three others. Among the authors whose contributions appear in this work, which was printed for Lintot, and 'William Lewis in Russell Street, Covent Garden,' were Dryden, Broome, Southcote, Edmund Smith, Fenton, and Betterton. Lewis, it

---

[4] Spence states that Pope said with reference to the 'Rape of the Lock,' 'I published the first draught of it (without the machinery) in a Miscellany of Tonson'—meaning Lintot.

may be mentioned, was an early friend of Pope's and was a Roman Catholic bookseller ; he also published the 'Essay on Criticism,' 1711.

In 1710 or 1711, Lintot grievously vexed the great Dean of St. Patrick's by publishing 'Noah's Dove,' a sermon by 'Tho. Swift, formerly Chaplain to Sir William Temple.' The 'Journal to Stella,' under date November 7, 1711, has the following entry :—'A bookseller has reprinted, or new-titled, a sermon of Tom Swift's, printed last year, and published an advertisement calling it Dr. Swift's sermon.'

Of the many not unimportant works which Lintot issued, perhaps John Urry's edition of Chaucer claims a place in the first rank. This edition, although it is of little commercial value at the present day, possesses some interest to bibliographers. The inception of the task began late in 1711, probably at the instigation of Dean Aldrich, and was continued with such ardour that on July 20, 1714, Urry was granted a patent for the exclusive right of printing the work. On December 17 of the same year he entered into an arrangement with Lintot, by which he himself was to have one-third of the proceeds, Christ Church College, Oxford, one-third, whilst the remaining portion was to accrue to Lintot, who was to pay for paper, copper-plates, and all incidental expenses. On January 19, 1714-15, Lintot issued the 'Proposals' for publishing the works 'of the celebrated and ancient English poet' by subscription, which included the following five proposals : '(1) This work is intended to be printed in one volume folio, and will contain near two hundred and twenty sheets.

(2) The cuts shall be engraved by the best gravers, and printed at the head of each Tale. (3) The price to subscribers will be thirty shillings for one complete book in sheets, fifteen to be paid in hand, the remainder upon delivery of each book. (4) A small number will be printed on a fine royal paper, which will be fifty shillings, half to be paid in hand; and (5) This work will be put into the press on Lady-day next, and is intended to be published the Christmas following. Subscriptions are taken in by the undertaker, Bernard Lintot, between the Temple Gates, assignee to Mr. Urry, and most booksellers in London and in the country.' But Urry died on March 19 following, his executor and intimate fellow-student, William Broome, undertaking the task, signing an agreement with Lintot to that effect on August 16, 1715. The agreement recites Urry's intention to apply part of the profits towards building Peckwater Quadrangle. Broome assigns his right to the Glossary and licence to Lintot for remainder of the term; the Dean and Chapter and Mr. Broome to deliver to Lintot a complete copy of Chaucer and Glossary, and to correct it, or get it corrected. Lintot was to print 1250 copies, 250 on royal paper and 1000 on demy, at his own charge, and to furnish a number of copies not exceeding 1500. The net result of this publication would be, at the rate stated, 2125*l.*, which would give Lintot 708*l.* 6*s.* 8*d.* The work was printed off early in 1719, but two years elapsed before the 'New Glossary' was finished, and it was 1721 when the work came forth, having been seven years in hand.

It is the publication of Pope's rendering of Homer's 'Iliad' that has prevented Lintot from being consigned to dim obscurity. Indeed, the episode itself was undoubtedly the greatest and most important event in the career of each man; perhaps, also, it was the happiest and most profitable. Arrangements were entered into between Pope and Lintot for the issuing of 'Proposals for a Translation of Homer' in 1714. The edition was to be in six volumes, printed on the finest paper, in a 'new Dutch letter,' whilst ornaments were to be specially designed for the work. Lintot agreed to pay Pope not only 200*l*. for each volume, but undertook to gratuitously supply the poet with the copies for his subscribers. The subscribers paid a guinea a volume, and as 575 subscribers took 654 copies, Pope received a grand total of 5320*l*. 4*s*. 0*d*. But several wealthy persons paid a much larger sum than the price stated. These figures do not quite agree with the entries in 'Lintot's Account-Book,' where the sum of 215*l*. is written as paid for each volume at its completion. 'Of the quartos,' said Dr. Johnson, ' it was, I believe, stipulated that none should be printed but for the author, that the subscriptions might not be depreciated; but Lintot impressed the same pages upon a small folio, and paper perhaps a little thinner; and sold exactly at half the price, for half a guinea each volume, books so little inferior to the quartos, that, by fraud of trade, those folios, being afterwards shortened by cutting away the top and bottom, were sold as copies printed for the subscribers. Lintot printed some on royal paper in folio for two guineas a volume; but of this experiment he repented, as his son sold copies of the first volume with all their extent of margin for two shillings. It is unpleasant to relate that the bookseller, after all his hopes and all his liberality, was, by a very unjust and illegal action, defrauded of his profit. An English edition of the "Iliad" was printed in Holland, in duodecimo, and imported clandestinely for the gratification of those who were impatient to read what they could not yet afford to buy.' Lintot had, consequently, no alternative but to issue a duodecimo edition, which possessed the grand advantage over the pirated edition in having the notes subjoined to the text in the same page.

The *Postboy* of December 25, 1714, contained this announcement, directed to the subscribers to the forthcoming translation : 'Whereas it was proposed that the first volume of the translation should be published by the beginning of May next, the editor intends it shall be delivered two months sooner than the time promised.' But for some reason, apparently unexplained, this promise was not performed, and on April 7, 1715, Gay facetiously writes thus to Congreve : ' Mr. Pope's " Homer " is retarded by the great rains that have fallen of late, which causes the sheets to be long a-drying. This gives Mr. Lintot great uneasiness, who is now endeavouring to engage the curate of the parish to pray for fair weather, that his work may go on.' However, the *Postboy* of June 4 announced that 'the first volume is now finished, and will be ready to be delivered to them upon producing their receipts, or paying the subscription money, on Monday, the 6th day of June next, by Bernard Lintot, bookseller, at the Cross Keys, between the Temple Gates in Fleet Street, where the several pieces of Mr. Pope may be had.'

This was all well and good; but the *Postboy* of June 7th contained a startling advertisement, which ran as follows:—'To-morrow will be published the first book of "Homer's Iliad," translated by Mr. Tickell. Printed for Jacob Tonson at Shakespeare's Head, against Katherine Street, in the Strand.' To this attempt at rivalry we shall refer again presently.

Nichols states that, according to Bowyer's account-books, no more than 660 were printed for the subscribers in quarto; but besides that number Lintot printed of vol. i. in folio for ordinary sale, 250 on large paper, and 1750 on small paper. Of the following volumes the same number of large copies, but only 1000 of the small. Of the first duodecimo edition 2500 were printed, which were soon sold, and another edition of 5000 was immediately printed.

The *Postman* of March 24, 1716, announced the completion of the second volume of Pope's version of 'Homer's Iliad," which was then ready for delivery to subscribers. The third was issued in the autumn of 1717, and the fourth in the spring of the following year. The *Postboy* of March 16, 1719, in announcing the fact that the fifth volume 'now lies finished at the press,' also advertised that ' Mr. Pope, having made a greater progress in the remainder than he expected, or promised, hereby gives notice, that he shall deliver the whole to the subscribers by the beginning of next winter.' From Lintot's account-book it would seem that the fifth volume appeared some time in October, 1718, when the stipulated sum was handed over to the poet. These apparently irreconcilable facts may be explained by presuming that Lintot paid his money when he received the last consignment of 'copy;' and, as will also be seen by the account-book, the royal paper copies of vol. v. were not finished until the first week in April, 1719. Indeed, with the exception of the first volume, some months elapsed between the payment for and the receipt of the gratis copies of each issue. The *Whitehall Evening Post* of May 14, 1720, announces: 'This day Mr. Pope's "Homer," the two last volumes (the whole work being now complete) will be delivered to the subscribers,' &c.

A brief reference must be made here to Tickel's projected translation, and of which only the first volume appeared. It was well known for at least twelve months before the work actually put in an appearance, that Pope was engaged in translating Homer's 'Iliad;' Tickel's work in that direction seems to have been kept remarkably close. It may be suggested that Tonson's cupidity had something to do with the preparation of a rival translation, but that is very unlikely. The actual cause was in all probability political jealousy. The almost simultaneous appearance of rival translations of Homer by the leading poets[5] of the two political parties, issuing from the shops of the two leading booksellers of the day, would to a dead certainty render a comparison certain

[5] We are assuming that Addison was largely concerned with Tickel's version.

and quite fatal to one of the two candidates. Pope knew this, and advertises to some extent more than he originally promised by professing to have added :— 'A critical preface, an essay on the life, writings and learning of Homer . . . . a map of Greece, a geographical table of the towns,' &c. But doubt did not long exist, and on June 10, 1715, Lintot writes to Pope thus :—'You have Mr. Tickel's book to divert one hour. It is already condemned here, and the malice and juggle at Button's is the conversation of those who have spare moments from politics.' Thus we see the Tickel-Addison-Tonson combination quite smashed and destroyed in two or three days.

The next big contract between Lintot and Pope was a translation of the 'Odyssey,' in five volumes, a work which was completed in 1725 or 1726, with the help of Broome and Fenton. Lintot paid in one way or another, over 4200*l.*, of which rather more than 3500*l.* fell to Pope's share, Broome received 500*l.* (100*l.* of which was for notes), and Fenton 200*l.* This undertaking was not so brilliant a success as the former; the bookseller pretended to have discovered some flaw in the agreement, or in the manner in which Pope had carried it out, and threatened the poet a suit in Chancery. But the threat was not carried into effect. It had, however, the very natural consequence of estrangement between the two, and Lintot became enrolled at a later date among the heroes of the 'Dunciad.' In addition to the sums which Lintot paid Pope for the Homeric renderings, the following will be read with interest :—For the nine poems inserted in the *Miscellany* of 1714, already referred to, Lintot paid him 88*l.* 14*s.* ; 'Temple of Fame,' (Feb. 1, 1714-5), 32*l.* 5*s.*; additions to the 'Rape of the Lock,' (Feb. 20, 1713-4), 15*l*; and the 'Key to the Lock,' (April 30, 1715), 10*l.* 15*s.* On the ground of payment we think Pope had nothing to grumble at.

In the great frost of January and February, 1715-16, the Thames was one solid block of ice, and shops of almost every description were erected on its surface, and Lintot is recorded as having had a stand erected there.

There is an amusing anecdote told by Dr. Young himself, recorded in Spence's 'Anecdotes,' which may be placed here :—Tonson and Lintot were both candidates for the printing of some work of Dr. Young. He answered both their letters in the same morning, and in his hurry misdirected them. When Lintot opened that which came to him, he found it begin : ' That Bernard Lintot is so great a scoundrel, that,' &c. It must have been very amusing, adds the Doctor, to have seen him in his rage, he was a great sputtering fellow. Tonson was described, much to his surprise, no doubt, as an old rascal. But neither Lintot nor Tonson made much out of Young, for the two names are absent from the title-pages of the Doctor's publications which we have examined.

Lintot on more than one occasion emulated Tonson's bold experimenting. This was the case, but in a very minor degree, with Shakespeare's works. At about the time Tonson issued Rowe's edition, Bernard published an edition of Shakespeare's poems in two volumes, which Malone rather unjustly consigned to oblivion as ' full of errors.' The first volume appeared on August 3, 1709, and was announced in the fifty-second number of the *Tatler*. It contains 'Venus and Adonis,' 'Rape of Lucrece,' 'Passionate Pilgrim,' and sonnets to sundry notes of music. The second volume came out about February, 1710-11, and contains 154 sonnets, and the 'Lover's Complaint.' Probably Congreve acted in some degree as editor of this work, which Lintot announced, in the *Postboy*, as 'correctly printed literatim,' and that ' some of these miscellanies were printed from an old edition which Mr. Congreve obliged me with ; others from an ingenious gentleman of the Middle Temple, who is pleased to leave his old copy with me to shew any person that has a mind to gratify his curiosity therewith.'

After Pope's Homer, perhaps nothing has conduced so much to handing down Lintot's name to posterity as Pope's famous letter to the Earl of Burlington. Nichols (' Lit. Anec.' viii. 304), considers this letter to have 'been written between September, 1715, when Lord Lansdown was committed to the Tower, and February 1716-17, when he was released.'

'MY LORD,—If your mare could speak, she would give an account of what extraordinary company she had on the road ; which, since she cannot do, I will.

' It was the enterprising Mr. Lintot, the redoubtable rival of Mr. Tonson, who, mounted on a stone horse (no disagreeable companion to your Lordship's mare), overtook me in Windsor Forest. He said, he heard I design'd for Oxford, the seat of the Muses, and would, as my bookseller, by all means, accompany me hither.

' I ask'd him where he got his horse ? He answer'd, he got it of his publisher : " For that rogue my printer " (said he) "disappointed me: I hoped to put him in good humour by a treat at the tavern, of a brown fricassee of rabbits, which cost two shillings, with two quarts of wine, besides my conversation. I thought myself, cock-sure of his horse, which he readily promis'd me, but said that Mr. Tonson had just such another design of going to Cambridge, expecting there the copy of a new kind of Horace from Dr. ——, and if Mr. Tonson went, he was pre-engaged to attend him, being to have the printing of the said copy."'

Shortly afterwards, when the ingenious publisher had made some remarks concerning a printer's devil who followed, and to whom Pope entrusted a small bag containing three shirts and an Elzevir Virgil, Lintot once more began, as follows :—

'" Now, damn them! what if they should put it into the newspapers how you and I went together to Oxford? what should I care? If I should go down into Sussex, they would say I was gone to the Speaker. But what of that? If my son were but big enough to go on with the business, by G—d, I would keep as good company as old Jacob."

'" The lad," continued Lintot, " has fine parts, but is somewhat sickly, much as you are—I spare for nothing in his education at Westminster . . . ."

'As Mr. Lintot was talking, I observed he sat uneasy on his saddle, for which I expressed some solicitude. " Nothing," says he, " I can bear it well enough; but since we have the day before us, methinks it would be very pleasant for you to rest awhile under the woods." When we were alighted, " See here, what a mighty pretty Horace I have in my pocket!

what if you amus'd yourself in turning an ode, till we mount again? Lord! if you pleased, what a clever miscellany might you make at leisure hours!"
"Perhaps I may," said I, "if we ride on : the motion is an aid to my fancy, a round trot very much awakens my spirits, then jog on apace, and I'll think as hard as I can." Silence ensued for a full hour ; after which Mr. Lintot lugg'd the reins, stopp'd short, and broke out, "Well, sir, how far have you gone?" I answer'd, "Seven miles." "Zounds, sir, I thought you had done seven stanzas. Oldisworth, in a ramble round Wimbleton-hill, would translate a whole ode in half this time."

'"Pray, Mr. Lintot, now you talk of translators, what is your method of managing them?" "Sir," reply'd he, "those are the saddest pack of rogues in the world ; in a hungry fit, they'll swear they understand all the languages in the universe : I have known one of them take down a Greek book upon my counter, and cry, 'Ay, this is Hebrew, I must read it from the latter end.' By G—d, I can never be sure in these fellows, for I neither understand Greek, Latin, French nor Italian myself. But this is my way ; I agree with them for 10s. per sheet, with a proviso that I will have their doings corrected by whom I please."'

When asked by Pope how he dealt with critics, Lintot replies :—'" I can silence the most formidable of them : the rich ones for a sheet a-piece of the blotted manuscript, which costs me nothing ; they'll go about with it to their acquaintance, and pretend they had it from the author, who submitted to their correction: this has given some of them such an air, that in time they come to be consulted with, and dedicated to as the top criticks of the town. As for the poor criticks, I'll give you one instance of my management, by which you may guess the rest. A lean man, that look'd like a very good scholar, came to me t'other day; he turn'd over your Homer, shook his head, shrugg'd up his shoulders, and pish'd at every line of it: 'One would wonder,' says he, 'at the strange presumption of some men; Homer is no such easy task, that every stripling, every versifier—' He was going on, when my wife call'd to dinner: 'Sir,' said I, 'will you please to eat a piece of beef with me?' 'Mr. Lintot,' said he, 'I am sorry you should be at the expense of this great book, I am really concern'd on your account.' 'Sir, I am much oblig'd to you: if you can dine upon a piece of beef, together with a slice of pudding.' 'Mr. Lintot, I do not say but Mr. Pope, if he would condescend to advise with men of learning—' 'Sir, the pudding is upon the table, if you please to go in.' My critick complies, he comes to taste of your poetry, and tells me in the same breath, that the book is commendable, and the pudding excellent.'"

'" Now sir," concludes Mr. Lintot, "in return for the frankness I have shown, pray tell me is it the opinion of your friends at Court, that my Lord Lansdown will be brought to the bar or not."' Mr. Pope informs the officious bookseller that he heard he (Lansdown) would not, and what is more, hoped it. But Mr. Lintot looked at it from a purely business point of view, and if Lansdown did not come before the bar, all friend Bernard could say was that he should lose the printing of a very good trial.

If this letter is really authentic, and it is necessary at all times to take Pope's statements with a very big grain of salt, Lintot was decidedly not a 'genteel man.' We may, however, assume that he was not a bad-hearted one, for he subscribed five guineas to the relief fund got up in aid of Bowyer, the printer, who suffered so greatly from the fire of January 30, 1712.

'George for Britain,' a 'poem' by one Lady Piers, was a handsomely printed octavo work of 44 pp. It was a timely production of Lintot's, if it had no other merit, for it was issued in 1714, the year of George the First's succession to the English throne. From John Nichols' quotations, the obnoxious flattery of the period must have very nearly reached its culminating point in this 'poem.'

Lintot's two efforts in the Miscellany direction were followed by one in 1717, and also by another in 1726. The former was entitled 'Poems on Several Occasions,' and contained contributions from the Duke of Buckingham, Wycherley, N. Rowe, Garth, Lady Winchelsea, and 'other eminent hands.' It was dedicated to the Earl of Orrery by Fenton, who was for some time the earl's tutor. The 1726 publication, in 2 vols. duodecimo, was entitled 'Miscellaneous Poems, Translations, and Imitations,' and the collection was formed by Lintot himself. The contributors included Buckingham, Gay, Pope, Betterton, Dryden, King, Smith, Dibben, Fenton, Yalden, Rowe, Southcote, Broome, Ward and Daniel.

P

This was probably the Miscellany at which Pope waxed so wroth in a letter to Christopher Pitt,⁶ July 23, 1726: 'If I have any [merit] in me, it really consists in an earnest desire to promote and produce, as far as I can, that of others. But as to my being the publisher, or in any way concerned in reviewing or recommending of 'Lintot's Miscellany,' it is what I never did in my life, though he (like the rest of his tribe), makes a very free use of my name. He has often reprinted my things, and so scurvily, that, finding he was doing so again, *I corrected the sheets as far as they went, of my own only.*'

Nichols suggests a very plausible theory which in absence of a better may be accepted. He says, 'perhaps Mr. Pope conceived that Lintot had risen *above his proper level*, for it appears that early in 1726, having, by successful exertions in business, acquired a decent competence, and made some additions to his paternal inheritance in Sussex, he was desirous of tracing the origin of his family.' He therefore consulted Humphrey Wanley, who had then the custody of the Earl of Oxford's heraldic manuscripts, and in whose diary is the following memorandum: 'Jan. 31, 1725-6. Young Mr. Lintot, the bookseller, came enquiring after arms, as belonging to his father, mother, and other relations, who now, it seems, want to turn gentle folks. I could find none of their names.'

One of the few lucrative Government appointments which fell to Lintot's share was the printing of the Votes, in conjunction, however, with Jacob Tonson

⁶ Of whom see Cibber's 'Lives of Poets,' v. 298—307.

and William Taylor, when the Hon. Spencer Compton was Speaker of the House of Commons, in 1715. The appointment held good until 1727. A namesake, of whom little is known, Joshua Lintot, Jacob Tonson, Timothy Goodwin, and John Roberts, printed them from 1708 until 1710, whilst Sir Richard Onslow was Speaker.

The very natural sequence of running across Pope's path followed Lintot, as well as every one else: he became enrolled in the 'Dunciad.' But, as Nichols justly points out, the principal delinquency Pope urged was that his late bookseller was a stout man, clumsily made, not a very good scholar, and that he filled his shops with rubric posts. Nothing is insinuated against Lintot's general character. Lintot makes his *début* in the first book, thus :—

> 'Hence Miscellanies spring, the weekly boast
> Of Curll's chaste press, and Lintot's rubric post.'
> (Lines 39, 40.)

In the famous race described in the second book, in honour of the Goddess of Dulness, Lintot and Curll are the two rival competitors :—

> 'But lofty Lintot in the circle rose :
> The prize is mine : who 'tempt it are my foes ;
> With me began this genius, and shall end.'
> He spoke: and who with Lintot shall contend ?
> Fear held them mute. Alone, untaught to fear,
> Stood dauntless Curll : Behold that rival here !
> The race by vigour, not by vaunts is won,
> So take the hindmost, hell (he said), and run,
> Swift as a band the bailiff leaves behind,
> He left huge Lintot and outstripped the wind.

> As when a dab-chick waddles through the copse
> On feet and wings, and flies, and wades, and hops.
> So lab'ring on, with shoulders, hands and head,
> Wide as a windmill all his figure spread,
> With arms extended Bernard'vows his state,
> And left-legg'd Jacob seems to emulate.'

Curll, however, wins the race.

Nichols quotes an extract from a 'poem' entitled 'Lintot's Lamentation,' which appeared in 'Gulliveriana,' (1728):—

> 'Well, then, all human things, henceforth, avast!
> Sawney the great is quite cut down at last.
> But I must say, this judgment was due to him,
> For basely murthering Homer's sacred poem;
> Due too, for dropping me, and running mad,
> To fall so foul on every friend he had.
> "So Fate and Jove require," and so, dear Pope,
> Either thy razor set, or buy a rope.'

But little now remains to tell concerning Bernard Lintot. He retired on an easy fortune in 1730, to Horsham, not far from Cuckfield, in Sussex, for which county he was nominated High Sheriff in November, 1735, but died on February 3 following, before he had actually entered on the duties of the office, to which his son, Henry, was appointed in his room, two days after his father's death. Henry's residence at that time was Southwater, two miles from Horsham.

From the entries published in *Notes and Queries*, referred to at the commencement of this sketch, we learn that Lintot's wife 'Katherine' was born by Temple Bar on January 2, 1664, that the marriage took place 'at St. Bartholomys by Smithfield' on

October 13, 1700, and that some time in 1703 'My son Henry was born.' Nichols incorrectly gives this last date as 'about August, 1709.' Henry Lintot was admitted to the freedom of the Company of Stationers, by patrimony, September 1, 1730, and obtained the Livery on the same day. Henceforth, until the death of his father, the business was carried on in the joint names of Bernard and Henry Lintot. The latter does not seem to have been much of a business-man, although he obtained the patent of Law Printer about 1748. In 1754 he was elected into the Courts of Assistants of his Company. In 1730 Henry was married to Elizabeth, daughter of Sir John Aubrey, Bart., of Llantrythed, in Glamorganshire, and by whom he had two children, 'born by Temple Barr,' (1) Aubrey Lintot, born 1731, died April 26, 1735, and (2) Catherine, born in 1732. Henry's wife died of consumption on January 21, 1734. He married a second time; and died suddenly, December 10, 1758. His widow survived until January 31, 1763. On October 20, 1760, Catherine Lintot[7] married Sir Henry Fletcher,[8] at Oxford Chapel.' Henry Lintot, like his father before him, came in for some hard words, but in the present instance we shall only quote one example, extracted from a letter of Warburton's dated June 20, 1744:—
'You will oblige me with telling me that beast

[7] She had a fortune of 45,000*l*.
[8] This entry is as transcribed in *N. and Q.*, but at the time of marriage her husband was a captain in the employ of the East India Company, and was not created a baronet until 1782, after which perhaps the entry quoted was only made.

Lintot's steps. I would do him all reason while he acts with decency and justice, and shall never print any part of his property with my notes and commentary without his leave ; but if he acts like a rogue, I have but one word with him, the Chancery and Mr. Murray.'

It is equally uncertain how long Henry Lintot remained in the trade, and the date at which he finally abandoned it.

One of the latest books we have noticed that contains his name is the 'Collection of English Precedents,' by James Harvey, Esq. (3rd ed.) 'In the Savoy: printed for Henry Lintot, Law Printer to the King's most Excellent Majesty, and sold by J. Shackburgh,* at the Sun between the two Temple-gates, Fleet Street, 1751.'

There are several descendants of the Lintots still living, notably Sir Henry Fletcher, Bart., of Clea Hall, Whitehaven, Cumberland.

* This person was in business as a printer or bookseller quite twenty years previous to 1751, but his whereabouts is not quite certain.

CHAPTER X.

EDMUND CURLL.

THERE is no more anomalous a name in the by-paths of English literature than Edmund Curll. His career is most singular and interesting. Indeed, he is almost the only one of the earlier booksellers who is allotted a niche in the various biographical dictionaries,—not so much because of his merits as of his demerits! He has received, also, perhaps even more than his due amount of attention from such accomplished antiquaries and bibliographers as the late Mr. W. J. Thoms, whose entertaining 'Curll Papers' will form the backbone of this sketch, and the late Mr. Solly.

John Nichols was the first to call into question the then almost universally accepted axiom that Curll was as black as he was painted. Nichols very truly observes that Curll's memory 'has been transmitted to posterity with an obloquy more severe than he deserved.' ('Lit. Anec.' I. 456). We do not, however, intend to whitewash Curll, or to attempt to show him up as a hero or a martyr. He was neither the one nor the other. He was, it must be honestly admitted, a sorry scamp, to whose unscrupulous dealings, trickery, and knavery there was absolutely no limit. But with all this, his is a fascinating history.

Mr. Thoms has pointed out that 'to form a just estimate of the character of Curll, the then state of literature and the law must be taken into account. We must remember how great were the restraints on the liberty of the press which existed in his days, when,—

'Ear-less on high stood pillory'd Defoe;'

how uncertain was the law of libel; and how heavy the' penalties for publications which were adjudged libellous. How undefined, or rather worse than undefined, how degraded, was the position of the mere author by profession: and, as a consequence of this state of things, what strange shifts were occasionally adopted to escape the risks which then awaited both authors and publishers, and adopted, too, by men of far higher social position than Edmund Curll.'

'Nearly everything connected with Curll is characterized by more or less mystery. His birth, parentage, and early career are shrouded in almost impenetrable gloom. The 'New and General Biographical Dictionary,' 1798, states that he 'was born in the west of England,' but gives no authority by which the remark can be verified. The question of Curll's parentage is one of importance, which has been considerably enhanced by a stray observation. In Curll's 'History of the Stage,' 1741, compiled perhaps in part by Betterton, whose name appears on the title-page, mention is made of the fatality which happens to the shedders of blood, and among other examples is the following:—'The last instance I shall produce is in the case of the late Lord Chief Justice Pine, of Ireland, who, when he was a

Edmund Curll.   217

student of Lincoln's Inn, in these walks killed the eldest son of one of the *finest gentlemen* in England, I beg to be excused naming him because he was *my near* relation.' This was not perhaps altogether an empty boast. It has been suggested (*Gents. Mag.*, 1858, 2,), and we are, after careful consideration and inquiry, strongly inclined to think that Curll really did claim relationship with the family of Dr. Walter Curll, who was born at Hatfield, Hertfordshire, who was at one time lord almoner to Charles the First, and successively Bishop of Rochester (1628), of Bath and Wells (1629), and of Winchester (1632). We have it on the authority of Anthony Wood ('Athenæ Oxon') that this eminent and worthy man died in reduced circumstances in the summer of 1647, leaving a widow and several children. At Edmund's death in 1747 he was seventy-two years of age, and was consequently born in 1675. No theory is more plausible than that these children were compelled to shift for themselves, and that Edmund, the much-abused bookseller, was a grandson to the good Bishop. Another coincidence which is, to say the least, curious, lies in the fact that one of his biographical publications was a 'Life' of the Bishop. The Curll family had for some time maintained a good social position, for in the list of counsel practising at the Bar in the time of James the First we find the name of 'E Curll' (Foss' 'Judges of England,' vi. 36). A few more links, missing as yet, are required either to clinch or to disprove the connection between the Bishop and the bookseller.

From the biographical dictionary already referred

[1] See also Collier's 'Annals of the Stage,' i. 320, n.

to we further learn that 'after passing through several menial capacities [he] arrived at the degree of a bookseller's man. He afterwards kept a stall, and then took a shop in the purlieus of Covent Garden.' Curll's master, it seems, was 'Mr. Smith, by Exeter Exchange,' an incident gleaned, as so many others have been gleaned, through the outcome of a quarrel. Curll's antagonist had advised, in connection with the bookseller's advertisement of a quack medical book, ' The Charitable Surgeon,' that his opponent's 'next advertisement, for the satisfaction of the publick, might be a certificate under the hand of Mr. Smith, by Exeter Change, his master, signifying, that he served him honestly during the whole of the time for which he was bound 'prentice to him.' The author of ' London's Medicinal Informer' (the rival publication), Curll's antagonist, quaintly concludes : 'but he has not, as yet, that I know of followed my advice.' Mr. Solly (*N. and Q*, 6th S., x. 204) has suggested that this Mr. Smith, 'was Richard Smith who had a shop at the sign of the Angel and Bible without Temple Bar,' that it was not unlikely that he was succeeded by Curll, and also that in the process of transfer, the sign of the shop was altered to 'the Peacock.' Mr. Solly draws his inferences from the fact that Capt. Bladen's edition of Cæsar's ' Commentaries' was originally printed in 1705, for Richard Smith, whilst the second edition was issued by Curll in the latter part of 1705 or else in 1706, at which period it is assumed that Smith resigned in favour of his apprentice. We have unimpeachable evidence that Curll was in business in 1706 and in 1707, and that, moreover, he published books in each of these years. It is not easy, therefore, to reconcile these facts with a statement of Curll's own, which he makes in 'An Apology for the writings of Walter Moyle, Esqr.' 1727, where, speaking of Dodwell,[2] he says :—' As to Mr. Dodwell, I had above twenty years intimate correspondence with him, and always believed him to be a learned and very pious man. . . . . he truly was, what the poet asserts :

> ' Stiff in opinions, *mostly* in the wrong,
> Was everything by starts, and nothing long.'

The first book I ever printed was the present of a manuscript he made me, in defence of his now sufficiently exploded doctrine of the Divine Immortalizing Spirit transferred by Baptism.' This was an octavo, price 2*s*. 6*d*., published in 1708. Curll made no entries of his books in the Stationers' Company Registers until 1710,—a fact, however, of but little moment. But this slight inconsistency of Curll's need not occasion surprise. From 1706 to 1708 Curll issued, among other books, and generally in part proprietorship with some other bookseller, ' A Letter to Mr. Prior,' 1706, occasioned by the Duke of Marlborough's victory at Ramilles; 'Prince Eugene, an Heroic Poem,' 1707, a translation of Boileau's ' Lutrin,' 1708, and Dodwell's work already referred to, ' An explication of a famous passage in the Dialogue of St. Justin the Martyr with Tryphon, concerning the immortality of Human Souls,' 1708 (2*s*. 6*d*.). ' Muscipula ' was also issued from the Peacock without Temple Bar, in 1709.

Three distinct and important episodes distinguish

[2] Henry Dodwell, 1641—1711, a learned theological writer.

Curll's career in 1710. First, he removed to the premises just vacated by J. Bosvill, at the Dial and Bible, against St. Dunstan's Church, in Fleet Street; secondly, he was already in hot water; and, thirdly, he published several books, the titles of which have been at least preserved, and in the compilation of which he must have had some share. (See *N. and Q.*, 6th S., xi. 381.)

The quarrel was an interesting one, and plainly showed that Curll was not only a man not easily put down, but that his education, for the time, must have been unusually good. Curll, like Newbery and many others, sold pills and powders for physical purposes, as well as food and medicine for mental. 'The Charitable Surgeon' (vide *ante*, p. 218) was 'reckoned up' in a 'scurrilous pamphlet' as quackery, etc. Mr. Curll does not trouble himself much about the attack made upon his book—perhaps for obvious reasons—but he takes exception to his opponent's logic. 'Whether,' says Curll, 'he can read or write is a query; but he has given the world a demonstration that he can't cast account; for he says the medicines sold at my shop come to between 3*l*. and 4*l*. a packet, which the author advises to be taken forty days, and will at that rate cost the patient about 20*l*.; but I am of the opinion that physick for forty days at 10*s*. per dose amounts to 120*l*. So much for his arithmetical learning. And for his grammatical, though he pretends in his book to understand Greek, I have five guineas in my pocket, which if John Spinke [the antagonist] can English so many lines out of any school-book, from " Sententia

Puerilis" to Virgil, he shall be entitled to.' This advertisement appeared in *The Supplement* newspaper of April 8, 1709, and was quoted in 'London's Medicinal Informer' (1710), the author of which was, it seems, the redoubtable Mr. Spinke. Taking him at his word, Spinke 'attended this ingenious E. Curll,' the day following that on which the challenge appeared, 'and in his shop Englished the first five lines of Virgil's first Eclogue, and made a demand for the said five guineas;' but he does not say whether he got them, so we may fairly conclude that the money was duly handed over. Even at this early period Curll's name was 'up' as the propagator of objectionable literature. Mr. Spinke grimly admits that if 'The Charitable Surgeon' were a scandalous book, 'then sure E. Curll would not sell it!'

Among the works issued partly or solely by Curll in 1710 were: 'A Complete Key to the Tale of a Tub,' a sixpenny pamphlet of 36 pp., which professed to give some account of the authors, in addition to an explanation as to the occasion and design of writing it. 'A Search after Principles, in a free conference between Timothy and Philatheus concerning the present times,' issued by Morphew, was one of the many productions in which Curll had a hand. The British Museum has a copy containing this statement in what is presumably Curll's own handwriting, which is, by the way, very neat: 'This I wrote at Farmer Lambert's, at Wanstead, in Surrey, whither I went with Mr. Gosling.[3]—E. CURLL.'

[3] A brother bookseller; the two were partners in numerous literary ventures.

'The Meditation upon a Broomstick, and Somewhat Beside of the same Author' (pp. 30, price 6*d*.), also contains a manuscript note, which states that the poems included in this volume—viz. 'Baucis and Philemon,' 'Mrs. Harris's Petition,' 'To Mrs. Biddy Floyd,' and 'The History of Vanbrugh's House'— were 'given and by John Cliffe, Esq., who had them of the Bp. of Kilolla, in Ireland, whose daughter he married, and was my lodger.—E. CURLL.' The Sacheverell controversy called forth, in 1710, three books from Curll, viz. 'The Case of Dr. Sacheverell' (pp. 32) and 'Some Considerations,' &c. (pp. 40). In the absence of anything proving the contrary, Curll's claims to the authorship of these and other works may be considered as genuine. The third work, 'Some Account of the Family of Sacheverell,' was entered in the books of the Stationers' Company, Sept. 13, 1710. This may have been, also, the work of the bookseller. 'The White Crow,' entered in the books of the Stationers' Company, Dec. 4, 1710, and published by Curll, professed to be an 'enquiry into some new doctrines broached by the Bishop of Salisbury [Dr. Burnet] in a pair of Sermons uttered in that Cathedral on the 5th and 7th days of November last, 1710; and his Lordship's Restauration Sermon, last 29th of May.' Betterton's 'The Amorous Widow' was printed for A. Bettesworth, of the Red Lion, London Bridge; R. Gosling, of the Mitre and Crown; and E. Curll, in 1710. 'Callipædia; or the Art of Getting Pretty Children,' translated by N. Rowe, was one of Curll's early publications, which was also issued by Tonson, and one or two other leading booksellers.

'The year 1716,' observes Mr. Thoms, 'was an unlucky year for Edmund Curll. The spring of it witnessed his first quarrel with Pope; and in the autumn—

"Himself among the storied chiefs he spies,
As from the blanket high in air he flies,"—

when the Westminster scholars avenged themselves upon him in a most characteristic manner for misprinting an oration delivered by one of their body.' The war between Pope and Curll was one of the most protracted in literary history. It arose through, comparatively speaking, nothing. Dignity was not one of Pope's failings. In March or April, 1716, James Roberts, who was for a long period connected more or less with Curll, but with whom, it seems, he subsequently quarrelled, issued a volume entitled, 'Court Poems,' which contained 'The Basset Table,' an eclogue, 'The Drawing-Room,' and 'The Toilet.' These were alleged to be 'published faithfully as they were found in a pocket-book, taken up in Westminster Hall the last day of the Lord Winton's trial.'[4] Curll was responsible for the publication of this work, and wrote the 'advertisement by the bookseller.' This curious piece of preface relates that the poems in question had been submitted to the inspection of the *literati* of St. James' Coffee House, by whom they were attributed to the pen of a 'Lady of

[4] The Earl of Winton or Wintoun was convicted of high treason, March 17, 1716.

Quality,' whilst the 'poetical jury' at Button's 'brought in a different verdict,' the 'foreman' strenuously insisting that 'Mr. Gay was the man.' But these two decisions were insufficient, and the bookseller resolved to call in an umpire, and accordingly chose 'a gentleman of distinguished merit,' who answered: 'Sir, depend upon it, these lines could come from no other hand than the laudable translator of Homer.' This was quite enough for Pope, who, perhaps not alone, manufactured the infamous 'Full and True Account of a Horrid and Barbarous Revenge by Poison on the Body of Mr. Edmund Curll,' which, with the 'Circumcision,' surpassed in foulness and indecency anything published by Curll himself; a fact which some of Pope's apologists deem proper to overlook. According to Pope, 'the said Mr. Edmund Curll, on Monday, the 26th instant, published a satirical piece, entitled "Court Poems,"' and on 'the Wednesday evening, between the hours of ten and eleven, Mr. Lintot, a neighbouring bookseller, desired a conference with Mr. Curll, about settling a title-page, inviting him at the same time to take a *whet* together. Mr. Pope, who is not the only instance how persons of bright parts may be carried away by the instigation of the devil, found means to convey himself into the same room, under pretence of business with Mr. Lintot, who, it seems, is the printer of his "Homer." This gentleman, with a seeming coolness, reprimanded Mr. Curll for wrongfully ascribing to him the aforesaid poems. He excused himself by declaring that one of his authors (Mr. Oldmixon by name) gave the copies to the press, and wrote the preface. Upon this Mr. Pope, being to all appearances reconciled, very civilly drank a glass of sack to Mr. Curll, which he as civilly pledged; and though the liquor, in colour and taste differed not from common sack, yet it was plain, by the pangs this unhappy stationer felt soon after, that some poisonous drug had been secretly infused therein.' It would be difficult to match what follows for foulness; and whether Pope intended it for humour or for satire, it will be difficult to find a more deplorable failure, if we except 'Dr. Norris's Narrative.'

Through this 'account,' however, we have at least one interesting fact concerning Curll's movements that would, perhaps, have been otherwise overlooked. We learn that Curll had a shop, depôt, or agency of some sort at Tunbridge Wells. In a frenzied address to his books, Curll is made to say, 'To my shop at Tunbridge ye shall go, by G—, and thence be drawn, like the rest of your predecessors, bit by bit, to the *passage-house.*' This was written in 1716. In connection with this Tunbridge Wells branch, a correspondent in *N.. & Q.*, 6th S., ii. 484, cites the following advertisement, 'dated July 15, 1712,' but without indicating its source:—

'By Edmund Curll, Bookseller, at his shop on the walk at Tunbridge Wells. Gentlemen and Ladies may be furnish'd with all the new Books and Pamphlets that come out; also French and Italian Prints, Maps, &c. Where may be had Mr. Rowe's Translation of " Callipædia, or the Art of getting Beautiful Children." A Poem in 4 Books. Price 4*s*. The Royal Paper,

7s. 6d. Catalogues are delivered gratis at Waghorn's and Brown's Coffee-House on the Walk.'

To return, however, to the unfortunate 'Court Poems.' Mr. Thoms thought it evident that Pope had circulated some libellous statement concerning Oldmixon before March 31, 1716, from an advertisement that appeared in the *Flying Post, or the Postmaster* of that date, in which Oldmixon declared that he never saw ' or heard of the title or preface to them till after the poems were published.' 'Witness, E. Curll.' 'The True and Full Account,' preposterous as it is in its present state, probably had its origin in a hoax resembling in some way that elaborated by Pope on Dennis. The 'Account,' although not published until some years afterwards, was not only written at the time, but amused all the wits about town for a long period,—much to Curll's chagrin. Probably Curll made only verbal objection to the 'Account' so long as it remained in manuscript state, but when this embryo stage was departed from, and smarting under the accumulated insults of an unsparing antagonist, Curll gives *his* version of the transaction in 'The Curliad,' which, professing to be 'a hypercritic upon the Dunciad variorum,' was issued at a shilling in 1729 (April 25). The title-page of this fierce onslaught contains the following remarks, which have, at least, the equivocal merit of candour :—

> ' Pope has less Reading than makes Felons 'scape,
> Less human Genius than God gives an Ape.'
> > Dunciad, b. i. v. 235-6.

> ' O may his Soul still Fret upon the Lee,
> And naught attune his Lyre but Bastardy ;

May unhang'd Savage all Pope's Hours enjoy,
And let his spurious Birth his Pen employ.'
                                    'Incerti Auth.'

Curll gives in 'The Curliad' a circumstantial and perhaps correct account of how the original 'Court Poems' came into his hands. He stigmatizes the 'Account' as false, and proceeds :—'About the year 1715, Mr. Joseph Jacobs (late of Hoxton, the founder of a remarkable sect called the Whiskers) gave to Mr. John Oldmixon three poems at that time handed about, entitled "The Basset Table," The Toilet," and "The Drawing-Room." ' These pieces were printed in octavo, and published by Mr. James Roberts, near the Oxford Arms in Warwick Lane, under the title of "Court Poems." The profit arising from the sale was equally to be divided between Mr. John Oldmixon, Mr. John Pemberton (a bookseller of Parliamentary note in Fleet Street, tho' he has not had the good fortune to be immortalized in the "Dunciad") and myself. And I am sure my brother Lintot will, if asked, declare this to be the same state of the case I laid before Mr. Pope, when he sent for me to the Swan Tavern in Fleet Street to enquire after this publication. My brother Lintot drank his half-pint of old hock, Mr. Pope his half-pint of sack, and I the same quantity of an emetic potion (which was the punishment referred to by our commentator), but no threatenings past. Mr. Pope, indeed, said that satires should not be printed (tho' he has now changed his mind). I answered, they should not be wrote, for if they were, they would be printed. He replied, Mr. Gay's interest at Court would be greatly hurt by publishing these pieces. This was all that passed in our Triumvirate. We then parted. Pope and my brother Lintot went together to his shop, and I went home and vomited heartily.'

It will be seen, therefore, that the 'Account' had some sort of foundation in fact. The 'Court Poems' were constantly before the public, being reprinted for 6d. among several other poems, in 1719, and it is included in the fourth volume of Curll's edition of 'Mr. Pope's Literary Correspondence,' in 12mo, 1736. In 1716, E. Smith, of Cornhill, issued in a broad-side form the well-known verses addressed by Pope 'To the ingenious Mr. Moore, Author of the Celebrated Worm-Powder.'

'Moore's Worms.
For the learned Mr. Curll, Bookseller,
Who, to be reveng'd on Mr. Pope for his Poisonous Emetick, gave him a Paper of Worm Powder, which caused that Gentleman to void a strange sort of Worms.'

Of this 'poem' there are twelve verses, of which the first four and concluding three alone are here given :—

'Oh learned CURLL! thy skill excels
    Ev'n Moore's of Abchurch Lane;
He only genuine worms expels,
    To crawl in print for gain.

From a Wit's brain thou mak'st worms rise,
    (Unknown in the worm-evil)
Fops, silkworms, beaus, and butterflies,
    With that old worm the Devil.

Ev'n Button's bookworms shall, with these,
    (Like these with dust decay'd)
In Grub-street rubbish rest in peace,
    Till Curlls their peace invade.

>   For booksellers vile vipers are,
>   On brains of Wits they prey:
>   The very worms they will not spare,
>   When Wits to worms decay.
>
>   *   *   *   *   *
>
>   Ah, Curl!![*] how greedy hast thou fed
>   (E'er worms gave food to thee)
>   Upon the late illustrous dead,
>   With worms of thy degree.
>
>   Why did the venom of a prude
>   Allure thy vicious taste?
>   Safer thou'dst feast on maggots crude,
>   Or with Tom D'Urfey fast.
>
>   For see! thy meagre looks declare
>   Some poison in thee lurks:
>   Let Bl[ackmo]re ease thy restless care,
>   Or who shall print his works?'

Curll's *fracas* with the indignant scholars of Westminster was not the least of the scrapes into which his ill-timed and ill-appreciated energy landed him. On Sunday, July 8, 1716, the learned and witty Robert South, Prebendary of Westminster, and Canon of Christ Church, Oxford, was gathered unto his fathers. 'Four days after his decease (says Mr. Thoms), his corpse, having for some time lain in a decent manner in the Jerusalem Chamber, was brought thence into the College Hall, where a Latin oration was pronounced over it by Mr. John Barber, then Captain of the King's Scholars. Of this funeral discourse Curll would appear, by some means or other, to have obtained a copy; and,

[*] 'Famous for printing the Lives and Last Wills of great men.'

"did th' Oration print
Imperfect, with false Latin in't."¹

Curll's 'seasonable' but luckless publication was in octavo form of 17 pages, the full title being,—' The Character of the Rev. and Learned Dr. Robert South. Being the Oration spoken at his Funeral on Monday, July xvi. 1716, in the College-Hall of Westminster. By Mr. Barber.' The irate scholars determined upon having revenge, and to this end decoyed the unsuspecting Curll into the Dean's Yard, on the pretence of giving him a perfect copy of the oration. The reception he met with is graphically told in a letter that appeared at the time in the *St. James's Post* :— 'King's College, Westminster, August 3rd, 1716. Sir,—You are desired to acquaint the public that a certain bookseller near Temple-bar, not taking warnings by the frequent drubs that he has undergone for his often pirating other men's copies, did lately, without the consent of Mr. John Barber, present Captain of Westminster School, publish the scraps of a Funeral Oration, spoken by him over the Corpse of the Rev. Dr. South. And being on Thursday last fortunately nabbed within the limits of Dean's Yard, by the King's Scholars there, he met with a college salutation, for he was first presented with the ceremony of the blanket, in which, when the skeleton had been well shook, he was carried in triumph to the school ; and after receiving a grammatical construction for his false concords, he was reconducted to Dean's Yard, and on his knees asking pardon of the aforesaid Mr. Barber for his offence, he was kicked out of the yard, and left to the huzzas of the rabble.' Poor Curll!

This episode was undoubtedly very fruitful in lampoons, the most noteworthy of which is that attributed to Samuel Wesley,[a] and entitled ' Neck or Nothing, a consolatory Letter from Mr. D—nt—n to Mr. C—rll, upon his being Tost in a Blanket,' &c. ' Prefixed is a plate, divided into three compartments: the first exhibits Curll being " presented with the ceremony of the blanket." In the second, he is prostrated on a table receiving a flagellation where one wound, 'tis said,

> "hurts honour more
> Than twenty when laid on before."

In the third he is on his bended knees between two files of the Westminster scholars,' asking pardon of the aforesaid Mr. Barber.' The whole of this poem is given in Mr. Thoms' 'Curll Papers,' but we can only afford space here for a few of the more salient passages.

> 'Lo! I that erst the glory spread
> Of Worthies, who for Monmouth bled,
> In letters black, and letters red;
> To thee, Dear *Mun*, Condolence write,
> As suff'rer from the Jacobite:
> For just as they were martyrs, so
> A glorious Confessor art thou;
> Else should this matchless pen of mine
> Vouchsafe thee not a single line;
> Nor wave its politicks for this,
> Its dark and deep discoveries,

---

[a] See 'Memoirs of the Society of Grub Street,' i., p. 16; and *N. & Q.*, 6th S., *passim.*

Nor for a moment should forbear
To charge the faction in the rear.
Could none of thy poetick band
Of mercenary wits at hand,
Fortell, or ward the coming blow,
From garret high, or cellar low?

For hat and gloves you call'd in haste,
And down to execution pass'd.
Small need of hats and gloves, I trow;
Thou mightst have left thy breeches too!

To see thee smart for copy-stealing,
My bowels yearn with fellow-feeling.
Have I alone oblig'd the press
With fifteen hundred treatises,
Printers and stationers undone,
A plagiary in ev'ry one?

I sweat to think of thy condition
Before that barb'rous Inquisition.
Lo! wide-extended by the crowd,
The Blanket, dreadful as a shroud,
Yawns terrible, for thee, poor *Mun*,
To stretch, but not to sleep upon.

" Confess," quo' they, ".thy rogueries.
What makes you keep in garret high
Poor bards tied up to Poetry?"
" I'm forc'd to load them with a clog,
To make them study:"—" Here's a rogue
Affronts the school, we'll make thee rue it:"
" Indeed, I never meant to do it!"
" No? didst thou not th' Oration print
Imperfect, with false Latin in't?"
'Tis vexatious, *Mun*, I grant,
To hear the passing truants taunt,
And ask thee at thy shop in jeer,
" Which is the way to Westminster?"

Why, POPE will make an epic on't!
BERNARD will chuckle at thy moan,

And all the booksellers in town,
From TONSON down to BODDINGTON.
Fleet Street and Temple-Bar around,
The Strand and Holborn, this shall sound :
For ever this shall grate thine ear :
" Which is the way to Westminster ? " '

The affair was by no means allowed to rest with a squib or lampoon or two, for up to very nearly the time of his death, good care was taken that Mr. Curll should not forget his excursions into space.

Pope's version of Homer afforded Curll an excellent pretext for attacking the poet, and accordingly on April 5, 1716, an advertisement appeared in the *Flying Post*, announcing that ' this day is published the Second part of Mr. Pope's Popish Translation of Homer. The subscribers having made great complaint that there were no pictures in the First part : This is to give notice, that to this Second part there is added a spacious map of the Trojan tents and rivers finely delineated. Translated into copper from the wooden original, as you have it in the learned Dr. Fuller's " Pisgah Sight," being the true travels of Moses and the Children of Israel from the land of Goshen to the land of Canaan. With an exact scale. Sold by E. Curll,' &c. The same issue contains another of Curll's advertisements, which stated that ' next week will be published, an excellent new ballad, called " The Catholic Poet, or Protestant Barnaby's Lamentation." To the tune of " Which nobody can deny."—

'Tho' of his wit the Catholick has boasted,
Lintot and Pope by turns shall both be roasted." '

Mr. Curll did not think he had 'laid it on' strong enough, and five days later, April 10, the same journal contained the following notice :—' To prevent any farther imposition on the public, there is now preparing for the press, by several hands, " Homer Defended," being a detection of the many errors committed by Mr. Pope in his pretended Translation of Homer, wherein is fully proved that he neither understands the original, nor the author's meaning, and that in several places he has falsified it on purpose. To which is added, a specimen of a Translation of the First Book of the Odysses, which has lain printed by Mr. Lintott some time, and which he intends to publish, in order to prejudice Mr. Tickell's excellent version. Any gentlemen who have made observations upon Mr. Pope's Homer, and will be pleased to send them to Mr. Curll . . . . shall have them faithfully inserted in this work.'

Much of the defamatory literature sent into the world by the 'Grubeans' on the appearance of Pope's Homer has been buried in oblivion, but among Curll's publications were 'An Epilogue to a Puppet-show at Bath, concerning the said Iliad, by Geo. Ducket, Esq.,' and 'Remarks upon Mr. Pope's Translation of Homer, by Mr. Dennis, 1717.' This latter, which also contained two letters concerning 'Windsor Forest,' and the 'Temple of Fame,' was issued by Curll in a modified form as 'The Popiad,' without author's or publisher's name, in 1728. But Curll was not the only bookseller who, by issuing libels on Pope prior to 1728, competed for a position in 'The Dunciad.'

Edmund Curll.

A more serious danger threatened Curll in 1716 than his 'differences' with Pope and the Westminster scholars. He was summoned to the Bar of the House of Lords to answer to a charge of violating the order of the House. The official order for printing and publishing the account of the protracted trial of Lord Wintoun, which was brought to a close March 19, 1715-6, was given to Jacob Tonson, who duly executed the work. Its price was prohibitive, and Sarah Popping published a popular account of the transaction for twopence. On April 13 an order was made to 'forthwith attach the said S. Popping.' Sarah, it appears, was indisposed, but their lordships were informed that 'a person is attending the door who can give an account concerning the said Paper.' This 'person' was one Elizabeth Cape, who, by some means or other, implicated Curll and Pemberton as the chief promoters of this outrage upon their lordships' privileges. On Tuesday, April 17, Sarah Popping presented a petition to the House, by which it appears that, during her illness, Messrs. Curll and Pemberton issued the account of Lord Wintoun's Trial without her knowledge, and placed her name as publisher on the title-page entirely upon their own responsibility, and without her consent. On Thursday, April 26, their lordships ordered that Sarah Popping and John Pemberton be forthwith discharged out of custody, without paying any fees; whilst poor Curll, with his usual share of ill-luck, was condemned to 'be continued in the custody he is now in.' Fate was indeed hard upon Edmund, for, still in durance vile, on Wednesday, May 2, Daniel Bridge, a printer in Paternoster Row, proved that he received the copy of the account of Lord Wintoun's Trial from E. Curll, and that he printed the same. On the following Tuesday (May 8) the unfortunate pair presented a joint petition praying for release, which, however, was not granted them until the following Friday, when, on their knees, they received a reprimand from the Lord Chancellor for their offence, and were discharged, after paying their fees.

But yet another quarrel needs recording. We find him in 1716 at loggerheads with Desaguliers, who in 1715 had employed Curll to publish a work entitled 'Fires Improved,' which professed to detail a 'new method of building chimneys so as to prevent their smoking.' It was a translation from the French, and Curll was allowed a share in the profits. In order to promote its sale, Curll ' puffed it off in a very gross manner,' which induced the irate author to publish a disclaimer in Steele's *Town Talk*, in which Desauliers informed the public that whenever his name hereafter was or should be printed with that egregious flatterer Mr. Curll's, either in an advertisement or at the title-page of a book, except that of " Fires Improved," he entirely disowned it.'

Neither the heaped-up insults of Pope, nor the 'orders' of the lords, spiritual and temporal, nor the blanketings of the scholars, had much permanent effect upon Curll, for in eleven days from his dismissal from the custody of the Black Rod, we find him busy getting through the press a new edition of Erdeswick's 'Survey of Staffordshire,' for the loan of Thoresby's manuscript copy of which the bookseller spontaneously offers two copies when it is finally published. We may turn aside for a short time from the incessant turmoil in which Curll was concerned, and consider some of the really useful work which he executed.

The Topographical works which Curll published are for the most part valuable even at the present day, and as few of his publications were issued in sizes larger than octavo, and at a correspondingly cheap rate, he was, apart from personal considerations, really instrumental in placing desirable literature in the hands of those whose purses were not long enough to bear the expense of the then costly and bulky folios and quartos. The following list, chiefly derived from Nichols' 'Lit. Anec.' v. 491, will prove that Curll's publications were not uniformly objectionable :—' History and Antiquities of Winchester,' 1715; ditto of Hereford, 1717; ditto of Rochester, 1717-23; ditto of the Churches of Salisbury and Bath, 1719-23; 'Inscriptions on the Tombs in Bunhill-Fields,' 1717; Aubrey's 'History of Surrey,' 1719, 5 vols.; Norden's ' Delineations of Northamptonshire,' 1720; ' History and Antiquities of Glastonbury,'Oxford,1722;and a ' Chorographical Description or Survey of the County of Devon,' &c., collected by the travail of Tristram Ridson, of Winscot, Gent,' 1714. The price of each volume averaged about 7s. 6d. Curll had a sort of certificate from the well-known antiquary, Browne Willis, who wrote to say that 'Mr. Curll, having been at great expense in publishing these books (now comprised under the title of "Anglia Illustrata," in 20 volumes), and adorning them with draughts of monuments, maps, &c., deserves to be encouraged by us all, who are well-wishers to this study'; no bookseller'—and was Mr. Willis here quietly satirical?—'in town having been so curious as he.' Mr. Curll is of course duly grateful for this tribute, which, he states in a P.S., 'was given upon a journey to Oxford, and has been greatly serviceable to me.'

A spirit of rivalry now and then prompted Curll to undertake some work which he would not have otherwise thought of. To this cause may be safely ascribed the reprint of Surrey's 'Songs and Sonnetts' issued by Tottell in 1567, &c. An edition of Surrey was issued in 1717 by W. Mears, of the Lamb, and J. Brown, of the Black Swan, within Temple Bar, and under the editorial care of George Sewell, M.D. Probably Curll got wind early of this undertaking, for he was not long in getting a rival edition in the market, but he omitted, in his haste perhaps, entirely those of 'Uncertain Authors' reprinted in Sewell's. The 'advertisement' to Curll's publication, dated April 13, 1717, and signed 'Vale,'—one of Curll's several *noms-de-plume*,—states: 'In order to give the publick as correct an edition as I could of these valuable poems, I procured among my friends these several editions, printed in the years 1565, 1567, and 1569, all which I found very full of typographical errors, but the most correct was that of 1567, from which this edition is printed. . . . When I had made the edition of 1567 as correct as I could from the other two, I heard of another copy in the Bodleian Library in Oxford, among Mr. Selden's books, wherein were many considerable amendments, sup-

Edmund Curll. 239

posed to be made by that eminent person : which I got collated by a learned gentleman there,' &c.

It does not appear that Curll was in very bad odour with the fraternity as a whole : it was the authors who 'could not stand' Curll, or *vice versâ*. Readers of the 'Account' of Curll's poisoning will observe that Pemberton is referred to as his partner. The connection between the two booksellers was probably not so close as the modern acceptation of the term would infer, but it lasted, off and on, for a term of several years. From Lintot's Account-Book, we find that Curll and Pemberton were paid, March 4, 1714-5, the sum of 3*l*. 4*s*. 6*d*. for 'half' of Noy's 'Rights of the Crown,' and on January 5, 1715-6, they were again paid 4*l*. 6*s*. for a half-share in West on 'Treasons.' It was a very common thing at this period for two or three booksellers to conjointly bear the expense and share the profits of any considerable work, and then to sell, in sheets, by auction or otherwise, a certain number of copies to various booksellers, whose names appeared on the title-page, and who bound their own copies.

It will be also interesting to learn that the scale of remuneration which Curll allowed 'his authors' was not quite so beggarly as has been imagined. Ed. Holdsworth was paid five guineas for, and allowed fifty copies of,' Muscipula ' (May 30, 1709) ; Susannah Centlivre, twenty guineas each for her three plays, 'The Wonder,' 'The Cruel Gift,' and 'The Artifice' (May 18, 1715) ; John Durant Breval, four guineas for 'The Art of Dress,' a poem (Feb. 13, 1716) ; Charles Beckingham, fifty guineas for 'King Henry IV. of France,'and the translation of Rapin's 'Christus Patiens'

(Nov. 13, 1719); Robert Samber, four guineas for, and twelve copies of, 'The Praise of Drunkeness' (Feb. 20, 1723); Thomas Stackhouse, ten guineas for 'The Life of Bishop Atterbury' (Sept. 16, 1723); Thomas Cooke, 5*l*. for writing Marvel's 'Life,' &c. (April, 1726); and John Clarke received two payments of one guinea each in part of the copy-money of two novels, 'The Virgin Seducer,' and 'The Batchelor's Keeper' (Oct., 1726).

Curll's famous quarrel with Mist dates from about April 5, 1718, when the *Weekly Journal* or *Saturday Post* afterwards rechristened *Mist's Journal*, contained an elaborate article on Curll and Curlicism. Curll was not a handsome man, unless overwhelming contemporary evidence be false. After a passage on the 'sin of Curlicism,' Mr. Mist's correspondent, 'H.,' goes on in this manner: 'There is indeed but one bookseller eminent among us for this abomination, and from him the crime takes the just denomination of *Curlicism*. The fellow is a contemptible wretch a thousand ways: he is odious in his person, scandalous in his fame; he is marked by Nature, for he has a bawdy countenance, and a debauched mien; his tongue is an echo of all the beastly language his shop is filled with, and filthiness drivels in the very tone of his voice.

'But what is the meaning that this manufacturer of ——— is permitted in a civilized nation to go unpunished, and that the abominable Catalogue is unsuppressed, in a country where religion is talked of (little more God knows!)? .... How can our Stamp Office take twelve pence a-piece for the advertisement of his infamous books, publishing the continued increase of lewd abominable pieces of bawdry, such as none can read even in miniature, for such an Advertisement is to a book. How can these refrain informing the government what mines are laid to blow up morality, even from its very foundation, and to sap the basis of all good manners, nay, and in the end, of religion itself?

'Where sleep the watchmen of Israel, that not one divine of the Church of England—not one teacher among the dissenters—has touched this crying curse? O Bangor! O Bradbury! how much better had the kingdom of Christ been established, had you attacked the agents of hell that propagate the kingdom of the devil, instead of snarling about who are, and who are not, vested with effectual power to act this way or that way in the Church, or in the State? How much more like "preachers of righteousness" had ye appeared, if, as far as became you, ye had laboured to establish our youth in virtue and piety, and so suppressed the spreading abominable vices by the agency of the printing-press!'

'In a word, Mist, record it for posterity to wonder at, that in four years past of the blessed days we live in, and wherein justice and liberty are flourishing and established, more beastly unsufferable books have been published by this one offender, than in thirty years before by all the nation; and not a man, clergyman or other, has yet thought it worth his while to demand justice of the government against the crime of it, or so much as to caution the age against the mischief of it.

'Publish this, Mist, as you value your promise, and

remember you'll be honoured with having put the first hand to correct a crime which begins to make us scandalous to our neighbours, and, in time, if not prevented, will make us detestable among all the Christian nations of Europe. Your friend, H.'

Curll was a Whig, and Mist was a Tory. It goes without saying that political animosities prompted the attack. So long as the Whig government could decently refrain from prosecuting an adherent possessing some amount of influence, as Curll did, they would naturally do so. Curll zealously promoted the Hanoverian succession, which was consummated nearly four years before Mist's attack, and the Whigs had the laughing side. Curll's reply was entitled 'Curlicism Display'd, or an Appeal to the Church. Being just Observations upon some Books published by Mr. Curll.' It was in the form of 'a letter to Mr. Mist' (6*d*.). Curll commences thus :—

'Mr. Mist,

'Your journal is now become the oracle of a discontented party, whose fruitless schemes and many disappointments make them kick against the pricks, and who like the deluded multitude of old had rather consult the Devil than not hear some responses in favour of their wandering (pretended) monarch :

> "Restless he rolls about from place to place,
> But will not look an army in the face."

Your superannuated letter-writer was never more out than when he asserted that CURLICISM was but of four years' standing. Poor Wretch ! he is but a mere novice in Chronology, and I do sincerely assure you, Mr. Mist, that CURLICISM (since it must be so called) dates its original from that ever memorable æra of the reign of the first monarch of the Stuartine race.'

After this short bit of introductory, Curll defends several of his publications, specifying at considerable length their nature and their origin. Following Mr. Thoms' excellent example, we shall not enter into that phase more fully than by quoting a representative example :—' The first piece of CURLICISM that appeared was that remarkable Tryal between Robert Earl of Essex and the Lady Frances Howard, who, after eight years' marriage, commenced a suit against him for impotency.' Curll concludes his defence with the following :—

'Thus, Mr. Mist, I have impartially laid before you and the world a full account of the books I have printed, which give your *religion mongers* so much uneasiness. I shall, in the next place, reduce all their trifling objections under four heads, and prove them false in every particular.

' 1. The first charge against me is, " That I am the inventor and introducer of a set of books into the world upon such subjects as were never before known to be brought under the pen."

' 2. " That no nation would permit the publication of such books but our own.'

'As to the first of these calumnies, I think I stand pretty clear, by the concurrent testimonies of the canonists and civilians, from the original institution of the law of nature and nations. And as to the latter, whenever any of these points have been debated in our own kingdom, the main support of the charge, as well as the judgment given, have been wholly confirmed by precedents cited from the ecclesiastical institutions, and the authority of the Fathers themselves.

'3. The other articles of the charge against me, are, " That these books would not have been suffered to be printed four years ago ;" when (if we may believe your old gentleman) none but persons of exemplary piety and virtue, such as the Ormonds, the Marrs, the Bolingbrokes, &c., and their agents the Swifts, the Oldisworths, the Sacheverells, &c., shared the royal favour, and defended that Church which has of late been so much in danger.

'4. And lastly, " That these books are now printed by the connivance of the present government."

'To which it is sufficient to answer, " That the five volumes of the *Cases of Impotency and Divorce* were all printed in the reign of her late *so pious* Majesty ; and that these books, which have given such grievous offence, were so far from appearing in public, by the connivance of this, or indeed any former government, that most of them were published by the immediate command and authority of the government itself."

' And now, Mr. Mist, having made good my promise, and refuted every particular of the charge against me, with relation to the publishing these books, I am farther to assure your old man, that they cannot by the laws of nature and nations be termed *bawdy* books, since they treat only of matters of the greatest importance to society, conduce to the mutual happiness of the nuptial state, and are directly calculated for antidotes against debauchery and unnatural lewdness, and not for incentives to them. For which reason I shall not desist from printing such books, when any occasion offers, nor am I either concerned or ashamed to have them distinguished by the facetious name of " CURLICISM."

'This, I think, Mr. Mist, an unexceptionable answer to the allegations of your antiquated letter-writer; and to prevent one objection, which he might otherwise possibly hereafter make, I shall frankly acknowledge to him, that as considerable a person as he may seem in the eyes of your admirers, nothing which either he or you could say of me, should have moved me to vouchsafe a reply, had not an opportunity thereby offered itself to me of publishing to the world the contents at large of these several pieces, which have of late been so severally inveighed against, and of demonstrating to your correspondent in particular (who I take for granted never read a syllable in either of them beyond the title-page[7]) that his zeal has been employed against such books, as are not only inoffensive, but very useful; and that his indignation against what he calls *Curlicism*, proceeds from a partial infatuated bigotry, and an implicit spirit of censoriousness, into which he has been led by what I call *Mysticism* and *Poperycism*. Whether he be really an old fellow, or only affects a formal gravity, to give his arguments the greater weight among the rabble of malcontents, to whose service alone his pen is de-

[7] 'Ay, there's the rub.' Mr. Curll's title-pages were the chief objection. They were foully suggestive, whilst the books were, in many cases, comparatively pure.

voted—I shall however be glad to see him in town, whither I suppose he is coming to some employment under you, either to solve cases of conscience, which your tattered customers are continually furnishing you with, or to strengthen your political reasonings and zealous insinuations against the government, with quotations from the fathers of the first four centuries, in which sort of learning the gentleman seems to me to be chiefly remarkable; and like the rest of his regular brethren in Christianity, to be passionately fond of their venerable errors, for the sake of their antiquity, and peremptorily to condemn the profane politeness of the classics, as much as he does the damnable conscientious sincerity of our modern prevailing freethinkers.

'Notwithstanding our present difference, Mr. Mist, I am willing to give you a piece of wholesome friendly advice: whereas you publicly declared in my presence, before several witnesses, who will attest it upon oath, that the first letter against me was inserted designedly to reflect on His Majesty under my cover; and likewise, that as for any passages in your *Journal*, whether they should be true or false, they equally conduce to the interest of the cause in which you are embarked, and to the reputation of your paper amongst the party your only constant readers. And whereas on another occasion you have made your boast, that whenever the government has thought fit to take an action of you, you have always brought them to your own terms, I wish you would accept the advice of a generous enemy, and take particular care lest your repeated insolences and treasonable glances on your indulgent superiors, should at length, contrary to their innate and unexampled clemency, prevail with them to put a stop to such flagrant enormities, and oblige them for once to bring you to their terms.

'Having thus given the world an impartial account of the books I have printed, which is the sole design of this letter; and being therefore resolved to enter into no future debate, either with yourself or your champion correspondent, I shall conclude all in the words of a late eminent and learned controvertist [the Dean of Chichester]:—"I now submit what I have said to the reader's judgment: whatever your letter-writer may be, the world, I am persuaded, is tired of such altercations, as I am sure I am."— E. CURLL, Fleet Street, May 26, 1718.'

The importance and interest of the subject, and the rarity of the pamphlet from which the foregoing is extracted, must be our excuse for the length of the excerpt. But notwithstanding his expressed determination not to notice any further attack from Mist, or his 'old man,' we find Curll once more in the heat of a combat, with 'An Answer to Mr. Mist's Journal of the Twenty Eighth of January, 1726.7.' *Mist's Journal*, we may mention, persistently attacked Curll.

Curll was nothing if not singular, and so we find in his lists of publications the most devout sermons issued in company with indecent tales and poems. All was grist for the mill, however, that came in his way. Next to his almost insane, and quite insatiable desire of publishing

'The speeches, verses, and last wills of Peers,'

may be classed his restless attempts at securing the

'copy' of some controversial Bishop's work, or that of any other eminent divine. He had a peculiar weakness for eminent persons, but more especially for Bishops. In 1718 he published a couple of works espousing Hoadly, the originator of the once famous but now forgotten Bangorian controversy. Each of these works was written by Nicholas Amhurst, the conductor of *Terræ-Filius*, a periodical issued twice weekly, January to June, during 1721, and subsequently of the *Craftsman*. The titles of Amhurst's two poems were 'Protestant Popery, or The Convocation,' and 'A Congratulatory Epistle from His Holiness the Pope to the Rev. Dr. Snape.' Both were anonymous publications, and were attributed to George Sewell who, however, inserted a denial in the *Evening Post*.

Pope, in his ' Narrative ' of the method by which his letters had been published, says, ' Mr. Pope's friends imagined that the whole design of E. Curll was to get him to look on the edition of Cromwell's Letters, and so print it as *revised* by Mr. Pope, in the same manner as he sent an *obscene* book to a reverend Bishop, and then advertised it as corrected and revised by him.' The obscene publication referred to was Rochester's ' Poems,' of which Curll issued several editions. But Curll denies Pope's account, and offered a hundred guineas if this 'narrative writer' can 'produce any such advertisement.' Curll's explanation of the transaction is, that he offered to give Dr. Robinson, Lord Bishop of London, an interleaved edition of Rochester, and 'whatever his Lordship saw amiss, if he would be pleased to strike out any lines or Poems therein, such leaves should be reprinted, and rendered conformable to his Lordship's opinion.' Upon being made acquainted with Curll's proposition, the Bishop smiled, and informed Henry Hoare, the medium, 'Sir, I am told that Curll is a shrewd man, and should I revise the book you have brought me, he would publish it as approved by me.'[8] Where two such men as Pope and Curll volunteer as many different stories of one transaction, it is not an easy matter to decide which is telling the truth, but in the present instance perhaps Curll's version is the more correct.

Between the years 1721-4, Curll struck up a correspondence with Bishop Kennett and Sir Robert Walpole. That with the former arose from the natural desire of publishing, after purchasing the copyright, of his Lordship's Translations of Erasmus's 'Praise of Folly,' first published in 1683, and Pliny's 'Panegyric,' 1686. Curll writes the Bishop, Nov. 4, 1721, to inform him of his intention, and also to offer him the opportunity of revising the publications. A prompt reply, dated Nov. 6, was received, in which the Bishop of Peterborough desires to know of whom the copyrights were purchased, as the author had only invested the original booksellers with the right of a single impression; winding up with a very broad hint 'that property and privilege are valuable things,' and discountenancing altogether the bookseller's project. The following day Curll

[8] A story identical with this is related of Wilkes and the 'Essay on Women,' and also of Samuel Foote and 'The Minor.'

was again 'at' his Lordship, and, in a rather lengthy epistle, which need not be here quoted, makes a general defence against the charge of publishing indecent books,—a charge which he ascribes to rumour only, 'or some idle paragraphs, inserted against me in that sink of scandal, *Mist's Journal*, wherein the best characters have been traduced.' He further obliges his Lordship with his catalogue, which 'will in some measure convince your Lordship, that I have been ready, and shall always be, to promote any work of religion or learning, as any other person of our profession.' But Mr. Curll did not obtain Kennett's sanction, and the reissue was not undertaken.

The year 1721 opened inauspiciously for Curll, and in the latter part of January we see him again at loggerheads with the members of the House of Lords. The *Daily Journal* of Monday, January 22, contained an advertisement announcing the speedy publication of the 'Works' of John Sheffield Duke of Buckinghamshire, prose and verse, with a 'true copy of his last Will and Testament.' On Tuesday, Jan. 23, Curll attended, 'according to order,' the House of Lords; he came out of the threatened conflict without hurt, but their lordships anticipated any future contacts by adding to the Standing Orders of the House the resolution that if the works, life, or last Will of any Lord of that House be published without the consent of his heirs, executors, administrators, or trustees, 'the same is a Breach of the Privilege of this House.' This order was vacated July 28, 1845.

Like many other skirmishers, Curll professed a

devoted attachment to his party when in power; but this devotion has almost invariably personal gain for its ulterior object. In 1723, Curll and Henley (who seven years later started *The Hyp-Doctor* to further Walpole's cause) seem to have gleaned some information respecting a projected fifth volume of Mrs. Manley's 'Atalantis,' which never seems to have appeared, but the design of which was 'to give an account of a sovereign and his ministers who are endeavouring to overturn that Constitution which their pretence is to protect; to examine the defects and vices of some men who take a delight to impose upon the world by the pretence of public good, whilst their true design is only to gratify and advance themselves.' These, according to Curll, writing to Walpole from the Strand, on March 2, 1723-4, were Mrs. Manley's own words. Curll's patriotism was not undiluted, for within a few lines of the above quotation he says, 'As your Honour was formerly pleased to promise me your friendship, I now hope to feel the effect of it for what I can, without vanity, call my unwearied diligence to serve the Government, having in a manner left off my business for that purpose. Mr. Goode told me, that I might depend upon having some provision made for me, and that he had named something in the Post-Office to your Honour for my purpose. And I hope that, either in that or some of the many others over which your Honour presides, I shall be thought on.' And also, in a P.S, 'Lord Townshend assured me he would recommend me to your Honour for some provision in the Civil List. In the Stamp Office,' Mr. Curll modestly suggests,

'I can be serviceable.' His patriotism and devotion not only availed him nought,—for none of the Government offices had the advantage of his zeal,—but were probably an additional if unexpressed reason for the Government prosecution of a couple of years later.

This prosecution was commenced in November, 1725, the trial itself having taken place on the 30th of that month. The whole transaction was a very singular one, inasmuch as Curll was indicted for the publication of certain libels, whereas the books 'were made the subject of prosecution because they were obscene.' Why it had taken so long for the Government to arrive at the conclusion that Curll was a proper object for prosecution, it would be very difficult to say, but the episode is only one of the many erratic movements made by English Governments. Of the five books held up to execration, the larger number had been in circulation at least a couple of years before receiving this gratuitous advertisement at the hands of His Majesty's custodians of morals and good manners. The title-pages of these books, however, sufficiently indicate their nature, and are as follows: (1) 'The Translation' of Meibomius, and 'Tractatus de Hermaphroditus,' 1718; (2) 'Venus in the Cloister, or the Nun in her Smock,' which was 'done out of French by Mr. Samber, of New Inne' (who also 'did' 'One Hundred Court Fables' from the French of Le Motte for Curll in 1721); (3) 'Ebrietatis Encomium' (vide *ante*, p. 240), 1723; (4) 'Three New Poems,' *i.e.* 'Family Duty,' 'The Curious Wife,' and 'Buckingham House ;' and (5) 'De Secretis Mulierum,' 1725. Apparently nothing daunted by this unexpected difficulty, which, if his political services to his party were of any value at all, ought never to have arisen, the ill-starred object of the prosecution published 'The Humble Representation of Edmund Curll,' Bookseller and Citizen of London, concerning five books complained of to the Secretary. Mr. Thoms states that 'Curll was found guilty, but moved an arrest of judgment, on the ground that the offence was not a libel; but if punishable at all, was an offence *contra bonos mores*, and punishable only in the spiritual courts.' The case is reported at considerable length in Strange's 'Reports,' and concludes thus: 'Curll not having attended me in time, I acquainted the Court I was not prepared: and my want of being ready proceeding from his own neglect, they [the Judges] refused to indulge him to the next turn. And in two or three days they gave it as their unanimous opinion, that this was a temporal offence. . . . . In this case they gave Judgment for the King. And the defendant was afterwards set in the pillory, as he well deserved.'

But even here Curll bore up with becoming fortitude, and came off in flying colours, as will be seen from the 'State Trials' (xvii. p. 160):—

'This Edmund Curll stood in the pillory at Charing Cross, but was not pelted nor used ill; for being an artful, cunning (though wicked) fellow, he had contrived to have printed papers dispersed all about Charing Cross, telling the people that he stood there for vindicating the memory of Queen

Anne; which had such an effect on the mob, that it would have been dangerous even to have spoken against him: and when he was taken out of the pillory, the mob carried him off, as it were in triumph, to a neighbouring tavern.'

Another prosecution was commenced in May or June, 1726, and this time it was occasioned through purely political motives, which the Government might have anticipated, but unwisely omitted doing. It transpires from what Curll says in ' The Curliad,' that during a five months' imprisonment in 1726, in the King's Bench, one of his fellow-prisoners was John Ker of Kersland, Esq., ' revered by Queen Anne.' Ker resolved to publish his ' Memoirs and Secret Negociations' at the Courts of Great Britain, Vienna, Hanover, &c., and desired his fellow-prisoner, the bookseller, to examine his papers. 'I returned them to him,' says Curll, ' after I had gone carefully through them, with a very short answer, but my real opinion,—that *the facts they contained, were too true to be borne.* However, he pressed me to engage in the affair, which I told him I durst not venture at, unless he would give me leave to communicate his intentions to the ministry. This he most readily acquiesced in, adding withal, that he intended to put himself under the patronage of Sir Robert Walpole. Upon which the contents of all his manuscripts were accordingly transmitted to the Secretary of State, neither from whom, nor from his patron, did Mr. Ker ever receive any the least countermand to his intended purpose.' The first volume was issued in May, 1726, and a few days afterwards the author was served with a warrant in which his book was called a 'scandalous and a seditious libel.' Ker generously took the sole responsibility, but was unable to obey the warrant, being confined to his bed through lameness; and as he died in July, nothing came of the prosecution so far as he was personally concerned. Curll was naturally pounced upon, whether culpable or no. According to promise, the second and third volumes of Ker's 'Memoirs' were published 'upon Oath.' And soon after this, says Edmund in 'The Curliad,' 'a warrant was issued out against me for publishing the three volumes, an information was filed against me, and a true copy of the said Information I both printed and translated, that my *Crime* might not be *forgotten*. For this misdemeanor I was likewise fined twenty marks and the corporal punishment of (what the Gentlemen of the long Robe are pleased jocosely to call) mounting the Rostrum for one hour, which I performed with as much alacrity as Mr. Pope ever pursued his spleen against Mr. Theobald; and tho' he is pleased to say that this machine *will lengthen the face of any man, tho' it were ever so comely*, yet will it not make the *crooked* straight. However, I have always been of opinion, that it is the *Crime*, not the *punishment*, or the *shape* of a man, which stamps his *ignominy*.'

It would be difficult, if Curll's account be true, as there is every reason to suppose it is, to instance a more diabolical piece of injustice. His motives for publishing the work were probably purely mercenary, but it is most obvious that the persecution was animated throughout by the desire to suppress, not obscene books, but Ker's 'Memoirs,' in which there were certain statements not very palatable to those in power. The ministerial bungling is now patent to all; but it had the one good feature of extensively advertising the book, which ran through at least three editions within a few months.

We shall do no more than refer to Curll's publishing, in six volumes, the 'Cases of Impotence and Divorce,' attributed to the pen of Sir Clement Wearg, whilom Solicitor-General, which caused a declamatory letter to be inserted in the *London Journal,* Nov. 12, 1726, signed 'A. P.'

The charge which held ground for so long a time against Curll, that he starved William Pattison to death, has been sufficiently exploded. The scandalous statement was first circulated in print by Pope, and so far from starving him, it is certain that Curll not only provided him with an asylum in his own house, but defrayed the expenses of medical attendance. Pattison's 'Poetical Works' were printed in 1728 for 'H. Curll,' and published at 6s.; whilst to the posthumous 'Memoir' it appears that Pope and Eusden, among others, were subscribers.

Reference has already been made to Curll's insatiable desire for publishing the last Wills of peers, which caused Arbuthnot to wittily observe to Swift that Curll was 'one of the new terrors of death;' but from an announcement in 'An Impartial History, &c., of Mr. John Barber,' 1741, we learn that the Lives and last Wills and Testaments of no less than thirty-one more or less eminent persons were published by him, and included those of Tillotson, Atterbury, Burnet (Bishop

Walter), Curll, Halifax, Talbot, Price, Congreve, Addison, Prior, Locke, Tindal, South, Partridge (the astrologer), John Gay, Wilks, Ashmole, Walter Moyle, William King, Mrs. Manley, &c.

The only one of these publications which involved Curll in a lengthy correspondence was that of Dr. Matthew Tindal, which was alleged to have been altered by Eustace Budgell in his own favour. The controversy between Budgell and Pope, in which Curll also figures, is of much too abstract a character to be here fully discussed. It must, therefore, suffice us to say that a very short time only elapsed between Tindal's death and the publication by Curll of 'A True Copy of the Last Will and Testament .... of Matthew Tindal,' 1733, which was perhaps followed shortly afterwards by 'Memoirs of the Life and Writings of Matthew Tindal.' Curll's energy was naturally offensive to Budgell, who, in the *Bee* of October 6, characterized Curll's 'Life of Dr. Tindall' as a 'scandalous imposition upon the public.' 'The person who wrote and published this senseless piece of stuff, was a fellow whose character all mankind are acquainted with; who, we are credibly informed, has been obliged several times to walk about Westminster Hall with a label about his neck, and has once already stood in the pillory. We are sorry to see ourselves obliged to stain our pens with the name of such a creature, yet since it must out, we will name at once the most perfect compendium of impudence and wickedness by naming CURLL the bookseller.' The 'Memoirs' are dedicated by 'E. C.,' September 10, 1733, to Mrs.

S

Lucy Price, relict of Mr. Justice Price, and it is from this lady that Curll obtained his materials. Much literary warfare, arising chiefly on side-issues, was the outcome of the contact between Budgell and Curll; and on one occasion, it is said, that when the former was passing through Fleet Street, he met a shabby fellow, who set upon him in the open street, calling him the rogue who scribbled in the *Bee*, the villain who wrote against the Government, and the fellow that forged a Will. This pugnacious person is stated to be Henry Curll, who was, if this rumour be true, on the high way to rivalling his father in notoriety. Mr. Budgell is reported to have retired into a shop, whilst Henry challenged him to fight, and further promised that if he and his father caught him in Burleigh Street, he should never more get out of it. Probably the entire story was a fabrication.

Concerning Henry and his movements scarcely anything is known. Nichols quotes an advertisement from the *Daily Post* of August 7, 1730, which announced that 'Henry Curll, bookseller, in Bow Street, Covent Garden, leaving off business at Michaelmas next, hereby gives notice, that the following books may (till that time) be had at his house above mentioned, at the following prices, after which they will be raised;' and then comes an enumeration of the topographical works named *ante*, p. 237. Henry is said to have kept a separate shop in Henrietta Street. (See *Post Boy*, July 26, 1726.)

Curll's frequent removals from one shop to another can scarcely be regarded as indications of success. During rather less than forty years he had in succession no fewer than seven habitations. The first was at the Peacock, without Temple Bar, but from here he seems to have moved in 1710 to the Dial and Bible against St. Dunstan's Church in Fleet Street, where he remained for ten years, having published Hale's ' Discourse of the Several Dignities and Corruptions ' ' next the Temple Coffee-house ' in 1720. He then tried Paternoster Row, where, in 1720, he published Jacob's ' Lives of the Poets ; ' but this locality seems to have soon disgusted him, as he did not remain there more than a year or so. Humphrey Broadbent's ' Domestick Coffee-man,' 1722, was dated from 'against Catherine Street' in the Strand, and the stay at this locality was one of six or seven years. The *Daily Post*, February 7, 1729-30, contained an advertisement from Curll of the publication of some original MSS. in the Heralds' Office and the Bodleian Library, in three volumes octavo, which were ' Printed only for E. Curll, at his *Literatory*, in Bow Street, Covent Garden, next door to Will's Coffee-house.' In 1733 we find him publishing, *inter alia*, ' The Life of that Eminent Comedian, Robert Wilks, Esq.,' at Burghley Street, in the Strand ; but about a couple of years later he again removed to the vicinity of Covent Garden, in Rose Street, and at the sign of Pope's Head,—and he seems to have remained here to the end of his busy, if not prosperous, life.

Mr. Curll's intentions in the famous Miscellany line were no doubt good enough from one point of view. But his efforts were not highly praised by some ; for instance, Swift writes, May 14, 1711, ' That villain

Curl has scraped up some trash, and calls it Dr. Swift's "Miscellanies," with the name at large, and I can get no satisfaction of him.' This feeling of animosity was heightened as time went on, so that on August 30, 1716, he says: 'I had a long design upon the ears of that Curl, when I was in credit, but the rogue would never allow me a fair strike at them, although my penknife was ready drawn and sharp.' Curll's scheme of making up a 'Miscellany' that would appeal to a wide circle was simple enough, and, it must be confessed, dishonest enough. He was constantly on the alert in the hope of picking up something smart or smutty in the way of verse, and if it bore the remotest resemblance to any work of Swift, or Pope, or Gay, or indeed of anybody else of note, the piece in question was duly secured. The particular Miscellany to which Swift alludes in the above extract was probably 'A Meditation upon a Broom-Stick, and somewhat beside, of the same Author,' which was issued in 1710 from the Dial and Bible, against St. Dunstan's Church in Fleet Street. This was again published, in 1711, with six other tracts by Swift, under the generic title of 'Miscellanies,' by Dr. Jonathan Swift. And this rule of including something stale among that which was new was almost always observed by Curll,—perhaps as much from force of circumstances as from choice. When Pope and Swift published their own authorized 'Miscellanies in Prose and Verse,' (1727), Curll brought out 'Miscellanea' in five volumes, and the last one of these Mr. Curll modestly declares, in the dedication to Dr. Towne, to be 'the pin-basket of my collections for the year seventeen hundred and twenty-six.' Many of the pieces in these volumes, labelled 'by Dr. Swift,' and 'by Mr. Pope,' were not written by either, as Curll must have very well known. (See *Antiquarian Magazine*, vii. 157 and 268.)

'The Dunciad' appeared in 1727, and that Curll received plenty of attention will be quite understood, for of all Pope's enemies none was more pertinacious than the bookseller. The honour of the most frequent reference is about equally divided between Curll and John Dennis, the critic. Of all the Dunces, Curll takes precedence, being mentioned, in connection with his 'chaste press,' in the fortieth line of Book I. The second book opens with these lines:—

> 'High on a gorgeous seat, that far outshone
> Henley's gilt tub, or Fleckno's Irish throne,
> Or that whereon her Curls the public pours,
> All-bounteous, fragrant grains and golden show'rs,
> Great Cibber sate.'

Pope, in a note, explains the reference to Curll, whom, he says, 'stood in the pillory at Charing Cross, in March 1727-8,' which Curll states was in February and not March. Perhaps even Pope wrote nothing more 'beastly' than that concerning the bookseller which follows the quotation given *ante*, pp. 211-212. Pope's note to this last reference is one of the most characteristic in the whole poem. It is much too good to be omitted here, particularly as the greater part of it is not included in most modern editions of Pope's 'Works.' 'We come to a character of much respect, that of Mr. Edmund Curll. As a plain repetition of great actions is the best praise of them, we shall only say of this eminent man, that he carried the trade many lengths beyond what it ever before had arrived at ; and that he was the envy and admiration of all his profession. He possessed himself of a command over all authors whatever ; he caused them to write what he pleased ; they could not call their very *names* their own. He was not only famous among these ; he was taken notice of by the State, the Church, and the Law, and received particular marks of distinction from each.

'It will be owned that he is here introduced with all possible dignity : He speaks like the intrepid Diomed ; he runs like the swift-footed Achilles ; if he falls, 'tis like the beloved Nisus ; and (what Homer makes to be the chief of all praises) he is *favoured of the Gods ;* he says but three words, and his prayer is heard ; a Goddess conveys it to the seat of Jupiter : Though he loses the prize, he gains the victory ; the great Mother herself comforts him, she inspires him with expedients, she honours him with an immortal present (such as Achilles receives from Thetis, and Æneas from Venus) at once instructive and prophetical : After this he is unrivalled and triumphant.

'The tribute our author here pays him is a graceful return for several unmerited obligations : Many weighty animadversions on the public affairs, and many excellent and diverting pieces on private persons has he given to his name. If ever he owed two verses to any other, he owes Mr. Curll some thousands. He was every day extending his fame, and enlarging his writings : Witness innumerable instances ; but it shall suffice only to mention the " Court Poems," which he meant to publish as the work of the true writer, A Lady of Quality; but being first threatened, and afterwards punished for it by Mr. Pope, he generously transferred it from *her* to *him*, and ever since printed it in his name. The single time that he ever spoke to C. was in that affair, and to that happy incident he owed all the favours since received from him.'

It can hardly be a matter of surprise if the 'favours' increased rather than diminished after the appearance of ' The Dunciad,' considering that Pope remarked of his old enemy,—

> ' Obscene with filth the miscreant lies bewray'd,
> Fall'n in the plash his wickedness had laid:
> Then first (if poets aught of truth declare)
> The catiff vaticide conceiv'd a pray'r,' &c.

In the same book (the second), the bookseller is again referred to as the 'shameless Curll.' In a note to the 142nd line of Book II., *re* the expression ' his rueful length of face' used in the context, Pope grimly remarks, after a quotation from *Mist's Journal*, to the effect that a decrepid person or figure of a man are no reflections upon his genius : ' This genius and man of worth, whom an honest man should love, is Mr. Curll. True it is, he stood in the Pillory, an incident which will lengthen the face of any man, tho' it were ever so comely, therefore is no reflection on the natural beauty of Mr. Curll.' Concerning those ' damn'd to Fame,' in the third book, we read :—

> ' Some strain in rhyme ; the Muses, on their racks,
> Scream like the winding of ten thousand jacks :
> Some free from rhyme or reason, rule or check,
> Break Priscian's head, and Pegasus's neck ;

> Down, down they larum, with impetuous whirl,
> The Pindars, and the Miltons of a Curl.'

This famous satire called forth from Curll's press or shop 'A Compleat Key to the Dunciad,' ¦which ran through several editions; 'The Popiad,' of Dennis; 'The Curliad,' by Curll, who also assisted in collecting materials for 'The Female Dunciad,' which contained 'The Metamorphosis of Mr. Pope into a Stinging Nettle,' by Mr. Foxton, who was not honoured with a place in 'The Dunciad,' and who was, perhaps, angry in consequence; 'The Dunciad Dissected,' by Curll, and Mrs. Thomas ('Corinna'); 'Remarks on the Dunciad,' by Dennis, in addition to several others not enumerated. Nearly all of the foregoing were issued in a popular form and at a popular price.

The last great literary battle that took place between Pope and Curll was concerning the publication of the former's letters,—a transaction which for its involved trickery has scarcely any rival in literary annals. The squabble really originated in 1727, when Curll gave Mrs. Thomas, a cast-off mistress of Henry Cromwell, the sum of ten guineas for some letters which Pope had in his early career addressed to this distant relative of the whilom Lord Protector. Pope's poetical fame was still at its zenith, and from this and other circumstances the unauthorized publication of his letters made a stir, and naturally sold well. This was highly gratifying to Pope's vanity, but he pretended to be angry. In 1728, his old enemy and rival, Lewis Theobald, edited the posthumous works of Wycherley, which furnished Pope with a groundless pretext for publishing the dramatist's correspondence. This was another example of his insatiable vanity.

From the success which his volume of Pope's letters had met with, Curll made the utmost efforts to obtain a further supply. He advertised, and gave it to be understood that he neither wanted to know nor cared where the letters came from, so long as he could get them. This offer was too generous; for he was imposed upon by purchasing some epistolary communications addressed by Voiture to Mdlle. Rambouillet as Pope's to Miss Blount. Curll's project received unexpected assistance from an extraneous quarter. But previous to this Pope had received Lord Oxford's sanction to allow the Wycherley letters to be deposited in his library, a fact to be duly mentioned in the preface. Pope further told Oxford that he had given his bookseller instructions to say that copies of the letters had been obtained from his Lordship,—a process which would at once appear as if Oxford and the bookseller were the sole and 'authorized' persons responsible for the publication. But this was hardly good enough, even for the weak, good-natured son of Queen Anne's famous minister. Another dodge was tried, and success was the result. After begging the return of his letters from various friends, upon various pretexts, he employed some one, a mysterious P. T., whose identity is still involved in the most complete obscurity, to sell them to Curll with a view to publication. P. T. wrote Curll in 1733, offering a collection of letters, 'from the early days of Pope to the year 1727.' The matter remained in abeyance for some time. In March, 1735, he writes thus to Pope:—'Sir,—To convince you of my readiness to oblige you, the enclosed is a demonstration. You have, as he says, disobliged a gentleman, the initial letters of whose name are P. T. I have some other papers in the same hand, relating to your *family*, which I will show, if you desire a sight of them. Your letters to Mr. Cromwell are out of print; and I intend to print them very beautifully, in an octavo volume. I have more to say than is proper to write; and if you will give me a meeting, I will wait on you with pleasure, and close all differences between you and yours, E. CURLL.'

This was a splendid opportunity for Pope, and the only return Curll got for his honest and well-meaning attempt at conciliation was an insulting advertisement in the *Daily Post Boy*, couched in these terms:— 'Whereas A. P. hath received a letter from E. C., bookseller, pretending that a person, the initials of whose name are P. T., hath offered the said E. C. to print a large Collection of Mr. P.'s letters, to which E. C. required an answer: A. P. never having had, nor intending to have, any private correspondence with the said E. C., gives it him in this manner: That he knows no such person as P. T.; that he believes he hath no such collection; and that he thinks the whole a forgery, and shall not trouble himself at all about it.' Curll replied, denying he had endeavoured to correspond with Mr. Pope, and affirms that he had written to him by direction.

The shadowy P. T. once again looms in the foreground, and accuses Curll of having betrayed him ' to Squire Pope, but you and he both shall soon be con-

vinced it was no forgery.' And further, as Curll had
not complied with the request to advertise, P. T. had
the letters printed at his own expense, and offers to
sell Curll some copies,—an offer which it is almost
needless to say was accepted. Still P. T. himself
holds back. According to Dr. Johnson, ' Curll said,
that one evening a man in a clergyman's gown, but
with a lawyer's band, brought and offered for sale a
number of printed volumes, which he found to be
Pope's epistolary correspondence ; that he asked no
name, and was told none, but gave the price demanded, and thought himself authorized to use this
purchase to his own advantage.' This ' short, squat '
go-between assumed the name of R. Smith, or
Smythe, and 240 copies of the work were delivered.

On May 12, 1735, the *Daily Post* contained the
following advertisement :—' This day are published,
and most beautifully printed, price 5s., Mr. Pope's
" Literary Correspondence for Thirty Years," from
1704 to 1734, being a collection of Letters regularly
digested, written by him to the Earls of Halifax and
Burlington; Craggs, Trumbull, Digby, Edward Blount,
Addison, Congreve, Wycherley, Walsh, Steele, Gay,
Arbuthnot, etc. With the respective answers of each
correspondent. Printed for E. Curll in Rose Street,
Covent Garden ; and sold by all the booksellers.
N.B. The original manuscripts (of which affidavit is
made) may be seen at Mr. Curll's House, by all who
desire it.' But, to quote D'Israeli, ' at this moment
Curll had not received many books, and no MSS. The
advertisement produced the effect designed ; it roused
public notice, and it alarmed several in the House of

Lords. Pope doubtless instigated his friends there. The Earl of Jersey moved, that to publish letters of Lords was a breach of privilege; and Curll was brought before the House. This was an unexpected incident; and P. T. once more throws his dark shadow across the path of Curll to hearten him, had he wanted courage to face all the lords. P. T. writes to instruct him in his answers to their examination, but to take the utmost care to conceal P. T.; he assures him that the lords could not touch a hair of his head if he behaved firmly; that he should only answer their interrogatories by declaring he received the letters from different persons; that some were given, and some were bought.'

On the very same day as that on which Curll's advertisement appeared in the *Daily Post Boy*, the following entry (reprinted by Mr. Thoms) was made on the *Lords' Journal:* 'Diè Lunæ, 12° Maij, 1735. *Books Printed for Curll to be seized.*—Notice was taken to the House of an Advertisement printed in the newspaper intituled *The Daily Post Boy*, Monday, May 12, 1735, in these words (videlicet),' and then follows the advertisement already quoted. After it had been read by the Clerk, it was ordered 'that the Gentleman Usher of the Black Rod attending this House, do forthwith seize or cause to be seized the impression of the said Book; and that the said E. Curll, together with J. Wilford, at the Three Flower de Luces behind the Chapter House near St. Paul's, for whom the said newspaper is said to be Printed, do attend this House to-morrow.' Accordingly 'to-morrow,' Tuesday, May 13, the two 'attended.' A postponement until the following day was agreed upon, after a special Committee had been formed. On Wednesday the examination actually took place, although their lordships were unable to discover anything tending towards a breach of their privileges; but Pope's friend, Lord Ilay, pointed out that the copy of the book under examination which he had, had, on the 117th page, a letter from Mr. Jervas which contained an abuse of the Earl of Burlington, but that letter the Committee were unable to find in the copy before them. When questioned as to whether the book delivered to the Committee contained the whole of what he published, Curll said that the particular book was more than he published, for this had a preface and a title-page, which he never saw before he came before the Committee. There were, he said, two parcels sent to him; the first he received himself, and the other parcel was left at his house with his wife, when he was not at home, which he had not opened when they were seized; those that he had sold had not the title and preface. Their lordships entered into a categorical examination as to the methods by which he came possessed of the letters, but adjourned the inquiry until 'to-morrow morning, 10 o'clock.'

The Committee met with no better success on Thursday, May 15, and proposed to report to the House that as they had not found any letter of a lord printed in the said book, they conceive that the printing of it is not contrary to the Standing Order, and are of opinion that the said Books should be delivered back to the said Curll. This Report was agreed to, and Curll once more came off in flying colours. On the same day, and just previous to his last appearance before the Lords, Curll writes this letter to 'the Rev. Mr. Smith:'—'Dear Sir,—I am just going to the Lords to finish Pope. I desire you to send me the *sheets* to *perfect* the first fifty books, and likewise the *remaining three hundred books*; and pray be at the Standard Tavern this evening, and I will pay you twenty pounds more. My defence is right; I only told the lords I did not know from whence the books came, and that my wife received them. This was strict truth, and prevented all further inquiry. *The lords declared they had been made Pope's tools.* I put myself on this single point, and insisted, as there was not any Peer's letter in the book, I had not been guilty of any breach of privilege. I depend that the books and the imperfections will be sent, and believe of P. T. what I hope he believes of me.'

This letter apparently irritated the reverend nonentity and his associate P. T., for they charge Curll with endeavouring to betray them to the Lords. Again Curll was duped, and promptly on Friday, May 16, 1735, he answers the charges preferred against him thus:—'Sir,—1st, I am falsely accused. 2. I value not any man's change of temper; I will never change my veracity for falsehood, in owning a fact of which I am innocent. 3. I did not own the books came from *across the water*, nor ever named you; and as you told me everybody knew you in Southwark, I bid him make a strict inquiry, as I am sure you would have done in such an exigency. 4. Sir, I have acted justly in this affair, and that is what I shall always think wisely. 5. I will be kept no longer in the dark; P. T. is *Will-o'-the-Wisp;* all the books I have had are imperfect; the first fifty had no titles nor prefaces; the last five bundles seized by the Lords contained but thirty-eight in each bundle, which amounts to one hundred and ninety, and fifty, is in all but two hundred and forty books. 6. As to the loss of a future copy, I despise it, nor will I be concerned with any more such dark suspicious dealers. But now, Sir, I'll tell you what I will do: when I have the *books perfected* which I have already received, and *the rest of the impression*, I will pay you for them. But what do you call this usage? First take a note for a month, and then want it to be changed for one of Sir Richard Hoare's. My note is as good, for any sum I give it, as the Bank, and shall be as punctually paid. I have always said *gold is better than paper*. But if this dark converse goes on, I will instantly reprint the whole book; and, as a supplement to it, all the letters P. T. ever sent me, of which I have exact copies, together with all your originals, and give them upon oath to my Lord Chancellor. You talk of *trust*—P. T. has not reposed any in me, for he has my money and notes for imperfect books. Let me see, Sir, either P. T. or yourself, or you'll find the old Scots proverb verified, *Nemo me impune lacessit.* Your abused humble servant, E. CURLL. P.S. Lord —— I attend this day. Lord Delawarr I sup with to-night. Where Pope has one lord, I have twenty.'

Pope had but little right to expect any leniency from the hardly-used bookseller, but he had the sympathetic assurances from those of his friends who could not see through his duplicity. For example, Swift, writing to Lady Betty Germain, on June 8, 1735, says: 'I detest the House of Lords for their indulgence to such a profligate villain as Curll.'

Curll's circumstantial account of the transaction concerning letters is to some extent strengthened by what Dr. Johnson records,—and the great lexicographer had but little respect for Curll, whom he designates 'a rapacious bookseller, of no good fame.' In speaking to Henry Lintot upon the subject, 'he declared his opinion to be, that Pope knew better than anybody else how Curll obtained the copies, because another parcel was at the same time sent to himself, for which no price had ever been demanded, as he made known his resolution not to pay a porter, and consequently not to deal with a nameless agent.'

It was now Curll's place to take up the offensive, which he did with commendable alacrity. 'He has,' exclaimed Edmund, 'a knack at versifying; but in prose I think myself a match for him.' The next 'move' was the following advertisement, which Mr. Thoms quaintly describes as 'saucy':—

'E. CURL TO THE PUBLIC.
 'From Pope's Head in Rose Street,
  'Covent Garden, July 26, 1735.

'Mr. Pope having put me under a necessity of using him as he deserves, I hereby declare that the first volume of his "Letters," which I published on the 12th of May last, was sent me ready printed by himself, and for six hundred of which I contracted with his agent, R. Smythe,⁹ who came to me in the habit of a clergyman. I paid the said R. Smythe half the sum contracted for, and have his receipt in full for three hundred books, tho' it has since, by him, been honestly owned that he delivered me but two hundred and forty books, and these all imperfect. For this treatment I shall have recourse to a legal remedy. Mr. Pope, in the *Grub Street Journal* (a libel[1] wherein he has been concerned from its original), the *Daily Journal*, and the *Daily Post Boy*, declared these letters to be forgeries, and complained of them to the House of Lords; which falsehood was detected before the most august assembly; and upon my acquittal, he publishes a very idle narrative of a robbery committed upon two manuscripts—one in his own, and the other in the Earl of Oxford's library. This fallacy being likewise exposed, he now advertises he shall *with all convenient speed* publish some " Letters " himself, particularly relating to his

⁹ Upon his own confession, it appears that James Worsdale, a painter, actor, and author, personated the Rev. Mr. Smythe, and was employed by Pope.

[1] Mr. Curll might have been excused had he spoken in much stronger terms of this witty newspaper, in which he was constantly satirized. The fourth number contained a letter, ascribed in the most serious strain to Curll, in which he is represented as applying for the post of bookseller to the Society. The fifteenth number contains a 'defence' of his manner of trading, and also the decision at which the learned members had arrived to appoint Capt. L. Gulliver as 'the most proper person to fill the place' of bookseller. The joke was carried still farther, for in No. 24, Mr. Curll is reported as resenting his disappointment at not being chosen, and had, since his rejection, spoken very disrespectfully of them.

T

correspondence with the Bishop of Rochester. But the public may be assured that, if any letters Mr. Pope himself, or any of his tools, shall think fit to publish, are the same, or any way interfere, with those I have published, that the same shall be instantly reprinted by me.'

Then follows the 'contents' of his second volume of Pope's correspondence, and an announcement of a third to be 'published next month,' the whole winding up with: 'I know not what honours Mr. Pope would have conferred on him:—1st, I have hung up his head for my sign; and, 2ndly, I have engraved a fine view of his house, gardens, &c., from Mr. Rijsbrack's painting, which will shortly be published. But if he aims at any farther artifices, he never found himself more mistaken than he will in trifling with me. E. CURLL.'

Curll did not stop at the third volume, for no less than six were issued at intervals; but several of these were composed for the most part of stale tracts and poems, which 'fell flat.' Still, the six volumes had the generic title of 'Mr. Pope's Literary Correspondence.' Pope probably more than once regretted that his vanity involved him in a scuffle with Curll, and he was, it may be inferred, only speaking the truth when, in a letter to Hugh Bethel, dated June 17, 1728, he wrote: 'After the publication of my boyish letters to Mr. Cromwell, you will not wonder if I should forswear writing a letter again while I live.' But although he makes substantially the same observation in several other letters, his correspondence does not seem to have fallen off. The quarrel had not much abated when Orrery wrote to Swift, March 18, 1736-7: 'Curll, like his friend the devil, glides through all key-holes, and thrusts himself into the most private cabinets.'

It will be quite unnecessary in this place to do more than to refer to the light which the late Mr. Dilke has thrown upon this subject of Pope's letters, and the trickery which has now become patent. Pope's own 'authorized' version was little more than a reprint of Curll's, and each alike contained a great number of falsifications, by Pope, which have been detected by comparing the exact copies of the originals which Caryll took before returning the letters addressed to him by the poet, according to Pope's request.

On October 29, 1735, we again find Curll 'on the rampage.' Stephen Duck, in a letter to Spence, records an interview he had with Curll, who visited the 'thresher poet' in company with some one else. The visitors inquired how the subscription was getting on for the new edition of his poems. Duck replied, as well as he could wish. 'Immediately one of the persons (who had more than an ordinary ill aspect) answered, that if I did not get a licence my book would be pirated in a week after 'twas published. I answered, that I did not see how even a licence would secure a man's property just now, when printers and booksellers, in defiance of all justice and honesty, pirated everything they could lay hands on: I added that I had been informed Mr. Pope's works which he had sold to Gilliver had not escaped this fate. As I mentioned your friend Mr. Pope, the gentleman put on a more terrible countenance, and with a particular emotion told me that I "talked quite out of my province, and that I knew nothing of Pope or Gilliver either, and that Gilliver had no more to do with Mr. Pope's works than he himself, or any other person." He then told me, with an air of insolence, that his name was Curl, and should be very glad to see me in Covent Garden.'

A few years later, in 1740 or 1741, we have still another example of Curll's restless desire of getting hold of something new. Mrs. Pilkington, in her 'Memoirs' (ii. p. 158), records an interesting fact to the effect that, when living in lodgings near White's Chocolate House about 1741, her landlady announced to her one morning that there was 'an ugly squinting old fellow' who requested an interview. When admitted, he informed the impecunious Mrs. Pilkington that a Mr. Clark had lately died at St. Edmondsbury and left her a legacy of 500*l*., which she could obtain by waiting on Counsellor Clark, of Essex Street, Strand. This was delightful news, which was, however, nullified by the 'old fellow' asking her to dine with him at Richmond. She refused to do that, whereupon he confessed that the windfall was a fabrication, and that his chief object of the visit was, being about to publish a life[2] of Alderman Barber, to whom her husband had been chaplain, he wished to embellish it with some letters of Dean Swift, which he had heard were in her possession.

We have had occasion already to lay before the reader a fact against which there can be no appeal, namely, that beauty was not one of Mr. Curll's natural

[2] Vide *ante*, p. 256.

endowments. But nothing that we have previously quoted surpasses in graphic minuteness the record which Thomas Amory, in a mad work entitled ' The Life of John Buncle' (1756), has bequeathed to a grateful posterity. 'Curll was,' he says, 'in person very tall and thin—an ungainly, awkward, white-faced man. His eyes were a light grey—large, projecting, goggle and purblind. He was splay-footed and baker-kneed.'

'He had,' continues candid Mr. Amory, 'a good natural understanding, and was well acquainted with more than the title-pages of books. He talked well on some subjects. He was not an infidel, as Mrs. Rowe represents him in one of her letters to Lady Hartford (afterwards Duchess of Somerset). He told me it was quite evident to him that the Scriptures of the Old and New Testaments contained a real revelation: there is for it a rational, a natural, a traditionary, and a supernatural testimony, which rendered it quite certain to him. He said he no more doubted the truth of the Christian religion than he did the existence of an independent supreme Creator; but he did not believe the expositions given by the divines. . . . .

'He was a debauchee to the last degree, and so injurious to society, that by filling his translations with wretched notes, forged letters, and bad pictures, he raised the price of a four-shilling book to ten. Thus, in particular, he managed Burnet's " Archæology." And when I told him he was very culpable in this and other articles he sold, his answer was, What would I have him to do? He was a bookseller; his translators in pay lay three in a bed at the Pewter Platter inn, in Holborn, and he and they were for ever at work to deceive the public! He likewise printed the lewdest things. He lost his ears for " The Nun in her Smock," and another thing. As to drink, he was too fond of money to spend any in making himself happy that way; but at another's expense he would drink every day till he was quite blind, and as incapable of self-motion as a block. This was Edmund Curll. But he died at last as great a penitent (I think in the year 1748)[3] as ever expired. I mention this to his glory.

'As Curll knew the world well, and was acquainted with several extraordinary characters, he was of great use to me at my first coming to town, as I knew nobody nor any place. He gave me the true characters of many I saw; told me whom I should avoid, and with whom I might be free. He brought me to the playhouses, and gave me a judicious account of every actor. He understood these things well. No man could talk better on theatrical subjects. He brought me likewise to Sadler's Wells; to the night-cellars, and to Tom King's, the famous night-house in Covent Garden. As he was very knowing and well known at such places, he soon made me as wise as himself in these branches of learning; and, in short, in the space of a month I was as well acquainted in London as if I had been there for years. My kind preceptor spared no pains in lecturing. But what of all things I thought most wonderful was the company I saw at Sieur Curll's. As he was intimate with all the high, &c., in town, many of them frequented his shop to

[3] It was in 1747.

buy his dialogues and other lively books. Some of these girls he often asked to dine with him, and then I was sure to be his guest.'

It is to be feared that much of Amory's narrative is correct, as he probably had no reason to vilify his old friend and *cicerone*. Probably, also, he drew upon his vivid imagination for some of the particulars, as it is exceedingly unlikely that a man like Curll would make such a weak statement when taxed about some of his 'culpable' articles. Amory perhaps got hold of a part of a fact, and supplied the other half himself. However that may be, it is simply impossible to reconcile his with Eliza Heywood's description (quoted in a note to the second book of 'The Dunciad'). This person, like Curll, had no character to lose. She celebrated Curll's undertakings for reformation of manners, and declares herself 'to be so perfectly acquainted with the *sweetness of his disposition*, and that *tenderness with which he considered the errors of his fellow-creatures*, that, though she should find the *little inadvertencies* of her *own life* recorded in his papers, she was certain it would be done in such a manner as she could not but approve.'

But we must now bring our memoir of Edmund Curll to a close. Like many other men who, from one cause or another, were constantly before the notice of the public in their early and middle age, Curll, the plucky enemy of Pope and Swift, the publisher of books good and bad, the smart stationer, the implacable opponent, and indomitable man of business, spent the last few years of his life in comparative obscurity, relinquishing his trade only at his death. He published but few books during his last seven years; among these perhaps the most notable was 'A History of the English Stage' (1741), which, although Thomas Betterton's name appears as author on the title-page, was, as we have already suggested, compiled partly by Curll himself, who, at all events, wrote the dedication to the Duke of Grafton. The last work which he entered on the books of the Stationers' Hall Company, August 20, 1746, was 'Achates to Varus. An epistle describing some wonderful appearances that ensued from a touch of Ithuriel's Spear, together with a large preface in the style and manner of some distinguished authors.'

Edmund Curll died on December 11, 1747, and if not quite 'unknelled, uncoffined, and unknown,' at least unwept and uncared-for.

CHAPTER XI.

JOHN DUNTON.

SINGULARITY is one of the most obvious characteristics of the old booksellers, viewed in the light of the present age, but in no individual, perhaps, is it so strongly apparent as in John Dunton, the eccentric 'dipper into a thousand books,' who 'formed ten thousand projects, six hundred of which he appears to have thought he had completely methodized.'

Dunton is the only bookseller of his period whose scribbling propensities resulted in giving to the world, among other things, an autobiography; but his *cacoëthes scribendi*, howsoever great a gain to English literature, was without doubt the greatest curse that beset this 'crack-brained' bookseller, for throughout his life it prevented him making progress in his calling, besides involving him in all manner of squabbles. 'The Life and Errors of John Dunton' is one of the most singular and interesting books published during the last century, which was so prolific in queer literature. From this we gather a very minute and detailed account of the future bookseller, told in a way that, but for the physical impossibility, would almost lead one to believe that the narrator had recollected every circumstance of his career, dating from the time and hour of his nativity. He modestly justifies this method when he naïvely suggests that there is nothing so small in itself which it is not interesting to know concerning a great man!

Before going any farther, it will be well to state that John Dunton was born at Graffham, Huntingdonshire, on May 14, 1659, of which place his father, the Rev. John Dunton, was rector. The Rev. John was a Fellow of Trinity College, Cambridge, and married a daughter, Lydia, of Mr. Daniel Carter, of Chesham; but she died on March 3, 1660, and her husband is said to have made a vow not to marry again for the space of seven years. He went into Ireland, whilst at an early age his son, the more famous John, was placed under the tuition of William Reading, a schoolmaster of Dungrove, near Chesham. The elder Dunton returned to England in 1669, when he obtained the rectory of Aston Clinton, where he married a second time, and took his son under his own immediate tuition, intending him for the Church. The Rev. John Dunton died Nov. 24, 1676, aged 48, and was interred in Aston chancel. He is described by his son as 'wonderfully fitted out by nature, and furnished with the acquirements for all the good ends of a useful life.'

Dunton's first appearance in this world did not by any means presage that striking restlessness which in after years made things so lively for the communities with which he came into contact. In fact, the excellent midwife was at first in great distress, being under the impression that he was still-born, but her joy was correspondingly great at young hopeful showing signs of life when sprinkled with a little cold water. 'The first appearance I made,' John candidly and perhaps accurately admits, 'was very mean and contemptible; and, as if nature had designed me to take up only some insignificant and obscure corner in the universe, I was so diminutive a creature that a quart pot could contain the whole of me with ease.'

> 'From such beginnings mighty things arise;
> So small a star can brighten all the skies.'

'In this condition,' he goes on, 'and long before I had any articulate use of my tongue, I gave the world sufficient evidence of a child of Adam, and the certain tokens of corrupt nature and passion were more and more apparent as I made advances in age and strength.' But the incidents of John's career before he became apprenticed to bookselling are not particularly interesting. The several accidents which befell him are much the same as other adventurous little boys are in the habit of meeting with: for example, he once fell into a pool of water, and the world would have been deprived of his valuable services but that, 'as Providence would have it, my cousin, John Reading, was lying on the bank and saved me.' Upon another occasion he unwillingly tried the digestive qualities of a leaden bullet, and when his sorrowing family and friends had given up all hopes of him, 'behold! up it bolted.' The 'third danger that my childish curiosity exposed me to' was the result of chewing a bearded ear of corn, which stuck in his throat, and which he could not get rid of. But even in this dilemma his luck did not desert him, for 'some of my relations, viz. Malmesey of Chesham, Aunt Reading, her daughter Anne, Mrs. Mary Gossam, Sarah Randal, &c., &c., who were walking in the fields, found me, speechless and gasping, and with much difficulty set me to rights again.' It gives him a sort of mournful pleasure to admit that it was easier for him to tell a lie than to utter the truth; whilst he is proud rather than ashamed to own that cowardice was one of his youthful characteristics,—certainly an attribute which did not entirely desert him in after life.

We have already said that John was designed for the ministry. His father seems to have desired that the dignity of 'Reverend' should be inherited by the 'John Duntons,' for he himself was the third in succession whose talents had been employed, successfully, we hope, in calling sinners to repentance. But John Dunton the fourth of that ilk was found to be too volatile for this purpose; he was, moreover, a bad scholar, for, although he acquired Latin easily enough, the natural difficulties of Greek were too much for him. Added to these disqualifications, even at the early age of fourteen or so, he contracted an additional one by forming 'a silent passion for a virgin in my father's house,' which 'quite unhinged all my resolutions of study.'

At the age of fifteen, John Dunton was apprenticed to Thomas Parkhurst, bookseller, of London, whom he subsequently describes as 'my honoured master,' . . . 'the most eminent Presbyterian bookseller in the three kingdoms, and now chosen Master of the Company of Stationers.' So placed, he should, as he truly observes, have at least an opportunity of becoming skilled in 'the outside of erudition—the shell and casks of learning.' The confinement to which he was now naturally subjected he felt at first to be very irksome; so much so, indeed, that once he fairly bolted, and made for his father's place in the country. The error of this movement was duly impressed upon him, and the lad returned to his master, after a few days' absence, with a determination to learn the intricacies of his trade, and his application to business thenceforth during his apprenticeship seems to have been commendable. The most noteworthy incident in his career when under Mr. Parkhurst was a joke perpetrated by a fellow-apprentice, who was evidently a bit of a wag, and knew John's failing in the matter of female-veneration. This young gentleman forged a letter to him in the name of a certain 'young virgin' then lodging with Parkhurst: it ran as follows :—'Dear Sir,—We have lived some time together in the same family, and your distant conversation has given me a little impatience to be a little better acquainted with you. I hope your good nature will not put any constructions upon this innocent address to my disadvantage; and should you discover it, it would certainly expose yourself at the expense of your SUSSANAH S—ING.' 'I was strangely surprised at this *billet-doux*,' says John, as well he might have been, considering the slender acquaintanceship. But 'so licentious and extravagant' was his folly that he gave her a *billet* the same day, in which he made an appointment to meet her in Grocer's Garden the next evening. She was likewise surprised in turn, but, evidently like Barkis, was quite 'willin',' for she duly attended, but, of course, expressed denial of inditing a letter. 'However, this romantic courtship gave both of us a real passion; but my master making a timely discovery of it, sent the lady into the country; and absence cooled our passions for us, and by little and little we both of us regained our liberty.' Thus ended love-affair number two. But another and perhaps rather more important event needs chronicling. During his apprenticeship he made himself conspicuous as principal leader of the Whig apprentices, and on one occasion addressed Sir Patience Ward, the Lord Mayor, but the young bloods were snubbed with the healthy advice to 'go home and mind your business, boys.' When his term of apprenticeship expired, John entertained a hundred apprentices to celebrate a 'funeral for it,' which he afterwards described as 'no more than a youthful piece of vanity.'

When he commenced business on his own account as bookseller, he took only 'half a shop, a warehouse, and a fashionable chamber.' At this juncture, he remarks, printing was 'the uppermost in my thoughts, and hackney authors began to ply me with 'Specimens' as earnestly, and with as much passion and concern, as the watermen do passengers with oars and scullers. 'I had some acquaintance with this generation in my apprenticeship, and had never any warm affection for them; in regard I always thought their great concern lay more in how much a sheet, than in any generous respect they bore to the commonwealth of learning; and, indeed, the learning itself of these gentlemen lies very often in as little room as their honesty; though they will pretend to have studied you six or seven years in the Bodleian Library, to have turned over the Fathers, and to have read and digested the whole compass both of Human and Ecclesiastic History : when, alas! they have never been able to understand a single page of Saint Cyprian, and cannot tell you whether the Fathers lived before or after Christ. And as for their Honesty, it is very remarkable : they will either persuade you to go upon another man's Copy, to steal his thought, or to abridge his book, which should have got him bread for his life-time. When you have engaged them upon some project or other, they will write you off three or four sheets perhaps ; take up three or four pounds upon an urgent occasion ; and you shall never hear of them more. I have offered thus much, as a character of these scribblers, that may give the caution to booksellers, and take off a most wretched scandal from the trade in general. However, though I have met with temptations enough of this nature, to grow rich by knavery, and a learned kind of theft, yet this I can say for myself (and I neither have, nor shall be too lavish in my own praise), that I never printed another's Copy, went upon his project, nor stole so much as his title-page, or his thought.'

And again: 'A man should be well furnished with an honest policy, if he intends to set out in the world now-a-days. And this is no less necessary in a bookseller than in any other tradesman! for in that way there are plots and counterplots, and a whole army of hackney authors that keep their grinders moving by the travail of their pens. These gormandizers will eat you the very life out of a Copy so soon as ever it appears; for, as the times go, original and abridgement are almost reckoned as necessary as man and wife; so that I am really afraid that a bookseller and a good conscience will shortly grow some strange thing in the earth. I shall not carry the reflection any farther, but only make this simple remark, that he who designs to be the best Christian, must dip himself the least in business.'

Dunton's first venture was 'The Sufferings of Christ,' by the Rev. Mr. Doolittle; it was a successful one, and fully answered the publisher's end, for, by 'exchanging it through the whole trade, it furnished my shop with all sorts of books saleable at that time;' but its publication also brought several of Mr. Doolittle's pupils to Mr. Dunton's shop. His second venture was 'Daniel in the Den, or the Lord President's Imprisonment and Miraculous Deliverance,' by Mr. Jay, Rector of Chinner; it was dedicated to Lord Shaftesbury, and published upon the occasion of his being acquitted by an 'ignoramus' jury. This work, being seasonable, sold well. These successes gave Dunton 'an ungovernable itch to be always intriguing that way.' The next thing he printed was a sermon by the Rev. John Shower, at the funeral of Mad. Anne Barnardiston, and this ran through three editions. He now determined to publish a collection of funeral discourses preached by his father, which were entitled 'The House of Weeping.'

His next move comes under quite a different category. His female friends not only urged upon John the importance of getting married, but they carried their friendship even farther by pointing out the most desirable young ladies of their acquaintance who would take John 'for better for worse.' There does not appear to have been the slightest supposition that either of the young ladies would refuse him,—or if any was so expressed at the time, he has dishonestly omitted to say so. Mrs. Seaton recommended Miss Sarah Day, of Greenwich, but without any result; 'another person' proposed Miss Sarah Doolittle, in addition to whose natural endowments there would be the chance of getting her father's 'Copies' for nothing; 'his Book on the Sacraments, you know, has sold to the twentieth edition, which would have been an estate for a bookseller.' But the claims of 'Sam. Crook' were too strong, and John stood no chance. At last, however, he met with Dr. Annesley's daughter, by whom he was 'almost charmed dead' when he saw her in her father's meeting-place. But she was pre-engaged, so his friends advised him to 'make an experiment upon her elder sister,' Elizabeth, and the result was marriage,—a consummation which took place on August 3, 1682, in All-hallows' Church. By this marriage he became brother-in-law of Samuel Wesley, the father of John Wesley, the founder of Methodism. He had now deserted his old quarters, and took a shop at the Black Raven, in Princes Street, and carried on business prosperously till the universal damp upon trade which followed Monmouth's defeat[1] in the West. 'Dear Iris' soon gave an early specimen of her prudence and diligence by acting in the capacity of cash-keeper, and managed the business, which left her 'Philaret' to his

[1] Monmouth was defeated at Sedgmoor on July 6, 1685.

'rambling and scribbling humours.' These were golden days for John and his wife, for they frequently visited their relations in the country together. But as a bright summer's day soon fades, so their happiness was short-lived. Having 500*l.* owing him in New England, he determined to make a voyage thither, and, in 1685, he found the fleet bound for that country lying at Gravesend. He procured stowage for his 'venture in two ships, that Neptune might have two throws at me, to make my ruin complete.' The name of the ship in which he himself took passage was the *Susannah and Thomas*, Captain Thomas Jenner, a 'rough covetous tarpaulin,' in command. 'Very sick, very miserable, and very cowardly is the bookseller on his tempestuous voyage. On one occasion he seems to have indulged in bragging, which he very soon repented, when, in a time of danger, the men called out, 'Where is Mr. Dunton, that was so valiant over-night?' 'This, I confess,' says John, 'put me into a cold sweat, and I cried, "Coming! coming! I am only seeking my ruffles,"—a bad excuse, you know, is better than none. I made my appearance at last, but looked nine ways at once; for I was afraid death might come in amongst the boards, or nobody knew where. This is the only instance I can give, when my courage failed me.' Although regretting the loss, value 500*l.*, of one of the two ventures in a storm, he 'cannot enough admire the good providence that saved' himself. They were over four months at sea, and were reduced to great straits more than once.

He arrived safe at Boston in March, 1685-6, and opened a bookseller's shop, which he stocked with the books contained in the second venture. He was, he admits, as welcome to the booksellers of Boston as 'sour ale in summer,' they looking upon his gain as their loss. No sooner had he arrived than he sent home a 'whole packet' of letters to dear Iris, and he duly transcribes one in his 'Life and Errors' for the benefit of his readers. Whilst in America he visited a number of places, such as Harvard College, the town of Salem, where he opened another warehouse for his books; Wenham, and also Ipswich, where he had an opportunity of seeing much of the customs of the Indians. He enters into a very particular account concerning those he met, especially the 'maids, wives, and widows,' nearly all of whom he describes in the most glowing and flattering terms; but there are some exceptions, to one only of which we shall refer. Mrs. D—— he mentions as 'having a bad face and a worse tongue; and has the report of being a Witch. Whether she be one or no, I know not, but she has ignorance and malice enough to make her one,' &c. But, notwithstanding all his charms,—and we may be sure he had many,—the American ladies all found him a 'true platonick.'

After a sojourn of several months, he once more turned his face towards home, and minutely describes his leave-taking. 'So soon as ever my friends were gone off to shore, our Captain ordered all his guns to fire, which were accompanied with huzzas, and shouts, and shaking of hats, till we had lost all sight of our friends.' And hereupon he drops down into verse:—

'Kind Boston, adieu; part we must, though 'tis pity,
But I'm made for mankind, and all the world is my city.

> Look how on the shore they hoop and they hollow,
> Not for joy I am gone, but for grief they can't follow.'

John's modesty does not even stop here, for he likens himself to Ulysses for the troubles he had undergone, but it will be a little difficult to find any great resemblance in the two wanderers' travels. He was sore afraid that his unexpected presence would prove fatal to his Penelope, so he commissioned his sister Mary to inform his wife that ' there was a gentleman waiting for her' at the Queen's Head Tavern, in Spitalfields, who would give ' some account of Philaret.' About an hour afterwards she came, and 'at the first interview we stood speechless, and gazing upon each other, whilst Iris shed a flood of tears,'—presumably of joy. His father-in-law received him with every mark of kindness and respect, and poor John expected nothing but 'a golden life of it for the future ;' but his hopes were soon withered, for he was 'so deeply entangled for my sister-in-law ; I was not suffered to step over the threshold in ten months, unless it was once under disguise.' He then relates a most amusing story, quite characteristic of the man. ' My confinement growing very uneasy to me, especially on Lord's-days, I was extremely desirous to hear Dr. Annesley preach ; and immediately this contrivance was started in my head, that dear Iris should dress me in woman's cloaths, and I would venture myself abroad under those circumstances. To make short of it, I got myself shaved, and put on as effeminate a look as my countenance would let me ; and being well-fitted out with a large scarf, I set forward ; but every step I took, the fear was upon me that it was made out of form,' &c. He got to the meeting, heard the sermon, and was returning home 'through Bishopsgate-street, with all the circumspection and the care imaginable (and I then thought I had done it pretty well), when an unlucky rogue cried out, "I'll be hanged if that ben't a man in a woman's cloaths." This put me into my preternaturals indeed, and I began to scour off as fast as my legs would carry me: there were at least twenty or thirty of them that made after me; but, being acquainted with all the alleys, I dropped them, and came off with honour.'

Finding his enforced retirement becoming more and more wearisome, he determines to make a trip to the Continent, and spends, accordingly, several months in Holland, Flanders, Germany, &c., and stayed four months at Amsterdam, whence he travelled to Cleves, Rhineberg, Dusseldorf, Cologne, Mentz, &c., and returned to London *viâ* Rotterdam on November 15, 1688. On the day the Prince of Orange came to London, Dunton opened shop at the Black Raven in the Poultry.

According to his own account, he here published no less than 600 books in a very short space of time. Dunton's experience must have been quite unique in the annals of bookselling, for of this great number he only repented of seven. The most noteworthy of these unfortunate 'specs.' was ' A Voyage around the World; or, a Pocket Library divided into several Volumes; the first of which contains the rare Adventures of Don Kainophilus, from his cradle to his 15th year, 1691.' This book is remarkable on account of its rarity, for two pieces of excellent poetry which it contains, and also in being probably the first of the long catalogue of his lucubrations. It has called forth some very interesting remarks from D'Israeli: 'It is a low rhapsody; but it bears a peculiar feature, a certain whimsical style, which he affects to call his own, set off with frequent dashes, and occasionally a banter on false erudition. These cannot be shewn without extracts. I would not add an idle accusation to the already injured genius of Sterne; but I am inclined to think he might have caught up his project of writing Tristram's life in "twenty-four cock-rambling" volumes; have seized on the whim of Dunton's style; have condescended even to copy out his breaks and dashes. But Sterne could not have borrowed wit or genius from so low a scribbler. The elegant pieces of poetry were certainly never composed by Dunton, whose mind had no elegance, and whose rhymes are doggrel.'

The six other books which Dunton repented having published are 'The Second Spira,' 'The Post-boy robbed of his Mail,' 'The New Quevedo,' 'The Pastor's Legacy,' 'The Heavenly Pastime,' and 'The Hue and Cry after Conscience.' These he heartily wished he had never seen, and advised all those who had them to burn them. We may as well here quote the titles of a dozen of his more successful publications, as indicating the general character of his works: 'The Morning Exercises,' Malebranche's 'Search after Truth' translated by Sault, Coke's 'Detection of the Court and State of England,' Lord Delamere's 'Works,' Dr. Burthogg's 'Essay on Reason,' Bishop Barlow's 'Remains,' 'The Life and Death of the

Reverend Mr. John Elliot,' 'The Bloody Assizes,' Joseph Stephens' 'Sermons,' 'Tradgedies of Sin' by Jay, Showers' 'Mourner's Companion,' and Madame Singer's 'Poems.' 'The History of the Edict of Nantes,' translated by several hands, attracted the attention of King William's Consort, and pleased her very much; it 'was the only book to which she ever granted her Royal License.' The License is dated June 30, 1693.

In 1692, having been 'put in possession of a considerable estate upon the decease of my cousin Carter, the Master and Assistants of the Company of Stationers began to think me sufficient to wear a Livery, and honoured me with the cloathing.' The first year he wore livery, Sir William Ashhurst was Lord Mayor, and 'I was invited by our Master and Wardens to dine with his Lordship.' The entertainment was a generous one. 'The world now smiled upon me. I sailed with wind and tide, and had humble servants enough among the booksellers, stationers, printers, and binders; but especially my own relations, on every side, were all upon the very height of love and tenderness, and I was caressed almost out of my five senses.'

'I have, it is true, been very plentifully loaded with the imputation of "Maggots," &c. And what is the reason? Why, because I have usually started something that was new; whilst others, like footpads, ply only about the high-roads, and either abridge another man's book, or one way or other contrived the very life and soul out of the Copy, which perhaps was the only subsistence of the first proprietor. I once printed a book, I remember, under the title of "Maggots,"[2] but it was written by a dignitary of the Church of England. . . . . My *first project* was the *Athenian Gazette*. As the Athenian Society had their first meeting in my brain, so it has been kept ever since religiously secret;' and he then enters into a lengthy account of what he terms this 'true discovery,' which may be summarized as follows:—The real origin of the 'venture' arose out of some thoughts which were caused by a 'very flaming injury loaded with aggravations,' and whilst labouring under a consequent perplexity, he was one day walking with Mr. Larkin and Mr. Harris over St. George's Fields, when on a sudden he made a stop and said, 'Well, Sirs, I have a thought I'll not exchange for fifty guineas!' Naturally his companions desired to be enlightened, but in vain. 'The first rude hint of it was no more than a confused idea of concealing the Querist, and answering his question.' When he arrived home he brought the idea into form, and hammered out a title for it, 'which happened to be extremely lucky.' He consulted his friend Mr. Rd. Sault (*ante*, p. 294) upon the matter 'over a glass of wine,' and that gentleman offered very freely 'to become concerned.' The design was well advertised, and the two at once 'settled to it' with great diligence, and produced by their own unaided efforts the first and second numbers of the *Athenian Gazette*. The first was published March 17, 1689-90. It appeared on Tuesdays and Saturdays, and was a 'newspaper' only

[2] 'Maggots, or Poems on Several Subjects never before handled,' 1685. This was by Samuel Wesley.

in the sense of advertisements. Each number consisted of a folio leaf printed on both sides. The matter consisted solely of questions on almost every conceivable subject, with answers according to the then state of knowledge on each particular phase. The project created a great sensation, so much so that its jubilant originator was overloaded with letters, sometimes finding several hundreds for him at Mr. Smith's coffee-house in Stocksmarket, 'where we usually met to consult about matters.' An additional helpmate was found by Sault in the person of Dr. Norris, 'the greatest prodigy of learning he [Sault] had ever met with.' To 'oblige authority' the title was altered to *Athenian Mercury*, and finding its popularity increasing every week, and with this the impatience of the querists, the Rev. Samuel Wesley, already mentioned as author of 'Maggots,' joined the staff.

Dunton's grand success soon created imitators, and 'Mr. Brown and Mr. Pate began to ape our design' by publishing the *Lacedemonian Mercury*, which John determined upon blowing up, 'one way or other.' The first step taken was to advertise that all the questions answered in the *Lacedemonian Mercury* should be answered over again in the *Athenian Mercury*, with amendments, and with the life of Tom Brown, the chief antagonist. 'This news startled them pretty much. At that time I was altogether unacquainted with Mr. Brown. However, one evening he comes to me with all the civility imaginable, and desires to take a glass with me.' Dunton, with his Athenian *confrères*, adjourned to the Three Cranes, and a good-tempered chat probably ensued, although Mr. Sault was inclined to be a bit pugnacious at first. Another imitator was the *London Mercury*, which commenced a short-lived career on February 1, 1691-2, to the authors of which Dunton's sign of a raven suggested the humorous idea of presenting their readers with a head-piece composed of Dunton's 'bird of dire presage bearing on its back Minerva's favourite attendant, the sapient, grave, and solemn owl.' The *Athenian Mercury* did not escape adverse criticism; but in spite of the difficulties it prospered, and Gildon wrote 'A History of the Athenian Society,' to which were prefixed several poems by such as Motteaux, Foe, Richardson, and Tate. 'Mr. Swift, a country gentleman, sent an Ode to the Athenian Society, which, being an ingenious poem, was prefixed to the fifth supplement of the *Athenian Mercury*.' This was a peculiarly ill-starred move of the morose Dean of St. Patrick's, for it called forth from Dryden the famous but true prognostication, 'Cousin Swift, you will never be a poet.' Dunton occasionally received communications for his paper from Sir William Temple, and several other men of eminence. The *Athenian Mercury* continued until it had swollen to twenty volumes folio, the last number being issued on February 8, 1695-6. 'A choice collection of the most valuable questions and answers' that appeared in the *Athenian Mercury* were reprinted in three volumes, and ran through several editions in the course of Dunton's lifetime. Dunton's *Mercury* was a sort of seventeenth-century *Notes and Queries*.

His second project was the *Athenian Spy*, the curious aim of which was to advocate the superior claims of platonic courtship and platonic matrimony. The third project for the promotion of learning was 'A Supplement to the *Athenian Mercury* afterwards rechristened the *Complete Library*, which existed for ten months, when it was driven out of the field by M. Lecrose's 'The Works of the Learned.' The *Post Angel* forms project number four. It commenced in January, 1701, and had upon its cover the following motto from Cowley:—

> 'Only that Angel was straight gone ; even so
> (But not so swift) the morning glories flow,
> (Quick post) that with a speedy expedition
> Flies to accomplish his divine commission,
> God's wingèd herald, Heaven's swift messenger,
> 'Twixt Heaven and Earth the true interpreter.'

'I don't know,' observes Mr. Dunton, 'what welcome this "Angel" will have, or how I came to write upon the subject, for I knew nothing of it till I dreamt of it, and I fell to write it as soon as I wak't.' 'Post Angels' Dunton defines as invisible inhabitants of the middle regions, who are continually employed about us either as friends or foes. This unlucky 'brat,'[3] as he calls it, was continued by him until June 1702, when, changing hands, and, to some extent, character, it expired 'in the clutches of the sheriff's officers.'

We shall do no more than name what he terms his fifth, sixth, and seventh projects respectively: 'The New Practice of Piety,' in imitation of Browne's

[3] The reader will find a full account of this most curious periodical, with numerous amusing extracts, in the *Gentleman's Magazine* for June, 1857, pp. 670-5.

'Religio Medici,' 'The Female War,' and 'The Post-boy robbed of his Mail.'

His eighth 'project' was of quite a different class to any others. It was entitled 'The Night Walker; or, Evening Rambles in Search after Lewd Women, with the various Conferences held with them.' Perhaps a more insane idea, to be carried out in such a novel fashion, never filtered itself through the human imagination. His chief object was to extirpate lewdness from London, a scheme, observes Nichols, highly creditable to the schemer, had it been practicable. 'Armed with a constable's staff, and accompanied by a clerical companion, he sallied forth in the evening, and followed the wretched prostitutes home, or to a tavern, where every effort was used to win the erring fair to the paths of virtue; but these, he observes, were 'perilous adventures,' as the Cyprians exerted every art to lead him astray in the height of his spiritual exhortations.

'The Merciful Assizes; or, a Panegyrick on the late Lord Jeffreys' Hanging so many in the West,' he describes as his last project, among many others left unmentioned. In 'The Bloody Assizes' (*ante*, p. 295), of which Dunton sold over six thousand copies, Jeffreys is 'made a very cruel man;' but, by an inherent spirit of contrariness, he ventures 'to praise that *nonsuchman*, George Lord Jeffreys,' and cites two justifications,—one in which a 'witty author' 'defended the bloody Nero,' and the other 'An Apology for the Failures of Dr. Walker.' 'The Merciful Assizes' had a good sale, and the author's friend, George Larkin, 'was pleased to explain the project by an ingenious poem.'

At or about the death of 'dear Iris,' which occurred on May 28, 1697, John got into difficulties, which increased as time went on. Probably the loss of her was to some extent the cause of his decline; for, apart from of her husband's constant endearments, she was presumably a good wife. His grief, however, was not very protracted; for, although he wrote 'A Comprehensive View of the Life and Death of Iris,' and put about twenty of their relations into mourning, he was not long before he married another, whose 'Duntonian' appellation was 'Valeria.' This lady's mother was probably a bit mean in parting with her cash; for upon an occasion when John was hard up, he applied to her, but without success. A parting thereupon took place between John and his wife, of whom, however, he always speaks in affectionate terms. John inundated his mother-in-law with pamphlets, in which her injustice was shown up in a truly terrible light. The only one of these squibs of which the title need be quoted here is 'The Case of John Dunton with Respect to Madame Jane Nicholas, of St. Albans, his Mother-in-Law, 1700.'

Not long after the death of his first wife he made a trip to Ireland, landing at Dublin in April, 1698, with a cargo of books, most of which he disposed of by auction; but he did not seem to be more welcome to the fraternity at Dublin than in America. Those at the former place he dressed off in 'The Dublin Scuffle; being a challenge sent by John Dunton, citizen of London, to Patrick Campbel, bookseller in Dublin; together with the small skirmishes of bills and advertisements. To which is added the *Billet Doux* sent him by a citizen's wife in Dublin, tempting him to lewdness, with his answers to her. Also some account of his conversation in Ireland, intermixed with particular characters of the most eminent persons he conversed with in that kingdom, but more especially in the city of Dublin. In several letters to the spectators of this scuffle. With a poem on the whole encounter, "I wear my pen as others do their sword," Oldam.' This queer publication, with its long-winded explanatory title, was dedicated to the Hon. Colonel Butler, a member of the House of Commons, in Ireland, and was dated from London, February 20, 1698-9. 'To those that are angry with me,' observes John, concerning his Irish scuffle, ' I answer here (with the ingenious Montaigne) "that constancy is not so absolutely necessary in authors as in husbands ; " and for my own part, when I have my pen in my hand, and subject in my head, I look as mounted my horse to ride a journey ; wherein, although I design to reach a town by night, yet will I not deny myself the satisfaction of going a mile or two out of my way, to gratify my senses with some new and diverting prospect.' In his ' Farewell ' to his acquaintances in Dublin, friends and enemies, dated from Dublin, Monday morning, December 26, 1698, he has the satisfaction of announcing the disposal of the 'venture of books I brought into this country, maugre all opposition.' His receipts were about 1500*l*. It is said that a clergyman told Mr. Penny, an English gentleman, that Dunton had done more service to learning, by his three auctions, than any one single man that had come into Ireland for the previous three hundred years.

Perhaps of all the books he published, the one best known at the present day, at least by name, is 'The Life and Errors of John Dunton, late citizen of London, written by himself in solitude. With an Idea of a New Life; wherein is shewn how he'd think, speak, and act, might he live over his days again: intermixed with the new discoveries the author has made in his travels abroad, and his private conversation at home. Together with the lives and characters of a thousand persons now living in London, &c. Digested into seven stages, with their own respective ideas.'

> 'He that has all his own mistakes confess'd,
> Stands next to him that never has transgress'd;
> And will be censured for a fool by none
> But they who see no errors of their own.
> *Foe's Satyr upon himself.*'

This work, which was published in 1705, is perhaps the maddest of all mad books, than which certainly never a more eccentric passed the bookbinder's hands. But its value to all students of the literary history of the eighteenth century can hardly be over-estimated. The principal classes with which it deals are licensers of the press, booksellers, and book auctioneers; and, as Mr. G. L. Craik once truly observed, 'never certainly, before or since, were all the graces, both of mind and body, so generously diffused among any class of men as among these old London booksellers.' Dunton's vagaries are scarcely ever to be trusted, especially when he has the 'biographicalizing' fit on.

The bad booksellers, &c., are about one per cent., but when dealing with them, John does not spare them. For instance :—'Mr. Fuller is not only a *villain*, but he is known to be so. He has something *peculiar* in his face that distinguishes him from the rest of mankind. However, he has been such a *mystery of iniquity* that the world had much ado to unriddle him. His books are so honest and innocent that you would think it was impossible that any mischief should be lodged in his heart. . . . *His penitence* and *his confession* . . . neither signify a farthing.' It is highly probable that Mr. Fuller was gathered unto his fathers before he had an opportunity of reading Dunton's character of him, or else a second 'scuffle' would have to be chronicled in Dunton's career.

Sir Roger L'Estrange comes at the head of the characters, as one of the licensers with whom Dunton had done business. He is characterized as 'a man that betrays his religion and country in pretending to defend it; that was made surveyor of the press, and would wink at unlicensed books if the printer's wife would but smile on him.' Mr. Fraser gets a better character for a like employment, in which he was engaged for several years, and during that period he licensed for Dunton the *Athenian Mercuries*, 'The Works of the Learned,' 'The Royal Voyage,' and 'such a numerous company of other books, as advanced his fees, for bare licensing, to thirty pounds per annum, which I paid him for several years together.' Than Fraser, also, 'no man was better skilled in the mystery of winning upon the hearts of booksellers, nor were the Company of Stationers ever blessed with an honester Licenser.' We have no space in which to quote further selections from these amusing characters, which, moreover, have been freely drawn upon in the course of this book. But his ingenious generalization of his country *confrères* certainly deserves a little room, as showing the brief and emphatic manner in which a 'great' man can deal with a heterogeneous subject :—' Of three hundred booksellers now trading in country towns, I know not of one knave or blockhead amongst them all.'

A short time previous to his writing his 'Life,' Dunton, from the unsuccessful results that attended his later efforts, had moved out of the bookselling trade ; but nothing, except the positive absence of pens, ink, and paper, or some other equally insurmountable difficulty, could keep the hero of the Dublin scuffle from publishing his projects and notions. To most of these he placed his name. One of the most curious was his series of 'Athenian Catechisms,' the first volume of which included twenty numbers, and contained a catechism for each of the following classes, among others :—The Atheist, Player, High Flyer, Bigoted Dissenter, Occasional Conformist, Nonconformist, Lady's (for paint and patches), (Late) Pamphleteer's, Coffee-house and Political.

'Whipping-post ; or, a Satire upon Everybody,' was published in 1706, a few months after the appearance of ' The Life and Errors.' It contained a ' panegyrick on the most deserving gentlemen and ladies in the three kingdoms ; the Living Elegy, or

Dunton's Letter to his few creditors ; with the character of a summer friend, and also the secret history of the weekly writers, in a distinct challenge to each of them.' This work was sold by, and printed for, B. Bragg, of the Black Raven, in Paternoster Row.

 The Sacheverell controversy, which, commencing soon after the assize sermon preached at Derby on August 14, 1709, and another at St. Paul's Cathedral on November 5, raged so furiously for a time, was one which Mr. Dunton was hardly likely to keep out of, and his eager and restless brain gave birth to at least three pamphlets : ' The Sacheverellite Plot,' written by the unknown author of ' Neck or Nothing,' and which forms part of another pamphlet, ' The Impeachment, or Great Britain's Charge,' both issued about 1710. The third one had a much more characteristic name than either of the others, being ' The Bull-baiting, or Sach————ll dress'd up in Fireworks, lately brought over from the bear-garden in Southwark ; and expos'd for the diversion of the citizens of London at six-pence a-piece. By John Dunton, author of the answer to Dr. Kennett, intituled " The Hazard of a Death-bed Repentance." Being remarks on a scandalous sermon bellow'd out at St. Paul's on the fifth of November last before the Right Honourable the Lord Mayor and Court of Aldermen, by Dr. Sach————ll,' 1709. On the 44th page of this peculiar pamphlet Dunton further promises ' The Second Bull-baiting, or Sach————ll dressed up again in Fireworks,' but this never seems to have been issued. J. Morphew was the bookseller of ' The Bull-baiting.'

At the end of the last-mentioned publication is an announcement of a forthcoming work, 'Athenianism,' at that time going through the press. Its sub-title, as is usual, runs to some length, and is as follows :—' The New Projects of Mr. John Dunton, author of the essay intituled " The Hazard of a Death-bed Repentance ;" being six hundred distinct treatises (in prose and verse) written with his own hand ; and is an entire collection of all his writings, both in manuscript and such as were formerly printed. To which is added " Dunton's Farewell to Printing," in some serious thoughts on those words of Solomon, " Of making many books there is no end; and much study is a weariness of the flesh." With the author's effigies, to distinguish the original and true copies from such as are false and imperfect.' The purchaser is further advised that the true copies have the woodcuts engraved by Knight and Vander Gucht. To this work, published by Morphew in 1710, is prefixed an heroic poem upon Dunton's projects by the Athenian Society. This volume as John Nichols truly observes, is a strange mixture of sense and folly, containing some good articles in prose and verse, a few of a licentious turn, and some deeply tinctured with insanity, a misfortune under which Dunton appears to have long laboured.

Dunton is also accredited with the authorship of ' The Preaching Weathercock,' which was 'written against William Richardson, once a dissenting teacher;' and ' Mordecai's Memorial, or, There's nothing done for him : a just representation of unrewarded services,' 1716. 'Athenian Sport,'—for John could never get over the idea of his being an Athenian,—or, 'Two thousand paradoxes merrily argued to amuse and divert the age,' appeared in 1707 ; and in the following year he had published 'The Hazard of a Death-bed Repentance,' which he so often quotes as being a production of his own pen. Lowndes mentions the following four pamphlets as being written by Dunton: 'Stinking Fish,' 'Queer Robin,' 'State Weathercocks,' and 'The Mob War.' A work for a long period associated with the name of Lord Somers, but which there seem to be good reasons for assigning to Dunton, is 'The Judgment of Kingdoms and Nations, concerning the rights, power, and prerogatives of kings, and the rights, etc., of the people.' It was published by T. Harrison, of the Royal Exchange, Cornhill, 1710. Dunton's own copy, with his autograph, is referred to at length in 'Censura Literaria,' vi. 247-250. This pamphlet has affixed to it sometimes the Sacheverell tract, 'The Impeachment' (*ante*, p. 306). 'Neck or Nothing,' in a letter to the Earl of Oxford, appeared in 1713, and called forth some banter, to be presently quoted, from Swift in his 'Public Spirit of the Whigs.' It should not be confounded with another publication, with the same primary title, referred to on page 231. Both an 'Essay on Death-bed Charity,' exemplified in Mr. Thomas Guy, bookseller; Madame Jane Nicholas, of St. Albans, and Mr. Fr. Bancroft, draper; and 'Religio Bibliopolæ, or religion of a bookseller,' appeared in 1728.

One of his later projects forms another illustration of political ingratitude. In 'An Appeal to George I.,' which he considered as 'in some sense' his 'Dying Groans from the Fleet Prison, or a Last Shift for Life,' he claims to have had the most distinguished share in bringing about the Hanoverian succession, the Pretender, he says, having sworn that 'John Dunton is the first man he will hang at Tyburn if ever he ascends the British throne, for his having writ forty books to prove him a Popish impostor, and all his adherents either fools, knaves, or madmen.' But not only did no good come of this 'Appeal,' but the 'literary gentlemen' retained by the Government in power taunted an already wretched man with poverty, and the 'high-flyers' among the Ministry exhibited their consummate high-breeding in heaping reproaches and insults upon poor old Dunton's head.

The last half-score years or more of Dunton's life were spent in great misery, which was fearfully enhanced by the maudlin, incoherent state in which his diseased intellect had placed him. It is not possible to entertain any great admiration for this quixotic scribe, but who can read the following,[1] which appeared on the title-page of what was perhaps his last work, without feeling a certain amount of sympathy and kindly consideration towards the author in his senile and lonely condition?—

'Upon this Moment depends Eternity; or, Mr. John Dunton's serious thoughts upon the present and future state, in a fit of sickness that was judged mortal; in which many new opinions are started and

[1] Quoted in 'Lit. Anec.,' v. 83, where it is stated that this advertisement appeared on October 17, 1723.

proved; in particular this, That the sincere practice of known duties, or dying daily to this life and world, would of itself resolve the most ignorant person in all the abstruse points of the Christian religion—being a new directory for holy living and dying; composed of the author's own experience in religion, politics, and morals, from his childhood to his sixty-third year (but more especially during his dangerous disease in Ireland in the year ninety-eight, when his life was despaired of); and completed in twenty essays upon such nice and curious points in divinity as were never handled before. To which is added, The Sick Man's Passing-bell, to remind all men of that death and eternity to which they are hastening. Containing, 1. God be merciful to me a Sinner; or, Dunton at confession, in which he discovers the secret sins of his whole life, with his resolution in what penitent manner (by the help of God) he'll spend the short time he has yet to live. 2. Dunton's Legacy to his Native Country; or, a dying farewell to the most remarkable persons and things both in Church and State, with his last prayer (or those very petitions to Almighty God) with which he hopes to expire. 3. A Living Man following his own Corpse to the Grave; or, Dunton represented as dead and buried, in an essay upon his own funeral; to which is added (for the oddness and singularity of it) a copy of his last Will and Testament; his living elegy wrote with his own hand, and the epitaph designed for his tombstone in the new burying-place. Together with, 4. The real Period of Dunton's Life; or, a philosophical essay upon the nature of the grand climacteric year sixty-three, in

John Dunton.

which (as few persons outlive that fatal time) he expects to be actually buried with the best of wives Mrs. Elizabeth Annesley, *alias* Dunton ; with their reasons for sleeping together in the same grave till the general resurrection, as contained in two letters that passed between Mr. Dunton and his wife a few days before she died. The whole directory and passing-bell submitted to the impartial censure of the Right Reverend Father in God, William Lord Bishop of Ely. By Mr. John Dunton, a member of the Athenian Society, and author of the essay intituled " The Hazard of a Death-bed Repentance."

> " We are all seiz'd with the Athenian itch,
>   News, and new things do the world bewitch."
>   *Dr. Wild.*

Printed for S. Popping, in Paternoster Row, price 1s. 6d.'

Truly religious melancholia had set its hard and uncanny grip upon the hero of six hundred books!.

Dunton has not been damned to everlasting fame by the satirists of his day. His own individuality was so strong as to have dispensed with extraneous help. Even Pope has only an incidental reference to 'Dunton's modern bed' (Dunciad, ii. l. 144), which is, however, an obvious hint at the old bookseller's poverty ; for 'a shaggy tapestry,' which the poet declares to be worthy of being 'spread on Codrus old,' will at once call to the reader's mind Codrus' poverty as described by Juvenal. From Swift, however, he gets some characteristic banter, which he was silly enough to consider as praise. In his ' Public Spirit of the Whigs '

(1714), the Dean grimly states that among the present writers on the Whig side, he only knows of three of any great distinction. These are Ridpath, the author of the *Flying Post*, Dunton, and Steele, author of ' The Crisis.' ' Mr. Dunton,' Swift goes on to say, 'hath been longer and more conversant in books than any of the three, as well as more voluminous in his productions: however, having employed his studies in so great a variety of other subjects, he hath, I think, but lately turned his genius to politicks. His famous track, " Neck or Nothing," must be allowed to be the shrewdest piece, and written with the most spirit, of any that hath appeared from that side since the change of Ministry: it is indeed a most cutting satire upon the Lord Treasurer and Lord Bolingbroke ; and I wonder none of our friends ever undertook to answer it. I confess, I was at first of the same opinion with several good judges, who from the style and manner suppose it to have issued from the sharp pen of the Earl of Nottingham ; and I am still apt to think it might receive his Lordship's last hand.' But in 1704, in the introduction to ' The Tale of a Tub,' Swift refers to Dunton in a manner which is unmistakably the reverse of flattering. Speaking of ' oratorical machines,' the pulpits, and the early publication of orators' speeches, which he looks ' upon as the choicest treasury of our British eloquence,' Swift continues,' I am informed, that worthy citizen and bookseller, Mr. John Dunton, hath made a faithful and a painful collection, which he shortly designs to publish in twelve volumes in folio, illustrated with copper-plates : a work highly useful and curious, and altogether worthy of such a hand !'

The 'praise' contained in the 'Public Spirit of the Whigs,' coming as it does from the 'Reverend and Learned Dr. Jonathan Swift, though a great Jacobite,' is gratefully welcomed as clearing the object of it from 'the undeserved slander of being crazed in his intel-'lectuals.'

Dunton died in 1733, but where and under what precise circumstances, are not now known.

CHAPTER XII.

THOMAS GUY.

THOMAS GUY, the philanthropic bookseller, and founder of Guy's Hospital, was, according to Maitland ('History of London,' 1739), born in the north-east corner-house of Pritchard's Alley, two doors east of St. John's Churchyard, in Fair Street, Horsleydown, Southwark, in the year 1645, but the exact date does not seem to have been discovered. Mr. Knight, in his 'Shadows of the Old Booksellers,' observes that Fair Street which still exists, is at the eastern extremity of Tooley Street, where Horsleydown begins, and at a short distance from the Thames. The 'Downs where horses once grazed, and where, probably, the child Thomas Guy once played, is now built over.'

His father, dying when Thomas was eight years old, was a lighterman and coal-dealer, and after his decease, the widow and her children left London for her native place in Staffordshire, Tamworth. A writer in the *Gentleman's Magazine*, 1784, p. 430, says that Tamworth was the place of young Guy's birth. Mrs. Guy, who married a second time shortly after the removal, took precaution, according to Maitland, 'to have her children carefully educated, and at a proper age put her son Thomas apprentice.' His education from between the ages of eight and fifteen was in all likelihood obtained in Tamworth. He was bound apprentice on September 2, 1660, to John Clark, a bookseller in the porch of Mercers' Chapel. After his apprenticeship had expired, he, in 1668, became a Freeman of the City of London, and of the Stationers' Company, and commenced business with a capital of about 200*l*. His first shop was at ' the little corner-house of Lombard Street and Cornhill.' The house, sometimes termed ' Lucky Corner' in more recent years, was a new one, for the Great Fire which raged a couple of years before he set on in business had devastated nearly all the surrounding structures. Guy's shop was hard by ' Stocks' Market,' which was for centuries a trading rendezvous of butchers and fishmongers, and its denomination is said to have arisen from the Stocks,—a form of punishment to which we were compelled to allude in our account of Mr. Curll's life and adventures. It is upon this area that the present Mansion House stands. ' Many persons,' remarked Mr. Knight, in 1865, ' now living will remember this little corner-house, when it was occupied by a noted lottery-office keeper, and scarcely a passer-by failed to fancy the lucky member that looked out upon him with seductive eyes out of that shop-window. When Guy settled here it must have been a capital situation, for the ruins of Sir Thomas Gresham's Exchange had been cleared away, and new dwellings had sprung up with the rapidity which the exigencies of trade never fail to command. Within a year after our Thomas had taken up his position, the second Exchange was opened with great pomp ; and it stood through all the changes and revolutions of thrones and institutions, of laws and commerce, till it was burnt down in 1838' (January 10). In the course of the improvements which were made in the neighbourhood of Cornhill and Lombard Street about 1833 or 1834, Guy's little corner-shop once for all became a thing of the past.

Guy was admitted a Liveryman of the Company of Stationers in 1673. His progress for some time was probably satisfactory. He seems to have been a bookseller, pure and simple, confining himself almost exclusively to retailing the publications of his more adventurous associates. He was not what we should now understand by the term 'publisher,'—such as Tonson, Lintot, Curll, and Dunton. Apparently he reserved his energy for the purpose of directing it into a channel as yet unworked by his rivals. The extreme rarity of coming across a work bearing Guy's imprint has already been remarked in *Notes and Queries* (4th S. vi.), where only two examples are quoted, viz.—a devotional book entitled 'Jacob's Ladder,' by Jo. Hall, B.D., 9th edition, 'London, printed by F. Collins for Thos. Guy, at the Oxford Arms in Lumbar Street,¹ 1698.' The other, a small quarto, is 'Death's Vision represented in a Philosophical Sacred Poem,' an anonymous production, 'London, printed for Thomas Guy, at the Oxford Arms in Lumbar Street, 1709.'

But this absence of his name as bookseller or publisher is not confined to general literature : it applies with equal, if not even greater, force to what he must have sold many thousands of during his

¹ That is, Lombard Street.

career,—we refer, of course, to the Bible. It is not known for certain at what period Guy commenced to devote his attention to producing better editions than those which were in circulation in the middle and latter part of the seventeenth century. It will not be necessary to quote here any of the innumerable inaccurate and stupid blunders. Barker's octavo of 1631, and Field's Pearl edition of 1653, showed how much a carefully printed edition was needed. Guy was aware of this fact, and was not slow in making capital out of it. A monopoly in the printing of the Bible had been granted to the Barker family by Queen Elizabeth, and their right remained undisturbed for about ninety years. This monopoly was not synonymous either with excellence or correctness. A long-suffering British public did on one or two occasions complain, particularly when, in 1631, Barker omitted the seventh commandment entirely : for this disgraceful and wanton slipshod method of going to work, Barker is said to have been fined 300*l.*, which he compounded by presenting a set of rich types to one of the Universities.

Maitland, in his capital article on the Hospital, referring to about the period when Guy had settled into business on his own account, observes that 'the English Bibles printed in this kingdom being very bad, both in the letter and paper, occasioned divers of the booksellers in this city to encourage the printing thereof in Holland, with curious types and fine paper, and imported vast numbers of the same, to their no small advantage. Mr. Guy, soon becoming acquainted with this profitable commerce, became a large dealer therein. But this trade proving not only very detrimental to the public revenue, but likewise to the King's printer, all ways and means were devised to quash the same; which being vigorously put in execution, the booksellers, by frequent seizures and prosecutions, became so great sufferers, that ,they judged a further pursuit thereof inconsistent with their interest.'

In addition to the King's printer, the Oxford University had also a claim upon the copyright, or rather right of publication, of the Bible. It was to the syndics of the University that he applied for an assignment of their privilege, which, after a time, it appears they granted. His next move was to buy a quantity of new type, and have his own Bibles printed in London. The project was highly successful. He was now a prosperous man of business. As time went on he was chosen Sheriff of London, but he paid the fine of 500*l.* consequent upon his refusal to act in this capacity.

Government securities of various sorts brought many thousands of pounds to the coffers of Guy. Nichols states that Guy realized large sums of money by purchasing seamen's tickets in the wars of Queen Anne, which are so frequently referred to in Pepys' 'Diary' during the first six or seven months of 1668; but Mr. Knight correctly points out that at the time this scandalous subterfuge was being prosecuted by an unscrupulous and dishonest Ministry, Guy was still an apprentice. The practice of paying seamen by ticket passed into desuetude in the reign of Charles the Second; but it was not, apparently, until 1757,

that a proposal was made in Parliament, by 'Mr.
Grenville, brother to Earl Temple,' to bring in a
bill 'for the encouragement of seamen .employed in
his Majesty's Navy, and for establishing a regular
method for the punctual, speedy, and certain payment of their wages, as well as for rescuing them
from the arts of fraud and imposition' (Smollet,
'Hist. of Eng.'). In 1758, a bill to that effect was
passed in the Commons, and, after the usual delay,
recrimination, and jealous regard to rights and
privileges, the House of Lords finally accepted it, and
it then passed into law. Pepys has no reference
in his 'Diary' to seamen's tickets later than July 17,
1668, and it is exceedingly unlikely that Guy speculated at that early date. What the other Government
securities were in which, upon the authority of
Maitland, Guy speculated, we need not stop to
inquire.

In 1695, Thomas Guy, the Whig, first entered Parliament as member for Tamworth, for which place he
sat in all Parliaments from the third of William III.
to the first of Queen Anne. Guy and penuriousness
have been popularly synonymous for a long period,
but like many other popular notions, the inconsis-
tencies are strong and numerous. He was what we
should now call stingy, and nothing more. He is
represented as acting as his own servant, whilst he
obtained his dinner from a cookshop, using his
counter as a table, and an old newspaper as a table-
cloth. Mr. Knight remarks upon this, that the Caro-
lian newspapers were only about the size of an
ordinary dish, and could scarcely have been used as

table-cloths. This anecdote was probably concocted years after Guy's death, as the reference to newspaper would seem to indicate. He is also described as being very careless about his personal appearance. But these statements are both apocryphal. An amusing story is that told concerning Guy and his servant, to whom he had promised marriage. In October, 1671, as Mr. Knight points out, an order was issued to the effect that all the streets within the City were to be paved round or causeway-fashion; the foot-pavements were to be provided at the expense of the occupier of each house. A fine would be inflicted upon those who did not carry out the order within a certain period. When the paviors were doing the portion which fell to Guy's share to have done, the prospective Mrs. Guy noticed a broken place which they had not repaired, and directed them to mend it. They answered, that Mr. Guy had requested them not to go so far. She persisted in having it mended, adding, 'Tell him I bade you, and I know he will not be angry.' But in this she was mistaken, for Guy was very much annoyed at finding his orders exceeded, and renounced his matrimonial scheme. Guy's character was thus delineated by John Dunton in 1705 :—
'Mr. Thomas Guy, in Lombard Street,' . . . . entertains a very sincere respect for English liberty. He is a man of strong reason, and can talk very much to the purpose upon any subject you will propose. He is truly charitable, of which his Almshouses for the poor are standing testimonies.'

Already Guy had 'come out' as a philanthropist, and his private acts of charity are described as many

Thomas Guy.

and great, especially to his poor relations. He frequently (according to the memoir prefixed to the annual syllabus of Guy's Hospital Medical School) accomplished the discharge from prison, and reinstatement in business, of Insolvent Debtors, who at that time were liable to very harsh treatment. He was constantly ready to advance money, without charge for interest, to enable young men, whom he knew to be deserving, to start in business. When he met with such (so runs the same memoir) diseased and friendless subjects as wanted the help of an Hospital, he used to send them to St. Thomas' (of which Institution he was a Governor), with directions to the Steward to supply them at his expense with clothes and such other necessaries as are not provided by the Hospital. Among his more public acts of benevolence the following may be mentioned:—He made large benefactions to the Stationers' Company, and to Christ's Hospital. He built, maintained during his life, and endowed by his Will, Almshouses, and a Free Library at Tamworth, and was a great benefactor to this town generally. In 1707 he built and furnished three wards on the north side of the outer court of St. Thomas' Hospital, for the reception of sixty-four patients, and gave to those wards 100*l.* yearly, for eleven years immediately preceding the foundation of his own hospital. Some time before his death, he removed the frontispiece of this hospital which stood over the gateway in the Borough, and erected it fronting the street; he also enlarged the gateway, rebuilt two large houses on its sides, and erected a fine iron gate between them.

Y

This work cost him 3000*l*. As an example of his charity, the following anecdote was communicated to the *Saturday Magazine* of August 2, 1834:—The munificent founder of Guy's Hospital was a man of very humble appearance, and of a melancholy cast of countenance. One day, while pensively leaning over one of the bridges, he attracted the attention and commiseration of a by-stander, who, apprehensive that he contemplated self-destruction, could not refrain from addressing him with an earnest entreaty not to let this misfortune tempt him to commit any rash act; then quickly placing in his hand a guinea, with the delicacy of genuine benevolence, he hastily withdrew. Guy, roused from his reverie, followed the stranger, and warmly expressed his gratitude, but assured him he was mistaken in supposing him to be either in distress of mind or of circumstances, making an earnest request to be favoured with the name of the good man, his intended benefactor. The address was given, and they parted. Some years after, Guy, observing the name of his friend in the bankrupt list, hastened to his house, brought to his recollection their former interview, found upon investigation that no blame could be attached to him under his misfortunes, intimated his ability and also his intention to serve him, entered into immediate arrangements with his creditors, and finally re-established him in a business which ever after prospered in his hands, and in the hands of his children's children, for many years in Newgate Street.

But it was in the infamous South Sea transactions that Guy made the bulk of his immense fortune. 'In

Thomas Guy.

the year 1710,' observes Maitland, 'when the debt of the navy was increased to divers millions, an Act of Parliament was made to provide for the payment of that and other men's dues from the Government by erecting the South Sea Company, into which the creditors of divers branches of the National Debt were empowered to subscribe the several sums due to them from the public.' Guy, possessing such securities to the amount of several thousands of pounds, subscribed the same into the South Sea Company, it being the condition that the subscribers should receive an annual interest of six per cent. upon their respective subscriptions, until the same was discharged finally. This bubble lasted for ten years. Maitland tells the story with sufficient clearness : ' It no sooner received the sanction of Parliament than the national creditors from all parts came crowding to subscribe into the said company the several sums due to them from the Government, by which great run one hundred pounds of the company's stock that before was sold at one hundred and twenty pounds (at which time Mr. Guy was possessed of forty-five thousand and five hundred pounds of the said stock), gradually rose to above one thousand and fifty pounds. Mr. Guy, wisely considering that the great rise of the stock was owing to the iniquitous management of a few, prudently began to sell out his stock at about three hundred (for that which probably at first did not cost him above fifty or sixty pounds), and continued selling till it arose to about six hundred, when he disposed of the last of his property in the said company.'

It is clear from this that the charge of stock-jobbing cannot be preferred against Guy, and in selling out he only followed the example of Sir Robert Walpole and several others. The bubble, as every one knows, burst in 1720, and many hundreds of families were completely wrecked. It would indeed have been a very queer sort of charity if Guy, foreseeing the ultimate bursting of the South Sea scheme, wilfully entered into it with the intention of fraud before him, and to have spent the proceeds he thus acquired in raising an everlasting monument to his name in the shape of an Hospital. But it does not appear to be understood with sufficient clearness that Guy was no stock-jobber; although, on the other hand, we do not hear that he refunded any of the money which he received from the infatuated individuals to whom he sold at different times his shares. Maitland relates that those best acquainted with Guy averred that he got more money in the space of three months, by the execution of the South Sea scheme, than what the erecting, furnishing, and endowing of the Hospital amounted to.

The idea of erecting a hospital at some time or other he had perhaps entertained for a long period. With this sudden and unexpected addition to his wealth in 1720, he at once commenced carrying his idea out by purchasing of the President and Governors of St. Thomas' Hospital, Southwark, a lease of a piece of ground opposite to that hospital, for a term of 999 years, for a ground-rent of 30/. per annum. This piece of ground was covered with small, old, and ill-tenanted houses, which were pulled down in 1721, and, erecting a house for his own residence, the foundation of the hospital bearing his name was laid in the spring of 1722. This 'vast fabric was completed before the death of its founder,' which occurred December 27, 1724. The only motive, says one writer, that induced Guy to erect this Hospital in so low and close a situation was his design of putting it under the management and direction of the Governors of that of St. Thomas, but by the advice of his friends he altered his resolution; it was then, however, too late to think of choosing another situation, for the building was raised to the second story, but he rendered the place as agreeable as possible by its elevation above the neighbouring streets. The expense of erecting and furnishing the hospital amounted to 18,793*l*. 16*s*., the greater part of which was spent before Guy's death. He endowed it with a sum of 219,499*l*., which, together with the cost of erection, &c., amounted to 238,292*l*. 16*s*., which was up to that time the largest amount left by one person to a single institution.

On August 5, 1717, he offered to the Stationers' Company, through the medium of his friend Richard Mount, the sum of 1000*l*., to enable them to add 50*l*. a year, by quarterly payments, to the poor members and widows, in augmentation of the quarterly charity; also 1100*l*., to be paid quarterly to such charitable uses as he should appoint by his Will in writing; and a further sum of 1500*l*., to have 75*l*. a year paid quarterly for another charitable purpose, to be appointed in a like manner; in default of such appointments the sum of 125*l*. to be paid annually by the Company to St. Thomas' Hospital. And, writes Nichols, no appointment having been made, the same is now regularly paid to the Hospital.

On September 24, 1724, Guy made his Will. He died on December 27 following, at the age of eighty years. In little more than a week afterwards Guy's Hospital was opened, and on Thursday, January 6, 1725, sixty patients were admitted. On April 6 of the same year the first Committee of Governors was held, and three days afterwards two physicians and two surgeons were formally appointed.

By his Will he bequeathed numerous legacies and annuities to a great number of his near and distant relations. To the Almshouses at Tamworth for fourteen poor men and women, and for their pensions, as well as for the putting out of poor children apprentices, Guy left 125*l*. a year. To Christ's Hospital he left 400*l*. per annum in perpetuity. The residue of his estate he left for the endowment of his own hospital, and to provide for the maintenance in it of four hundred patients. The sum of 75,589*l*. was left to be divided up in stated portions among his younger relations and executors. He also bequeathed a further sum of 1000*l*. for discharging poor prisoners within the city of London and the counties of Middlesex and Surrey who could be released for the sum of 5*l*.; by which sum, and the good management of his executors, there were over 600 persons set at liberty from the several prisons within the prescribed radius.

The Governors of his charity, in pursuance of the powers entrusted to them by Parliament, erected a noble monument of the founder, at a cost of 1000*l*., in the chapel, from a design of Bacon. A copy of the inscription appeared, with some other interesting particulars concerning Guy, in the *Gentleman's Magazine*, vol. 54, p. 430. It runs as follows :—

'Underneath are deposited the remains of Thomas Guy, a citizen of London, member of Parliament, and the sole founder of this hospital in his life-time. It is peculiar to this beneficent man to have persevered, during a long course of prosperous industry, in pouring forth to the wants of others all that he had earned by labour or withheld from self-indulgence. Warm with philanthropy, and exalted by charity, his mind expanded to those noble affections which grow but too rarely from the most elevated pursuits. After administrating with extensive bounty to the claim of consanguinity, he established this asylum for that stage of languor and disease to which the charities of others had not reached, he provided a retreat for hopeless insanity, and rivalled the endowments of kings.'

From the Annual Report and Syllabus of Guy's Hospital Medical School, 1886-7, we are enabled to give a few further particulars, which will bring the present sketch, so to speak, down to date. Guy's Hospital was the first of the London Hospitals designed and built for the special purposes which it fulfils. The original building is at present occupied by the surgical wards and operating theatre, the surgery, the library, and various offices. The east wing was commenced in the year 1738 : it contains the Treasurer's house, the Governors' court-room and offices, and, as at present arranged, the Superintendent's residence, and the House-Surgeons' and Dressers' rooms. It was not until more than thirty years later that the west wing was added, which now contains the chapel and the residences of the chaplain and the matron.

In 1744 the Lunatic House was built for the accommodation of twenty confirmed lunatics, in accordance with directions contained in Guy's Will. In 1859, the Governors of the Hospital, in the exercise of their discretion, provided for the reception of the then inmates elsewhere, and converted this house to general hospital purposes. It now contains the clinical wards and room, electrical department, private rooms for ovariotomy and other special cases, the House-Physicians' rooms, &c.

But, although additions were thus made to the original building, it would appear that during many years the internal arrangements and management of the Hospital were so far defective or faulty that the beneficent intentions of the founder were but imperfectly fulfilled. In 1797, Mr. Harrison was appointed Treasurer. He assumed and maintained until nearly the period of his death the almost absolute control and direction of the affairs of the Hospital, which was brought into a state of the highest efficiency. On February 8, 1828, William Hunt, merchant and citizen of London, a friend of Harrison's, and for many years an influential Governor of Guy's, added a codicil to his Will, by which, after providing for certain bequests and annuities, he left the residue of his property to the Treasurer and Governors of Guy's Hospital, for the benefit and purposes of the institution, on condition that, 'within three years after his decease, they should enlarge, extend, finish, and fit up such other buildings adjoining the said Hospital ; and also finish and provide the same with beds and all other conveniencies necessary to receive and entertain therein at least one hundred more persons than were provided for by the said Thomas Guy.' Hunt died September 23, 1829, and was buried in the chapel vault on October 2. His estate realized about 200,000*l*., of which 180,000*l*. came to the funds of the Hospital. Three windows of stained glass have been placed in the chapel by the Governors, commemorative of this munificent benefaction. In compliance with the conditions of Hunt's bequest, some temporary buildings, named together Hunt's House, were speedily prepared, at a cost of 3500*l*., and on December 23, 1830, the first patients were received into them. These buildings were removed when the new wards were built some years afterwards, and which are now known as 'The New Building, or Hunt's House.'

In 1768 it was resolved that the barrier between Guy's and St. Thomas' Hospitals be taken down, and that the pupils of each avail themselves of the advantages afforded by the other institution. This union of the two schools lasted until 1825.

INDEX.

'AD BIBLIOPOLAM,' 68.
Addison, Joseph, 128, 161, 171, 177, 179, 203, *n.*, 204, 257, 267.
'Advancement of Learning,' 75.
Aldine Magazine, The, 138, *n.*
Aldrich, Dean, 197.
Allestry, James, 107.
Allot, Robert, 56, 144.
Alphonsus, King of Naples, 6.
'Amadis de Gaul,' 108.
America, Dunton in, 290.
Amhurst, N., 248.
Amory, Thomas, 277—279.
'Anglia Illustrata,' 237.
Anjou, Countess of, 5.
Anstey's 'Munimenta Academica,' 14.
Antiquarian Magazine, 261.
Antiquarii, The, 10.
Arbuthnot, John, 256, 257.
'Art of Making Love,' 163.
Ashmole, Elias, 257.
Aspley, or Apsley, W., 50, 51, 52, 55, 63, 74, 144.
Astle, Thomas, 10.
Astley, Hugh, 136.
'Atalantis,' Mrs. Manley's, 251.
Athenian Gazette, The, 296.
Athenian Mercury, The, 297—299.
Athenian Spy, 298.
Athenianism, 307.
Athenian Society, The, 298.
'Athenian Sport,' 307.
Atkins, M., 144.

Atterbury, Bishop, 115, 240, 256.
Aubrey, John, 237.
Audeley, John, 119.
Authors, The status of early, 33.
Aylmer, Brabazon, 166.

BACON'S (Lord), booksellers, 72—77.
Baker, Alderman, 187.
Baker, Thomas, 189.
Bale, John, on the Monasteries, 16.
Ballards of Little Britain, The, 124, 127, 152.
Bancroft (not Sancroft), Archbishop, 63.
Bangorian Controversy, The, 241, 248.
Banks, John, 113.
Bankworth, R., 60.
Barber, Alderman, 256, 276.
Barber, John, 229, 230, 256.
Barker, Benjamin, 148.
Barker, Christopher, 31, 36.
Barker, Robert, 75.'
Barlow's (Bishop) 'Remains,' 294.
Barret, Hanna, 74, 76.
Barret, W., 48, 62, 74, 76.
Bartelet, Thomas, 34.
Bartlett, John, 144.
Bassett, T., 104, 153, *and note*.
Batemans of Little Britain, The, 122.
Bath, 'Churches' of, 237.
Bayle, Peter, 127.

Bayley, John, 165, *n.*
Beale, John, 73.
Beaumont and Fletcher, 48, 98, 180.
Beckingham, Charles, 239.
Bede, the Venerable, 2.
Bee, Cornelius, 119.
Bee, The, 257, 258.
Beeston, Hugh, 90.
'Beliarus of Greece,' 108.
Beloe's 'Ovid' 177.
Benedict Biscop, 2.
Benedictines, The, 2.
Bennet, Thomas, 114, 115.
Bentley, Richard (bookseller), 111—113.
Bentley, Dr. Richard, 113—115.
Bethel, Hugh, 274.
Bettesworth, Arthur, 136, 222.
Betterton, Thomas, 196, 209, 216, 222, 280.
Bibles, 83—85, 109, 317.
Bickerton, Thomas, 127.
Bill, John, 76.
Billingsley, S, 165, *n.*
Binneman, Henry, 43.
Birch, William, 144.
Blackmore, Sir Richard, 173.
Bladen, Captain, 218.
Blare, J., 134.
'Bloody Assizes,' The, 295, 300.
B.ount, or Blunt, Edward (bookseller), 54, 56, 62, 73.
Blount, Edward, 267.
Blount, Miss, and Pope, 265.
Boccaccio, 5, 73, 127.
Boethius' 'Consolation of Philosophy,' 11.
Boileau, 219, 164.
Bonian, R., 54, 63.
Boniface, St., 2.
Book, A 'Good,' 67.
Books, prices paid for, 5, 6, 83, 88; with valuable appendages, 8; peculiarities and sizes of early, 20—22; licenser of, 26; proscribed in 1531, 25; seditious and heretical, 27; fines for selling on Sunday, 37; unlicensed, 86; various methods for disposing, 93; lotteries, 93;

burnt at the Great Fire, 99; printed in England, 1471—1660, 103; 1666—1680, 102; dedicated to booksellers, 113; and quack medicines, 114.
Bookbinding, early, 22; and gilding and garnishing 15.
Book-borrowing in ancient times, 5, 12.
Bookseller, 'Epigram to my,' 92.
BOOKSELLING BEFORE PRINTING, 18—45.
Bookselling in France, 12.
BOOKSELLING, THE DAWN OF ENGLISH, 18—45.
BOOKSELLING IN THE TIME OF SHAKESPEARE, 46—77.
BOOKSELLING IN THE SEVENTEENTH CENTURY, 78—115.
BOOKSELLING IN LITTLE BRITAIN, 116—129.
BOOKSELLING ON LONDON BRIDGE, 130—139.
BOOKSELLING LOCALITIES, OTHER, 140—149.
Bostock, Robert, 144.
Bosvil, J., 220.
Bowyer, William, 201, 209.
Boyle *v.* Bentley, 114.
Bragg, B., 306.
Breton, N., 61, 67.
Breval, J. D., 239.
Brewer, Anthony, 108.
Bridge, Daniel, 235.
Broadbent, Humphrey, 259.
Brome, H., 89, 104, 144.
Brome, 'The Widdowe,' 104.
Broome, W., 196, 198, 203.
Brown, Dr. John, 105.
Brown, J., 238.
Browne, Sir Thomas, 299.
Browne, Tom, 146.
Bryde, 'A Singing Man,' 29.
Buckingham, Duke of, 191, 209, 250.
Buckley, Samuel, 128.
Budge, John, 63, 81, 144.
Budgell, E., 257—258.
Buncle, 'Life' of John, 277—279.
Bunhill Fields, 237.
Bunyan, John, 104—107.

Index.

Burbie, or Burby, C., 49, 50, .59, 60.
Burley, William, 60.
Burlington, Earl of, 205, 267, 269.
Burnet, Bishop, 164, 222, 256, 277.
Burre, Walter, 60, 144.
Burthogg's 'Essay on Reason,' 294.
Burton, F., 80.
Burton's 'Censure of Simonie,' 53.
Bury, Richard de, 13—14.
Busbie, T., 52.
Busby, John, 51, 59, 60.
Butler, Samuel, 107.
Butter, Nathaniel, 52, 82, 87, 90.

CADELL, T., 186, *n*.
Cadman, T., 59.
Cæsar's 'Commentaries,' 75, 176, 218.
Calvert, Giles, 145.
Cambridge printers and the Bible, 83.
Camden, W., 112.
Camden's 'Greek Accedence,' 85.
Campbel (Patrick), and Dunton, 301.
Cape, Elizabeth, 235.
Capell, E., 177, 181.
Caryll, John, 275.
Casaubon, I., 53, 74.
Catalogues, Maunsell's, 69; London's, 88; Clavel's, 102, 103.
'Cato,' Addison's, 177.
Caxton, W., 18, 19, 22—24, 32, 146.
Censorship of the Press, 24, 100, 101.
Centlivre, Mrs., 190, 193, 239.
Chamberlayne, William, 102.
Chapman, G., 63, 74.
Charlton, Jeffrey, 72, 145.
Chaucer, G., 197.
'Childe Harold and Cookeries,' 164, *n*.
Cholmondley, Ralph, 43.
Chudleigh, Lady, 189.
Cibber, Colley, 149, 189, 190, 193.
Clarke, John, author, 240.
Clarke, John, of Duck Lane, 128.
Clarke, John, Guy's master, 315.
Clarke, Dr. Samuel, 175.

Clavel, Robert, 102, 103.
Cocker's 'Arithmetic,' 131.
Coinage, Debased character of, 161.
Coke, Sir E., 53, 294.
Collier, Jeremy, 165.
Collins, B., 135.
Collins, James, 149.
Collins, Richard, 90.
Colton, Charles, 104.
Colwell, Thomas, 34.
Comber, Dr., 103.
'Complete Angler,' The, 89.
Condell, Henry, 56.
Congreve, W., 160, 168, 171, 174, 183, 184, 205, 257, 267.
Connoiseur, The, 67, *n*.
Conyers, George, 125—127, 152.
Cooke, Thomas, 240.
Copland, William, 32.
'Corinna,' *see* THOMAS, MRS.
Cornbury, Lord, 100.
Cornwall, Carew's 'Survey' of, 73.
Cotes, Thomas, 56.
'Court Poems,' The, 223, 224, 227, 228, 262.
Cowley, A., 180.
Craftsman, The, 248.
Craggs, James, 178, 267.
Craik, Mr. G. L., 303.
Creede, T., 50.
Crowder, Stanley, 138.
Crowne, John, 189.
Cromwell, Henry, 264, 266, 275.
Cunningham, P., 131, *n.*, 189.
CURLL, EDMUND, 211, 215—280.
Curll, Henry, 256, 258.
Curll, Bishop Walter, 217, 257.
'Curliad,' The, 226, 254, 255, 264.
Curlicisism, 240, *et. seq.*
'Curll Papers,' by W. J. Thoms, 215.

Daily Courant, The, 128.
Daily Journal, The, 273.
Daily Post, The, 258, 259, 267.
Daily Post Boy, The, 266, 268, 273.
Danish Invasions, 4.
Danter, J., 60.
D'Avenant, Charles, 153.
Davies, John, of Hereford, 63, 66.
Davis, Walter, 113.

334 *Index.*

Day, John, 29, 41, 42, 117—118.
Decker, T., 53, 67, 74.
Dedications, 90.
Defoe, Daniel, 143.
Delamere, Lord, 294.
Delawarr, Lord, 271.
Denham, Henry, 142.
Denham, Sir John, 180, 194.
Dennis, John, 163, 190, 234, 261, 264.
De Quincey, T., 97.
Desaguliers and Curll, 236.
Devon, 'Survey' of, 237.
Dibben, T., 209.
Dibden, T. F., 176, 180.
Digby, Hon. R., 267.
Dilke, C. W., 275.
D'Israeli, I., 191, 267.
'Diurnals,' 86.
Dodwell, Henry, 219.
Donne, John, 89.
Doolittle, Rev., 288.
Dorset, Earl of, 120.
Drayton, M., 53, 64, 65.
Dryden, Charles, 168.
Dryden, John, 79, 110—112, 120, 150—169, 174, 180, 183, 196, 298.
'Dublin Scuffle,' The, 301.
Duck, Stephen, 275.
Ducket, Geo., 234.
Duck Lane, Booksellers in, 128.
'Dunciad,' The, 211, 261—264; Key to the, 264; the 'Female,' 264; 'Dissected,' 264; Dennis's 'Remarks' on, 264.
'Duke of York,' the true tragedy of, 51.
DUNTON, JOHN, 103, 106, 110, 115, 122, 124, 125, 137, 148, 149, 185, 188, 194, 281—313, 320.
Dunton, Rev. John, 281.
D'Urfey, T., 193, 194.
Dyche's 'Youth's Guide,' 137.
'Dying Groans from the Fleet Prison,' 309.

EACHARD, L., 127.
Eadburga, The Abbess, 2.
Earle's 'Micro-cosmographie,' 44.

'Eikon Basilike,' The, 87.
Eld, G., 55.
Elizabeth and her Book Grants, 28.
'England's Helicon,' 34.
Englishman, The, 128.
Erasmus's 'Praise of Folly,' 249.
Erdeswick's 'Survey of Staffordshire,' 236.
'Essays' of Bacon, 72.
Etheridge, Sir George, 111.
Eusden, L., 256.
Evelyn, John, 99, 100, 113.
Everingham, Robert, 109.

FABER, F., 171.
'Faction Displayed,' 172.
Fairfax, E., 73.
Farquhar, G., 189, 190, 193.
Faulkener, F., 60.
Fennor, W., 69.
Fenton, E., 177, 190, 193, 194, 196, 203, 209.
Field, R., 46—47.
Filmer, Sir Robert, 113.
Fire, The Great, 99, 152.
Fisher, T., 50.
Flasket, John, 34, 62.
Fleet Street, 120.
Fletcher, Sir Henry, 213, 214.
Fletcher, J. P., 188.
Flower, Francis, 29.
Flying Post, The, 314.
'Folio,' Tom, 129.
Foote, Samuel, 249.
Ford, John, 79, 90.
Foxe's 'Book of Martyrs,' 42, 143.
Foxton's 'Metamorphosis of Mr. Pope,' 264.
Franklin, Benjamin, 128.
Froissart's 'Chronicles,' 43.

GARTH, SIR SAMUEL, 171, 209.
Garthwait, T., 88.
Gascoigne, G., 67.
Gay, John, 177, 184, 186, *n*., 190, 192, 196, 200, 209, 224, 227, 257, 260, 267.
Gazette, The, 179.
Germain, Lady Betty, 272.
'Gesta Romanorum,' 11.
Gibbon, E., 186, *n*.

Index.

Gibson's edition of Camden. 112
Gildon, Charles, 176.
Gilliflower, Matthew, 148.
Gilliver, Lawton, 275, 276.
Glastonbury, 'History' of, 237.
Godfrey, Abbot of Malmesbury, 8.
Godolphin, Francis Lord, 171.
Goodwin, Timothy, 211.
Googe's 'Eglogs, Epytaphes and Sonettes,' 34.
Gosling, R., 221, 222.
Gosson, H., 51, 54, 87, 136.
Gosson, T., 37.
Grafton, R., 41, 43.
Greene, R., 48, 53, 59.
Grimstone, Lord, 190.
Grub Street Journal, The, 128, 273.
Guardian, The, 178.
'Gulliveriana,' 212.
GUY, THOMAS, 308, 314—329.
Guy's Hospital, 317.

HACKETT, THOMAS, 60.
Haimon, Bishop of Halberstadt, 5.
Hale's 'Discourse,' &c., 259.
Halifax, Earl of, 267.
Hall, Bishop, 74.
Hall, J., B.D., 316.
'Hamlet,' 52, 53.
Harding, John, 188.
Hardyng's 'Chronicles,' 41.
Harris, John, 127.
Harris, T., 138.
Harrison, John (16th cent.), 47.
Harrison, John (19th cent.), 142.
Harrison, T., 308.
Harvey, James, 214.
Hawkins, Richard, 63.
Hayes, Laurence, 51.
Head, Richard, 107.
Heath, Robert, 92, 98.
Henley, John, 251.
Heminge, John, 56.
'Henry IV.,' 49, 50.
'Henry V.,' 51.
'Henry VIII.,' 149.
Herbert, G., 89.
Hereford, 'History and Antiquities of,' 237.
Herringman, H., 51, 107, 110—111, 155.

'Hey for Honesty,' 90.
Heywood, Eliza, 279.
Heywood, John, 43.
Heywood, T., 89, 90.
Hilyard, J., 97.
'Histriomastix,' 82.
Hitch, C., 136.
Hoare, Henry, 249.
Hodges, F., 134.
Hodges, Sir James, 134—136, 138.
Hogg, Alexander, 142.
Holdsworth, E., 239.
Hollier, John, 114.
Homer, 192, 199—203, 233.
'Homer defended,' 234.
Hooper, Humfry, 72, 73.
Hopkins, C., 163.
Horace, 192.
Houghton, John, 67.
'Hudibras,' 107.
Huggins, T., 75.
Hughes, 176.
Hume, Patrick, 167.
Hyde, Lord Clarendon, 100, 101.
Hyp-Doctor, The, 251.

ILAY, LORD, 269.
'Iliad,' The, *see* HOMER.
Imprint of a Book, The, 71.
Irving, Washington, 117.
Islip, Adam, 60, 90.

JACKSON, R., 48.
Jacob, Giles, 259.
Jacobs, Joseph, 227.
Jaggard, Isaac, 56, 73, 75.
James, Thomas, 109.
Jay, Rev., 288.
Jeffes, Abel, 37.
Jeffreys, Judge, 300.
John de Harpham, 7.
Johnson, Arthur, 52.
Johnson, Dr., 167, 177, 179, 267, 272.
Jones, Johnes, or Jhones Richard, 60, 61, 62.
Jones, Thos., 68.
Jones, W., 60.
Jonson, Ben, 63, 64, 68, 82, 90.
Jugge, John, 28.

KENNETT, Basil, 150, 164.
Kennett, White (Bishop), 164, 249, 250, 306.
Ker, John, 254—256.
Kettilby, Walter, 144.
King, C., 148.
King, Dr. W., 190, 192, 193, 196, 209, 257.
Kirkman, F., 107, 108.
Kirton, Joshua, 99, 144, 145.
Kit-Cat Club, 151, 169—175.
Knaplock, Robert, 127.
Kneller, Sir Godfrey, 165, 171, 174.
Knight, Charles, 22, 186.
Kyrkham, Henry, 145.

Lacedemonian Mercury, The, 297.
Lacy, Alexander, 118.
Ladvocat, M., 93.
La Mothe le Vayer, M. F. de, 35.
Lanfranc, Archbishop, 7.
Lansdown, Lord, 205.
Lant, Richard, 118.
Law, Matthew, 51, 52.
Leake, W., 47, 48, 63.
'Lear,' 53.
Lee, N., 112.
Lee, W., 76.
'Left-Legged Jacob,' 184.
'Legenda Aurea,' 146.
Leland, John, 16.
L'Estrange, Sir Roger, 101, 148, 304.
Lewis, William, 196.
Library, The Complete, 299.
Librarii, The, 10.
Lilburne, John, 81.
Lilly's 'Euphues,' 48.
Ling, N., 52, 53, 60, 63.
Lingard, Thomas, 188.
LINTOT, BERNARD, 126, 152, 188 —214, 224, 227, 234, 239.
Lintot, Henry, 210, 212—214, 272.
Lintot, John, 188.
Lintot, Joshua, 211.
Lintot, Katherine, 212.
Lisle, Laurence, 63.
Lister's 'Journey to Paris,' 163.
'Literary Anecdotes,' *see* NICHOLS, JOHN.

Literary Quarrels, 33.
'Literatory,' Curll's, 259.
LITTLE BRITAIN, BOOKSELLING IN, 116—129, 133.
Littleton's 'Tenures,' 43.
Lock, John, 113, 257.
LONDON BRIDGE, BOOKSELLING ON, 133—139.
London Magazine, The, 128.
London Mercury, The, 298.
London Journal, The, 128, 256.
London, W., 88, 89.
Lotteries of Books, 93, 94.
Louis XI., 5.
'Loves Labour Lost,' 49, 52.
Lownes, Hugh, 75, 90.
Lownes, Matthew, 74, 75, 76.
Luttrell, Narcissus, 154.

MACAULAY, Lord, 145, 161, *n*.
Machyn's 'Diary,' 146.
'Maggots,' 296.
Mainwaring, Arthur, 171.
Maitland, Rev. S. R., 4, 6.
Maitland, W., 314, 317.
Malebranche's 'Search after Truth,' 294.
Malone, E., 159, 161, *n*., 162, 172, 204.
Malthus, Thomas, 106.
Manley, Mrs., 251, 257.
Markham, Gervase, 48, 138.
Marlborough, Duke of, 219.
Marlow, C., 48, 56, 62, 108.
Marriot, John, 89, 91.
Marriot, Richard, 89, 107.
Marsh, Henry, 107.
Marsh, Thomas, 29.
Martyn, John, 107.
Marvel, Andrew, 240.
Massinger, P., 79.
Masson, Professor, 95, 96.
Maunsell, Andrew, 69, 70.
Mears, William, 238.
Medical books, Quack, 218.
Medicines sold by Booksellers, 114, 220.
Meighen, R., 68.
'Merchant of Venice,' 51.
Mercurius Librarius, 108.
Mercury's, 86.

'Merry Wives of Windsor,' The 52.
Middleton, W., 43.
'Midsummer Night's Dream,' 50.
Midwinter, D., 127.
Midwinter, Ed., 138.
Miller, Andrew, 186, *n*.
Miller, Simon, 107.
Millington, T., 51.
Mills and Scott, 123.
Milton, John, 79, 90, 94—98, 144, 165, 194.
Mist's Journal, 240—247, 250, 263.
Miscellanies, Tonson's, 154, 155, 156—158, 184; Lintot's 155, 194—196, 203, 209; Curll's 259—261; Fenton's 194.
Monasteries, Dissolution of, 16.
Monks as booksellers, 3.
Montaigne, 74.
Monthly Review, The, 128.
Moore, Richard, 145.
'Moore's Worms, 228.
More, John, 77.
Morphew, John, 221, 306, 307.
Mortlock, H., 148.
Moseley, Humphry, 94, 98, 99.
Motteaux, P., 298.
Motte, B., 180, 195.
Mount, John, 179.
Moyle, Walter, 219, 257.
'Much Ado About Nothing,' 50.
Murray, John, 164, *n*.
'Muscipula,' 219, 239.

Nash, T., 52, 57, 60, 61, 64, 144, 146.
'Neck or Nothing,' 149, 231, 306, 308, 312.
Newbery, R., 34.
Newcastle, Duke of, 178.
Negus, Samuel, 133, 134.
Nevill, Henry, 107.
Newman, Dorman, 124.
Newman, Hugh, 125.
Newman, Thomas, 34.
News, Ben Jonson's 'Staple' of, 82.
Newsletters, 101, 102.
Newspapers, 54, 113, 319.

Newton, J., 127.
Nichols, John, 129, 171, 175, 182, 185, 189, 191, 196, 211, 215, 237.
Nicholson, John, 127.
Nikke, Robert, 140.
Norden's Northamptonshire, 237.
Norriss, Thomas, 133.
Norris', Dr., 'Narrative,' 225.
North, Francis, 121.
North, Dr. John, 123.
North, Roger, 121—123.
Norton, Fœlix, 74.
Norton, George, 81.
Norton, W., 37.
Notarii, The, 10.
Noy's 'Rights of the Crown,' 239.
'Novum Organum,' 76.

Ogilby's 'Book on Roads,' 93.
Okes, J., 90.
Okes, N., 81, 90.
Oldisworth, W., 207.
Oldmixon, J., 224, 226, 227.
'Oratorical machines,' Swift on, 312.
Orrery, Earl of, 209, 275.
Osborne, T., 97.
Oswald, J., 127.
Otway, T., 153, 194.
Ovid, 156, 157, 158, 177.
Oxford, bookselling at, 14.
Oxford, the Pope-Lintot journey to, 205—209.

Pamphlets, the war of, 91, 101.
'Paradise Lost,' 95—97, 120, 148, 165—167, 172.
Parchemineurs, The, 10.
Parkhurst, Thomas, 284.
Parnell, T., 190.
Parr, Thomas, 137.
'Parrome,' 6.
Partridge, the Astrologer, 257.
Parrot, Henry, 68.
'Passionate Pilgrim,' The, 48.
Passinger, Charles, 138.
Passinger, Thomas, 114, 138.
Paternoster Row, 120, 140—143.
Pattison, W., 256.
Pavier, T., 51.

Z

338   Index.

Peele, George, 60.
Peele, Stephen, 60.
Pekerynge, William, 36.
Pemberton, John, 227, 235, 237.
Pepwell, H , 41.
Pepys, Samuel, 99, 111, 141, 144, 147, 318, 319.
'Pericles,' 51, 54.
Petet, Thomas, 32.
'Petite Palace ot Pettie's Pleasure,' A, 66.
'Philobiblon,' 13.
Philips, J., 194.
Phillips, Sir Richard, 170, 171.
Pickering, W., 136.
'Pierce Penilesse,' *see* NASH, THOMAS.
Piers, Lady, 209.
'Pier Plowman,' 118.
'Pilgrim's Progress,' 104—106.
Pilkington, Mrs., 276.
Pitt, Christopher, 210.
Pitt, Moses, 125.
Pillory, Prynne in the, 81 ; Curll do., 253.
Plays, prices paid for, 69.
Pliny's 'Panegyric,' 249.
Ponder, Nathaniel, 104—106.
Ponder, Robert, 106.
Ponsonby, or Posonbie, William, 58, 59, 63.
Pope, Alexander, 155, 177, 184, 196, 199, 211, 223—228, 233—236, 248, 249, 255, 256, 260—276, 311.
'Popiad,' The, 234.
Popping, Sarah, 235, 311.
Pordage, S., 153.
Powell, Stephen, 137, *n.*
Portlock, W., 168.
Post Angel, The, 299.
Postboy, The, 258.
'Postboy robbed of his mail,' 294, 300.
Poulson, M., 180.
Press, Censorship of the, 24.
Price, Mrs. Lucy, 258.
Printers, The early, 20.
Printing patents, 32.
Prior, M., 164, 194, 219, 257.
Proscribed books, 25, 27.

Prynne, W., 81, 82.
'P. T.' and Pope, 265—268, 270, 271.
Publishers' Circular, The, 108.
Pulteney, William, 171.
Pynson, Richard, 24, 40, 43.

QUARITCH, Mr. B., 22, 53.
Quintius Curtius, 11.

RAFFLES, book, 94.
Raleigh, Carew, 99.
Raleigh, Sir Walter, 99, 148, 153.
Rambouillet, Mdlle., 265.
Randolph, T., 90, 91.
'Rape of Lucreece,' 47, 48.
Rapin's works, 127, 239.
Rasis, 5.
Rawlinson, Tom, 129.
Raworth, R., 90, 137.
Ray, John, 114.
Rea, Roger, 138.
Redman, R., 40, 41, 43, 64.
Reformation (the) and books, 28.
Relieurs, The, 10.
'Religio Bibliopolæ,' 308.
'Religio Medici,' 300.
Renn, J., 149.
Reynault, or Reynold, Francis, 31.
Rich, Barnaby, 64.
'Richard III.' 49, 50, 51.
Richardson, W., 307.
'Richardsoniana,' 174.
Ridpath, Geo., 312.
Ridson, T., 237.
Rimbault, E. F., 189.
Roberts, James (16th century bookseller), 29, 50, 52, 60.
Roberts, James (18th century bookseller), 223, 227.
Roberts, John, 211.
Robinson, Bishop of London, 248.
'Robinson Crusoe,' 143.
Robinson, Humphrey, 76, 98.
Rochester, 'History,' &c., of, 237.
Rochester's 'Poems,' 248.
Rogers, Owen, 118.
'Romeo and Juliet,' 49, 52, 53.
Rowe, N., 174, 175, 176, 193, 204, 209, 222, 225.
Royston, Richard, 87.

Index. 339

Rymer, T., 153, 154.

SACHEVERELL, Henry, 222, 306.
Sadler's Wells Theatre, 278.
Sage, Thomas, 179.
St. Maur, Raymond de, 97, 98.
St. Paul's Cathedral, 140.
ST. PAUL'S CHURCHYARD, BOOK-
SELLING IN, 143, 145.
Salisbury, Churches of, 237.
Salmon, Dr. William, 114.
Samber, Robert, 240, 252.
Sandford's ,' Genealogical History,'
127.
Sandys, G., 74.
Sault, R., 294, 296, 297.
Schlosser's 'Literary History,' 97.
Scoloker, Anthony, 118.
Scott, Robert, 123.
'Scintilla,' 83, 85, 101.
Scribes at work, 9.
Scriptorium, The, 9.
'Secunda Secundæ,' 22.
Sedley, Sir Charles, 153.
Seile, H., 90.
Selden, John, 238.
Seres, William, 29, 42, 118.
Settle, Elkanah, 189, 193.
Sewell, George, 238, 248.
Shadwell, T., 158, *n*.
SHAKESPEARE, BOOKSELLING IN
THE TIME OF, 46—77.
Shakespeare, W., 149, 165, 176,
177, 181, 204.
Shears, W., jun., 148.
Shepherd, H., 90.
Shippen, W., 172.
Shirley, Benjamin, 153.
Short, P., 47.
Shower, Rev. John, 288.
Sidney's ' Astrophel and Stella,' 34.
Signatures, 21.
Simmes, Valentine, 49, 50.
Simmons, Samuel, 94—96, 121, 165.
Simon, *See* MILLER, SIMON.
Sloane, Hans, 114.
Smethwick, J., 53.
Smith, E. (author), 190, 193, 196,
209.
Smith, E. (bookseller), 228.
Smith, Richard (book-hunter), 119.

Smith, Richard (bookseller), 218.
Smith, J. Moore, 193.
Smyth, Hy., 43.
Smythe, or Smith (R.) and Pope,
267, 270, 271, 273, *and note*.
Snodham, T., 81.
'Society News' in the 18th century,
178, *n*.
Solly, Professor Edward, 215, 218.
'Sonnets' of Shakespeare, 54, 55.
Sophocles, 192.
Sorbière's 'Journey to England,'
120.
Southcote, or Southcott, 196, 209.
Spark, Michael, 81.
Spectator, The, 128. 167, 178.
Spence, Joseph, 167, 174, 177, 183,
196, 204.
Spenser, Edmund, 58, 95.
Spinke, John, 220, 221.
Sprint, Benjamin, 127.
Sprint, J., 127.
Stackhouse, Thos., 240.
Stagg, J., 148.
Stansby, W., 63.
Star-chamber, 81, 119.
Starkey, John, 96.
Stationarii, The, 10.
Stationers'; Company, The, 27—30,
31, 32, 36, 79.
Stebbing's edition of Sandford's
'History,' 127.
Steele, Sir R., 127, 128, 163, 171,
179, 193, 236, 312.
Sterne, L., 294.
Steevens, G., 186.
Stow, John, 43, 48, 118, 140.
Strahan, Geo., 180, 190.
Surrey, Aubrey's 'History' of, 237.
Surrey's ' Poems,' 34, 238.
Swall, Abel, 154.
Swift, Dean. 94, 123, 179, 195, 197,
222, 256, 259, 260, 261, 276,
298, 308, 311.
Swift, Tho., 197.

TACHYGRAPHOI, The, 13.
'Tale of a Tub,' 221, 312.
'Taming of the Shrew,' 52.
Tap, John, 138.

Index

Tarleton, Richard, 53.
Tasso, 180.
Tate, N., 153, 163, 298.
Tatler. The, 178.
Taylor, John, 137.
Taylor, John, 'the Water poet,' 62, 87.
Taylor, Randal, 97, 163.
Taylor, W., 143, 211.
Temple, Sir W., 298.
Terræ-Filius, 248.
Theobald, L., 177, 191, 252, 264.
Theatres, Selling books at, 69.
Thomason, George, 61.
Thomas, Mrs. ('Corinna'), 264.
Thoms, W. J., 215, 216, 226, 253.
Tickel, T., 201—203, 234.
Thorpe, Thomas, 55, 63.
Tillotson, Archbishop, 256.
Tindal, M., 257.
Titles of books, 67, 245.
'Titus Andronicus,' 51.
Toland, John, 190, 191.
Tomes, Henrie, 74, 75.
TONSON, JACOB, I., 104, 111, 150—187, 191, 196, 204, 206, 210, 211, 223.
Tonson, Jacob, II., 178, *and note*, 179, 182.
Tonson, Jacob, III., 167, 186.
Tonson, Richard, I., 152, 153, 165, 178.
Tonson, Richard, II., 185, 187.
Tonson, Samuel, 182, 185.
Tooke, Ben., 179.
Topographical works published by Curll, 237.
Tothill, R., 28, 36, 43, 238.
Towne, Dr., 260.
Tracy, H., 137.
Transcribing by secular students, 9.
Translators, Curll's, 276, 277.
'Troilus and Cressida,' 54.
Trumbull, Sir W., 261.
Trundell, J., 52.
Tuberville, George, 142.
Tuke, Sir Samuel, 99.
Tully's ' Five Books of Morals,' 163.
Turner, William, 66.
Tusser's ' Husbandrie,' 43.
Tyus, Charles, 138.

UNIVERSITIES (the), and bookselling, 11, 14.
Urry, John, 197, 198.

VANBRUGH, Sir John, 171, 173, 175, 183.
Vander Gucht, 174, 307.
Vandyke's 'Charles I.,' 184.
Varilla's ' History of Heresies,' 164.
Vautrollier, T., 29, 47.
Ventris, Sir Peyton, 164.
'Venus and Adonis,' 46, 48.
Virgil, Dryden's, 150, 159, 160.
Virgil, Ogilby's, 160, *an l n te*.
'Visions of Bellay,' The, 58.
' Visions of Petrarch,' The, 58.
Vives, Io. Lod., 55.
Voiture, 2, 65.

WALEY, John, 32.
Walker, R., 181.
Waller, Edmund, 180.
Walleworth, Thomas (canon of York), 7.
Walley, or Whalley, H., 54, 63.
Wallington, Nehemiah, 137.
Walpole, Sir Robert, 171, 249, 251, 254.
Walton, I., 89.
Walsh, W., 267.
Wanley, Humphrey, 210.
Warburton, W., 177, 213.
Ward, Aaron, 127.
Ward, Edward, 169.
Ward, Sir Patience, 286.
Ward, T., 127.
Ward, Dr., 209.
Warde, Roger, 30, 59.
Warren, Earl of, 7.
Washington, W., 75.
Watkyns, R., 29.
Watts, Isaac, 127.
Watts, John, 179.
Wearg, Sir Clement, 256.
Webbe's 'Discourse of English Poetrie,' 38.
Weekly Advertisement of Books, 109.
Weekly Journal or Saturday Post. See MIST'S JOURNAL.
Wesley, Samuel, 231, 289, 296, *n*.

Index.

WESTMINSTER HALL, BOOKSELL-
  ING IN, 145—149, 257.
Westminster Scholars and Curll,
  229—233.
West on 'Treasons,' 239.
Whalley, Peter, 177.
'Whipping-Post,' Dunton's, 305.
'Whiskers,' The, 227.
Whitaker, Rev. J., 10.
White, E., 49, 51, 59.
Whitehall Evening Post, 128.
Whitgift, Archbishop, 63.
Whittaker, John, 74.
Whittaker, Richard, 76.
'Whole Duty of Man,' The, 88.
Wilcocks, Geo., 127.
Wilford, J., 218.
Wilkes' 'Essay on Women,' 249, *n*.
Wilkes, Oliver, 36.
Wilks, Robert, 257, 259.
Wilkinson, Mr., 114.
Wilkins, W., 128.
Williams, John, 125.
William II., heavy tax levied by, 8.
William III., 162.
William de Longchamp, 8.
Williamson, John, 138.
Willis, Browne, 237, 238.

Willis' Current Notes, 119.
Wills and last Testaments published
  by Curll, 256, 257.
Wilson, William, 110.
Winchelsea, Lady, 209.
Winchester, 'History,' &c., of, 237.
Windet, John, 70.
Wintoun, Lord, 235, 236.
'Wisdom of the Ancients,' 75.
Wise, Andrew, 48—52.
Withers, Geo., 79, 80, 81.
Wolfe, John, 30, 35, 36, 145.
Wood, Anthony à, 58, 119, 217.
Wood, Dr. John, 73.
Woodcock, Thomas, 59.
Wright, John, 55.
Wright, William, 60.
Writing materials, 3.
Wycherley, W., 209, 264, 265, 267.
Wynkyn de Worde, 24, 32.

YALDEN, T., 209.
Yates, James, 67.
Young, Edward, 204.

ZAROT, Anthony, inventor of signatures, 22.

THE END.

LONDON:
PRINTED BY GILBERT AND RIVINGTON, LIMITED,
ST. JOHN'S HOUSE, CLERKENWELL ROAD.

A Catalogue of American and Foreign Books Published or Imported by MESSRS. SAMPSON LOW & CO. *can be had on application.*

St. Dunstan's House, Fetter Lane, Fleet Street, London, September, 1888.

A Selection from the List of Books
PUBLISHED BY
SAMPSON LOW, MARSTON, SEARLE, & RIVINGTON,
LIMITED.

ALPHABETICAL LIST.

A BBOTT *(C. C.) Poaetquissings Chronicle.* 10s. 6d.

—— *Waste Land Wanderings.* Crown 8vo, 7s. 6d.
Abney (W. de W.) and Cunningham. Pioneers of the Alps. With photogravure portraits of guides. Imp. 8vo, gilt top, 21s.
Adam (G. Mercer) and Wetherald. An Algonquin Maiden. Crown 8vo, 5s.
Adams (C. K.) Manual of Historical Literature. Cr. 8vo, 12s. 6d.
Agassiz (A.) Three Cruises of the Blake. Illustrated. 2 vols., 8vo, 42s.
Alcott. Works of the late Miss Louisa May Alcott :—
Eight Cousins. Illustrated, 2s.; cloth gilt, 3s. 6d.
Jack and Jill. Illustrated, 2s.; cloth gilt, 3s. 6d.
Jo's Boys. 5s.
Jimmy's Cruise in the Pinafore, &c. Illustrated, cloth, 2s.; gilt edges, 3s. 6d.
Little Men. Double vol., 2s.; cloth, gilt edges, 3s. 6d.
Little Women. 1s. } 1 vol., cloth, 2s. ; larger ed., gilt
Little Women Wedded. 1s. } edges, 3s. 6d.
Old-fashioned Girl. 2s.; cloth, gilt edges, 3s. 6d.
Rose in Bloom. 2s.; cloth gilt, 3s. 6d.
Silver Pitchers. Cloth, gilt edges, 3s. 6d.
Under the Lilacs. Illustrated, 2s.; cloth gilt, 5s.
Work: a Story of Experience. 1s. } 1 vol., cloth, gilt
—— Its Sequel, "Beginning Again." 1s. } edges, 3s. 6d.
Alden (W. L.) Adventures of Jimmy Brown, written by himself. Illustrated. Small crown 8vo, cloth, 2s.
Aldrich (T. B.) Friar Jerome's Beautiful Book, &c. 3s. 6d.
Alford (Lady Marian) Needlework as Art. With over 100 Woodcuts, Photogravures, &c. Royal 8vo, 21s. ; large paper, 84s.
Amateur Angler's Days in Dove Dale : Three Weeks' Holiday in 1884. By E. M. 1s. 6d.; boards, 1s.; large paper, 5s.

A

Andersen. Fairy Tales. An entirely new Translation. With over 500 Illustrations by Scandinavian Artists. Small 4to, 6s.

Anderson (W.) Pictorial Arts of Japan. With 80 full-page and other Plates, 16 of them in Colours. Large imp. 4to, £8 8s. (in four folio parts, £2 2s. each); Artists' Proofs, £12 12s.

Angler's Strange Experiences (An). By COTSWOLD ISYS. With numerous Illustrations, 4to, 5s. New Edition, 3s. 6d.

Angling. See Amateur, "British," "Cutcliffe," "Fennell," "Halford," "Hamilton," "Martin," "Orvis," "Pennell," "Pritt," "Senior," "Stevens," "Theakston," "Walton," "Wells," and "Willis-Bund."

Annals of the Life of Shakespeare, from the most recent authorities. Fancy boards, 2s.

Annesley (C.) Standard Opera Glass. Detailed Plots of 80 Operas. Small 8vo, sewed, 1s. 6d.

Antipodean Notes, collected on a Nine Months' Tour round the World. By Wanderer, Author of "Fair Diana." Crown 8vo, 7s. 6d.

Appleton. European Guide. 2 Parts, 8vo, 10s. each.

Armytage (Hon. Mrs.) Wars of Victoria's Reign. 5s.

Art Education. See "Biographies," "D'Anvers," "Illustrated Text Books," "Mollett's Dictionary."

Artistic Japan. Illustrated with Coloured Plates. Monthly. Royal 4to, 2s.

Attwell (Prof.) The Italian Masters. Crown 8vo, 3s. 6d.

Audsley (G. A.) Handbook of the Organ. Top edge gilt, 42s.; large paper, 84s.

—— *Ornamental Arts of Japan.* 90 Plates, 74 in Colours and Gold, with General and Descriptive Text. 2 vols., folio, £15 15s.; in specially designed leather, £23 2s.

—— *The Art of Chromo-Lithography.* Coloured Plates and Text. Folio, 63s.

—— *and Tomkinson. Ivory and Wood Carvings of Japan.* 84s. Artists' proofs (100), 168s.

Auerbach (B.) Brigitta. (B. Tauchnitz Collection.) 2s.

—— *On the Heights.* 3 vols., 6s.

—— *Spinoza.* 2 vols., 18mo, 4s.

BADDELEY (S.) Tchay and Chianti. Small 8vo, 5s.

Baldwin (James) Story of Siegfried. 6s

—— *Story of the Golden Age.* Illustrated by HOWARD PYLE. Crown 8vo, 6s.

Baldwin (James) Story of Roland. Crown 8vo, 6s.
Bamford (A. J.) Turbans and Tails. Sketches in the Unromantic East. Crown 8vo, 7s. 6d.
Barlow (Alfred) Weaving by Hand and by Power. With several hundred Illustrations. Third Edition, royal 8vo, £1 5s.
Barlow (P. W.) Kaipara, Experiences of a Settler in N. New Zealand. Illust., crown 8vo, 6s.
Barrow (J.) Mountain Ascents in Cumberland and Westmoreland. Crown 8vo, 7s. 6d.; new edition, 5s.
Bassett (F. S.) Legends and Superstitions of the Sea. 7s. 6d.

THE BAYARD SERIES.

Edited by the late J. HAIN FRISWELL.

Comprising Pleasure Books of Literature produced in the Choicest Style.

"We can hardly imagine better books for boys to read or for men to ponder over."—*Times.*

Price 2s. 6d. each Volume, complete in itself, flexible cloth extra, gilt edges, with silk Headbands and Registers.

The Story of the Chevalier Bayard.
Joinville's St. Louis of France.
The Essays of Abraham Cowley.
Abdallah. By Edouard Laboullaye.
Napoleon, Table-Talk and Opinions.
Words of Wellington.
Johnson's Rasselas. With Notes.
Hazlitt's Round Table.
The Religio Medici, Hydriotaphia, &c. By Sir Thomas Browne, Knt.
Coleridge's Christabel, &c. With Preface by Algernon C. Swinburne.
Ballad Poetry of the Affections. By Robert Buchanan.

Lord Chesterfield's Letters, Sentences, and Maxims. With Essay by Sainte-Beuve.
The King and the Commons. Cavalier and Puritan Songs.
Vathek. By William Beckford.
Essays in Mosaic. By Ballantyne.
My Uncle Toby; his Story and his Friends. By P. Fitzgerald.
Reflections of Rochefoucauld.
Socrates: Memoirs for English Readers from Xenophon's Memorabilia. By Edw. Levien.
Prince Albert's Golden Precepts.

A Case containing 12 Volumes, price 31s. 6d ; or the Case separately, price 3s. 6d.

Baynes (Canon) Hymns and other Verses. Crown 8vo, sewed, 1s.; cloth, 1s. 6d.
Beaugrand (C.) Walks Abroad of Two Young Naturalists. By D. SHARP. Illust., 8vo, 7s. 6d.
Beecher (H. W.) Authentic Biography, and Diary. [*Preparing*
Behnke and Browne. Child's Voice: its Treatment with regard to After Development. Small 8vo, 3s. 6d.
Beyschlag. Female Costume Figures of various Centuries. 12 reproductions of pastel designs in portfolio, imperial. 21s.
Bickersteth (Bishop E. H.) Clergyman in his Home. 1s.
—— —— *Evangelical Churchmanship.* 1s.

*Bickersteth (Bishop E. H.) From Year to Year: Original
Poetical Pieces.* Small post 8vo, 3s. 6d.; roan, 6s. and 5s.; calf or
morocco, 10s. 6d.
—— *The Master's Home-Call.* 20th Thous. 32mo, cloth
gilt, 1s.
—— *The Master's Will.* A Funeral Sermon preached on
the Death of Mrs. S. Gurney Buxton. Sewn, 6d.; cloth gilt, 1s.
—— *The Reef, and other Parables.* Crown 8vo, 2s. 6d.
—— *Shadow of the Rock.* Select Religious Poetry. 2s. 6d.
—— *The Shadowed Home and the Light Beyond.* 5s.
*Bigelow (John) France and the Confederate Navy. An Inter-
national Episode.* 7s. 6d.
Biographies of the Great Artists (Illustrated). Crown 8vo,
emblematical binding, 3s. 6d. per volume, except where the price is given.

Claude le Lorrain, by Owen J. Dullea.	Mantegna and Francia.
Correggio, by M. E. Heaton. 2s. 6d.	Meissonier, by J. W. Mollett. 2s. 6d.
Della Robbia and Cellini. 2s. 6d.	Michelangelo Buonarotti, by Clément.
Albrecht Dürer, by R. F. Heath.	Murillo, by Ellen E. Minor. 2s. 6d.
Figure Painters of Holland.	Overbeck, by J. B. Atkinson.
Fra Angelico, Masaccio, and Botticelli.	Raphael, by N. D'Anvers.
Fra Bartolommeo, Albertinelli, and Andrea del Sarto.	Rembrandt, by J. W. Mollett.
	Reynolds, by F. S. Pulling.
Gainsborough and Constable.	Rubens, by C. W. Kett.
Ghiberti and Donatello. 2s. 6d.	Tintoretto, by W. R. Osler.
Giotto, by Harry Quilter.	Titian, by R. F. Heath.
Hans Holbein, by Joseph Cundall.	Turner, by Cosmo Monkhouse.
Hogarth, by Austin Dobson.	Vandyck and Hals, by P. R. Head.
Landseer, by F. G. Stevens.	
Lawrence and Romney, by Lord Ronald Gower. 2s. 6d.	Velasquez, by E. Stowe.
	Vernet and Delaroche, by J. Rees.
Leonardo da Vinci.	Watteau, by J. W. Mollett. 2s. 6d.
Little Masters of Germany, by W. B. Scott.	Wilkie, by J. W. Mollett.

Bird (F. J.) American Practical Dyer's Companion. 8vo, 42s.
—— *(H. E.) Chess Practice.* 8vo, 2s. 6d.
Black (Robert) Horse Racing in France: a History. 8vo, 14s.
Black (Wm.) Novels. See "Low's Standard Library."
—— *Strange Adventures of a House-Boat.* 3 vols., 31s. 6d.
—— *In Far Lochaber.* 3 vols., crown 8vo., 31s. 6d.
*Blackburn (Charles F.) Hints on Catalogue Titles and Index
Entries,* with a Vocabulary of Terms and Abbreviations, chiefly from
Foreign Catalogues. Royal 8vo, 14s.
Blackburn (Henry) Breton Folk. With 171 Illust. by RANDOLPH
CALDECOTT. Imperial 8vo, gilt edges, 21s.; plainer binding, 10s. 6d.
—— *Pyrenees.* Illustrated by GUSTAVE DORÉ, corrected
to 1881. Crown 8vo, 7s. 6d. See also CALDECOTT.

Blackmore (R. D.) Lorna Doone. Édition de luxe. Crown 4to,
very numerous Illustrations, cloth, gilt edges, 31s. 6d.; parchment,
uncut, top gilt, 35s.; new issue, plainer, 21s.; small post 8vo, 6s.
—— *Novels.* See "Low's Standard Library."
—— *Springhaven.* Illust. by PARSONS and BARNARD. Sq.
8vo, 12s.
Blaikie (William) How to get Strong and how to Stay so.
Rational, Physical, Gymnastic, &c., Exercises. Illust., sm. post 8vo, 5s.
—— *Sound Bodies for our Boys and Girls.* 16mo, 2s. 6d.
Bonwick. British Colonies. Asia, 1s.; Africa, 1s.; America,
1s.; Australasia, 1s. One vol., cloth, 5s.
Bosanquet (Rev. C.) Blossoms from the King's Garden: Sermons
for Children. 2nd Edition, small post 8vo, cloth extra, 6s.
—— *Jehoshaphat; or, Sunlight and Clouds.* 1s.
Boussenard (L.) Crusoes of Guiana. Gilt, 2s. 6d.; gilt ed, 3s. 6d.
—— *Gold-seekers.* Sequel to the above. Illust. 16mo, 5s.
Boyesen (F.) Story of Norway. Illustrated, sm. 8vo, 7s. 6d.
Boyesen (H. H.) Modern Vikings: Stories of Life and Sport
in Norseland. Cr. 8vo, 6s.
Boy's Froissart. King Arthur. Knightly Legends of Wales.
Percy. See LANIER.
Bradshaw (J.) New Zealand of To-day, 1884-87. 8vo.
Brannt (W. T.) Animal and Vegetable Fats and Oils. 244
Illust., 8vo, 35s.
—— *Manufacture of Soap and Candles, with many Formulas.*
Illust., 8vo, 35s.
—— *Metallic Alloys. Chiefly from the German of Krupp*
and Wilberger. Crown 8vo, 12s. 6d.
Bright (John) Public Letters. Crown 8vo, 7s. 6d.
Brisse (Baron) Ménus (366). A *ménu,* in French and English,
for every Day in the Year. 2nd Edition. Crown 8vo, 5s.
British Fisheries Directory. Small 8vo, 2s. 6d.
Brittany. See BLACKBURN.
Browne (G. Lennox) Voice Use and Stimulants. Sm. 8vo, 3s. 6d.
—— *and Behnke (Emil) Voice, Song, and Speech.* N ed., 5s.
Bryant (W. C.) and Gay (S. H.) History of the United States.
4 vols., royal 8vo, profusely Illustrated, 60s.
Bryce (Rev. Professor) Manitoba. Illust. Crown 8vo, 7s. 6d.
—— *Short History of the Canadian People.* 7s. 6d.
Burnaby (Capt.) On Horseback through Asia Minor. 2 vols.,
8vo, 38s. Cheaper Edition, 1 vol., crown 8vo, 10s. 6d.

Burnaby (Mrs. F.) High Alps in Winter; or, Mountaineering in Search of Health. With Illustrations, &c., 14*s*. See also MAIN.
Burnley (J.) History of Wool and Woolcombing. Illust. 8vo, 21*s*.
Burton (Sir R. F.) Early, Public, and Private Life. Edited by F. HITCHMAN. 2 vols., 8vo, 36*s*.
Butler (Sir W. F.) Campaign of the Cataracts. Illust., 8vo, 18*s*.
—— *Invasion of England, told twenty years after.* 2*s*. 6*d*.
—— *Red Cloud; or, the Solitary Sioux.* Imperial 16mo, numerous illustrations, gilt edges, 3*s*. 6*d*.; plainer binding, 2*s*. 6*d*.
—— *The Great Lone Land; Red River Expedition.* 7*s*. 6*d*.
—— *The Wild North Land; the Story of a Winter Journey* with Dogs across Northern North America. 8vo, 18*s*. Cr. 8vo, 7*s*. 6*d*.

CABLE (G. W.) Bonaventure: A Prose Pastoral of Acadian Louisiana. Sm. post 8vo, 5*s*.
Cadogan (Lady A.) Illustrated Games of Patience. Twenty-four Diagrams in Colours, with Text. Fcap. 4to, 12*s*. 6*d*.
—— *New Games of Patience.* Coloured Diagrams, 4to, 12*s*. 6*d*.
Caldecott (Randolph) Memoir. By HENRY BLACKBURN. With 170 Examples of the Artist's Work. 14*s*.; large paper, 21*s*.
California. See NORDHOFF.
Callan (H.) Wanderings on Wheel and on Foot. Cr. 8vo, 1*s*. 6*d*.
Campbell (Lady Colin) Book of the Running Brook: and of Still Waters. 5*s*.
Canadian People: Short History. Crown 8vo, 7*s*. 6*d*.
Carleton (Will) Farm Ballads, Farm Festivals, and Farm Legends. Paper boards, 1*s*. each; 1 vol., small post 8vo, 3*s*. 6*d*.
—— *City Ballads.* Illustrated, 12*s*. 6*d*. New Ed. (Rose Library), 16mo, 1*s*.
Carnegie (A.) American Four-in-Hand in Britain. Small 4to, Illustrated, 10*s*. 6*d*. Popular Edition, paper, 1*s*.
—— *Round the World.* 8vo, 10*s*. 6*d*.
—— *Triumphant Democracy.* 6*s*.; also 1*s*. 6*d*. and 1*s*.
Chairman's Handbook. By R. F. D. PALGRAVE. 5th Edit., 2*s*.
Changed Cross, &c. Religious Poems. 16mo, 2*s*. 6*d*.; calf, 6*s*.
Chaplin (J. G.) Three Principles of Book-keeping. 2*s*. 6*d*.
Charities of London. See LOW'S.
Chattock (R. S.) Practical Notes on Etching. New Ed. 8vo, 10*s*. 6*d*.
Chess. See BIRD (H. E.).

Children's Praises. Hymns for Sunday-Schools and Services.
Compiled by LOUISA H. H. TRISTRAM. 4d.

Choice Editions of Choice Books. 2s. 6d. each. Illustrated by
C. W. COPE, R.A., T. CRESWICK, R.A., E. DUNCAN, BIRKET
FOSTER, J. C. HORSLEY, A.R.A., G. HICKS, R. REDGRAVE, R.A.,
C. STONEHOUSE, F. TAYLER, G. THOMAS, H. J. TOWNSHEND,
E. H. WEHNERT, HARRISON WEIR, &c.

Bloomfield's Farmer's Boy.	Milton's L'Allegro.
Campbell's Pleasures of Hope.	Poetry of Nature. Harrison Weir.
Coleridge's Ancient Mariner.	Rogers' (Sam.) Pleasures of Memory.
Goldsmith's Deserted Village.	Shakespeare's Songs and Sonnets.
Goldsmith's Vicar of Wakefield.	Tennyson's May Queen.
Gray's Elegy in a Churchyard.	Elizabethan Poets.
Keat's Eve of St. Agnes.	Wordsworth's Pastoral Poems.

"Such works are a glorious beatification for a poet."—*Athenæum.*

Chreiman (Miss) Physical Culture of Women. A Lecture at the
Parkes Museum. Small 8vo, 1s.

Christ in Song. By PHILIP SCHAFF. New Ed., gilt edges, 6s.

Chromo-Lithography. See AUDSLEY.

Cochran (W.) Pen and Pencil in Asia Minor. Illust., 8vo, 21s.

Collingwood (Harry) Under the Meteor Flag. The Log of a
Midshipman. Illustrated, small post 8vo, gilt, 3s. 6d.; plainer, 2s. 6d.

—— *Voyage of the " Aurora."* Gilt, 3s. 6d. ; plainer, 2s. 6d.

Cook (Dutton) Book of the Play. New Edition. 1 vol., 3s. 6d.

—— *On the Stage: Studies.* 2 vols., 8vo, cloth, 24s.

Cowen (Jos., M.P.) Life and Speeches. 8vo, 14s.

Cowper (W.) Poetical Works: A Concordance. Roy. 8vo, 21s.

Cozzens (F.) American Yachts. 27 Plates, 22 × 28 inches.
Proofs, £21 ; Artist's Proofs, £31 10s.

Crew (B. J.) Practical Treatise on Petroleum. Illust., 8vo, 28s.

Crouch (A. P.) On a Surf-bound Coast. Crown 8vo, 7s. 6d.

Crown Prince of Germany : a Diary. 2s. 6d.

Cudworth (W.) Life and Correspondence of Abraham Sharp.
Illustrated from Drawings. (To Subscribers, 21s.) 26s.

Cumberland (Stuart) Thought Reader's Thoughts. Cr. 8vo., 10s. 6d.

—— *Queen's Highway from Ocean to Ocean.* Ill., 8vo, 18s. ;
new ed., 7s. 6d.

Cundall (Joseph) Annals of the Life and Work of Shakespeare.
With a List of Early Editions. 3s. 6d. ; large paper, 5s.; also 2s.

—— *Remarkable Bindings in the British Museum.*

Curtis (W. E.) Capitals of Spanish America.. Illust., roy. 8vo.

Cushing (W.) Initials and Pseudonyms. Large 8vo, 25s. ;
second series, large 8vo, 21s.

Custer (Eliz. B.) Tenting on the Plains; Gen. Custer in Kansas and Texas. Royal 8vo, 18s.
Cutcliffe (H. C.) Trout Fishing in Rapid Streams. Cr. 8vo, 3s. 6d.

DALY *(Mrs. D.) Digging, Squatting, and Pioneering in* Northern South Australia. 8vo, 12s.
D'Anvers. Elementary History of Art. New ed., 360 illus., cr. 8vo, 2 vols. (5s. each), gilt, 10s. 6d.
—— *Elementary History of Music.* Crown 8vo, 2s. 6d.
Davidson (H. C.) Old Adam; Tale of an Army Crammer. 3 vols. crown 8vo, 31s. 6d.
Davis (Clement) Modern Whist. 4s.
Davis (C. T.) Bricks, Tiles, Terra-Cotta, &c. Ill. 8vo, 25s.
—— *Manufacture of Leather.* With many Illustrations. 52s. 6d.
—— *Manufacture of Paper.* 28s.
Davis (G. B.) Outlines of International Law. 8vo. 10s. 6d.
Dawidowsky. Glue, Gelatine, Isinglass, Cements, &c. 8vo, 12s. 6d.
Day of My Life at Eton. By an ETON BOY. 16mo. 2s. 6d.
Day's Collacon: an Encyclopædia of Prose Quotations. Imperial 8vo, cloth, 31s. 6d.
De Leon (E.) Under the Stars and under the Crescent. N. ed., 6s.
Dethroning Shakspere. Letters to the Daily Telegraph; and Editorial Papers. Crown 8vo, 2s. 6d.
Dictionary. See TOLHAUSEN, "Technological."
Dogs in Disease. By ASHMONT. Crown 8vo, 7s. 6d.
Donnelly (Ignatius) Atlantis; or, the Antediluvian World. 7th Edition, crown 8vo, 12s. 6d.
—— *Ragnarok: The Age of Fire and Gravel.* Illustrated, crown 8vo, 12s. 6d.
—— *The Great Cryptogram: Francis Bacon's Cipher in the* so-called Shakspere Plays. With facsimiles. 2 vols., 30s.
Doré (Gustave) Life and Reminiscences. By BLANCHE ROOSEVELT. Illust. from the Artist's Drawings. Medium 8vo, 24s.
Dougall (James Dalziel) Shooting: its Appliances, Practice, and Purpose. New Edition, revised with additions. Crown 8vo, 7s. 6d.
"The book is admirable in every way. . . . . We wish it every success."—*Globe.*
"A very complete treatise. . . . Likely to take high rank as an authority on shooting."—*Daily News.*
Dupré (Giovanni). By FRIEZE. With Dialogues on Art. 7s. 6d.

EDMONDS *(C.) Poetry of the Anti-Jacobin.* With additional matter. New ed. Illust., crown 8vo.
Educational List and Directory for 1887-88. 5s.

Educational Works published in Great Britain. A Classified Catalogue. Third Edition, 8vo, cloth extra, 6s.
Edwards (E.) American Steam Engineer. Illust., 12mo, 12s. 6d.
Eight Months on the Argentine Gran Chaco. 8vo, 8s. 6d.
Elliott (H. W.) An Arctic Province: Alaska and the Seal Islands. Illustrated from Drawings; also with Maps. 16s.
Emerson (Dr. P. H.) Pictures of East Anglian Life. Ordinary ed., 105s.; édit. de luxe, 17 × 13¼, vellum, morocco back, 147s.
—— *Naturalistic Photography for Art Students.* Crown 8vo.
—— *and Goodall. Life and Landscape on the Norfolk Broads.* Plates 12 × 8 inches, 126s.; large paper, 210s.
English Catalogue of Books. Vol. III., 1872—1880. Royal 8vo, half-morocco, 42s. See also "Index."
English Etchings. Published Quarterly. 3s. 6d. Vol. VI., 25s.
English Philosophers. Edited by E. B. IVAN MÜLLER, M.A.
Crown 8vo volumes of 180 or 200 pp., price 3s. 6d. each.
Francis Bacon, by Thomas Fowler. | Shaftesbury and Hutcheson.
Hamilton, by W. H. S. Monck. | Adam Smith, by J. A. Farrer.
Hartley and James Mill. |
Esmarch (F.) Handbook of Surgery. Translation from the last German Edition. With 647 new Illustrations. 8vo, leather, 24s.
Etching. See CHATTOCK, and ENGLISH ETCHINGS.
Etchings (Modern) of Celebrated Paintings. 4to, 31s. 6d.
Evans (E. A.) Songs of the Birds. Analogies of Spiritual Life. New Ed. Ilust., 6s.
Evelyn. Life of Mrs. Godolphin. By WILLIAM HARCOURT, of Nuneham. Steel Portrait. Extra binding, gilt top, 7s. 6d.

FARINI (G. A.) Through the Kalahari Desert. 8vo, 21s.

Farm Ballads, Festivals, and Legends. See CARLETON.
Fawcett (Edgar) A Gentleman of Leisure. 1s.
Fenn (G. Manville) Off to the Wilds: A Story for Boys. Profusely Illustrated. Crown 8vo, gilt edges, 3s. 6d.; plainer, 2s. 6d.
—— *Silver Cañon.* Illust., gilt ed., 3s. 6d.; plainer, 2s. 6d.
Fennell (Greville) Book of the Roach. New Edition, 12mo, 2s.
Ferns. See HEATH.
Field (H. M.) Greek Islands and Turkey after the War. 8s. 6d.
Field (Mrs. Horace) Anchorage. 2 vols., crown 8vo, 12s.
Fields (J. T.) Yesterdays with Authors. New Ed., 8vo, 10s. 6d.
Fitzgerald (P.) Book Fancier. Cr. 8vo. 5s.; large pap. 12s. 6d.

Fleming (Sandford) England and Canada : a Tour. Cr. 8vo, 6s.
Florence. See YRIARTE.
Folkard (R., Jun.) Plant Lore, Legends, and Lyrics. 8vo, 16s.
Forbes (H. O.) Naturalist in the Eastern Archipelago. 8vo. 21s.
Foreign Countries and British Colonies. Cr. 8vo, 3s. 6d. each

Australia, by J. F. Vesey Fitzgerald.
Austria, by D. Kay, F.R.G.S.
Denmark and Iceland, by E. C. Otté.
Egypt, by S. Lane Poole, B.A.
France, by Miss M. Roberts.
Germany, by S. Baring-Gould.
Greece, by L. Sergeant, B.A.

Japan, by S. Mossman.
Peru, by Clements R. Markham.
Russia, by W. R. Morfill, M.A.
Spain, by Rev. Wentworth Webster.
Sweden and Norway, by Woods.
West Indies, by C. H. Eden, F.R.G.S.

Foreign Etchings. From Paintings by Rembrandt, &c., 63s.; india proofs, 147s.
Fortunes made in Business. Vols. I., II., III. 16s. each.
Frampton (Mary) Journal, Letters, and Anecdotes. 8vo, 14s.
Franc (Maud Jeanne). Small post 8vo, uniform, gilt edges :—

Emily's Choice. 5s.
Hall's Vineyard. 4s.
John's Wife : A Story of Life in South Australia. 4s.
Marian ; or, The Light of Some One's Home. 5s.
Silken Cords and Iron Fetters. 4s.
Into the Light. 4s.

Vermont Vale. 5s.
Minnie's Mission. 4s.
Little Mercy. 4s.
Beatrice Melton's Discipline. 4s.
No Longer a Child. 4s.
Golden Gifts. 4s.
Two Sides to Every Question. 4s.
Master of Ralston. 4s.

Also a Cheap Edition, in cloth extra, 2s. 6d. each.

Frank's Ranche ; or, My Holiday in the Rockies. A Contribution to the Inquiry into What we are to Do with our Boys. 5s.
Freeman (J.) Lights and Shadows of Melbourne Life. Cr. 8vo. 6s.
French. See JULIEN and PORCHER.
Fresh Woods and Pastures New. By the Author of " An Amateur Angler's Days." 1s. 6d.; large paper, 5s. ; new ed., 1s.
Froissart. See LANIER.
Fuller (Edward) Fellow Travellers. 3s. 6d.
——— *Dramatic Year* 1887-88 *in the United States.* With the London Season, by W. ARCHER. Crown 8vo.

GANE (D. N.) New South Wales and Victoria in 1885. 5s.

Gasparin (Countess A. de) Sunny Fields and Shady Woods. 6s.
Geary (Grattan) Burma after the Conquest. 7s. 6d.
Gentle Life (Queen Edition). 2 vols. in 1, small 4to, 6s.

THE GENTLE LIFE SERIES.

Price 6s. each ; or in calf extra, price 10s. 6d. ; Smaller Edition, cloth extra, 2s. 6d., except where price is named.

The Gentle Life. Essays in aid of the Formation of Character.
About in the World. Essays by Author of " The Gentle Life."
Like unto Christ. New Translation of Thomas à Kempis.
Familiar Words. A Quotation Handbook. 6s.
Essays by Montaigne. Edited by the Author of " The Gentle Life."
The Gentle Life. 2nd Series.
The Silent Hour: Essays, Original and Selected.
Half-Length Portraits. Short Studies of Notable Persons. By J. HAIN FRISWELL.
Essays on English Writers, for Students in English Literature.
Other People's Windows. By J. HAIN FRISWELL. 6s.
A Man's Thoughts. By J. HAIN FRISWELL.
The Countess of Pembroke's Arcadia. By Sir PHILIP SIDNEY. 6s.

Germany. By S. BARING-GOULD. Crown 8vo, 3s. 6d.
Gibbon (C.) Beyond Compare: a Story. 3 vols., cr. 8vo, 31s. 6d.
―――― *Yarmouth Coast.*
Gisborne (W.) New Zealand Rulers and Statesmen. With Portraits. Crown 8vo, 7s. 6d.
Goldsmith. She Stoops to Conquer. Introduction by AUSTIN DOBSON ; the designs by E. A. ABBEY. Imperial 4to, 48s.
Goode (G. Brown) American Fishes. A Popular Treatise. Royal 8vo, 24s.
Gordon (J. E. H., B.A. Cantab.) Four Lectures on Electric Induction at the Royal Institution, 1878-9. Illust., square 16mo, 3s.
―――― *Electric Lighting.* Illustrated, 8vo, 18s.
―――― *Physical Treatise on Electricity and Magnetism.* 2nd Edition, enlarged, with coloured, full-page, &c., Illust. 2 vols., 8vo, 42s.
―――― *Electricity for Schools.* Illustrated. Crown 8vo, 5s.
Gouffé (Jules) Royal Cookery Book. New Edition, with plates in colours, Woodcuts, &c., 8vo, gilt edges, 42s.
―――― Domestic Edition, half-bound, 10s. 6d.
Grant (General, U.S.) Personal Memoirs. 2 vols., 8vo, 28s. Illustrations, Maps, &c. 2 vols., 8vo, 28s.
Great Artists. See " Biographies."

Great Musicians. Edited by F. HUEFFER. A Series of Biographies, crown 8vo, 3s. each :—

Bach.	Mendelssohn.	Schubert.
English Church Com-	Mozart.	Schumann.
posers. By BARRETT.	Purcell.	Richard Wagner.
Handel.	Rossini.	Weber.
Haydn.		

Groves (*J. Percy*) *Charmouth Grange.* Gilt, 5s.; plainer, 2s. 6d.

Guizot's History of France. Translated by R. BLACK. In 8 vols., super-royal 8vo, cloth extra, gilt, each 24s. In cheaper binding, 8 vols., at 10s. 6d. each.

"It supplies a want which has long been felt, and ought to be in the hands of all students of history."—*Times.*

—————— *Masson's School Edition.* Abridged from the Translation by Robert Black, with Chronological Index, Historical and Genealogical Tables, &c. By Professor GUSTAVE MASSON, B.A. With Portraits, Illustrations, &c. 1 vol., 8vo, 600 pp., 5s.

Guyon (*Mde.*) *Life.* By UPHAM. 6th Edition, crown 8vo, 6s.

HALFORD (*F. M.*) *Floating Flies, and how to Dress them.* Coloured plates. 8vo, 15s.; large paper, 30s.

—————— *Dry Fly-Fishing in Theory and Practice.* Col. Plates.

Hall (*W. W.*) *How to Live Long; or,* 1408 *Maxims.* 2s.

Hamilton (*E.*) *Recollections of Fly-fishing for Salmon, Trout,* and Grayling. With their Habits, Haunts, and History. Illust., 6s.; large paper, 10s. 6d.

Hands (*T.*) *Numerical Exercises in Chemistry.* Cr. 8vo, 2s. 6d. and 2s.; Answers separately, 6d.

Hardy (*Thomas*). See LOW'S STANDARD NOVELS.

Hare (*J. S. Clark*) *Law of Contracts.* 8vo, 26s.

Harley (*T.*) *Southward Ho!* to *the State of Georgia.* 5s.

Harper's Magazine. Published Monthly. 160 pages, fully Illustrated, 1s. Vols., half yearly, I.—XVI., super-royal 8vo, 8s. 6d. each.

"'Harper's Magazine' is so thickly sown with excellent illustrations that to count them would be a work of time; not that it is a picture magazine, for the engravings illustrate the text after the manner seen in some of our choicest *éditions de luxe.*"— *St. James's Gazette.*

"It is so pretty, so big, and so cheap. . . . An extraordinary shillingsworth— 160 large octavo pages, with over a score of articles, and more than three times as many illustrations."—*Edinburgh Daily Review.*

"An amazing shillingsworth . . . combining choice literature of both nations."— *Nonconformist.*

Harper's Young People. Vols. I.-IV., profusely Illustrated with woodcuts and coloured plates. Royal 4to, extra binding, each 7s. 6d.; gilt edges, 8s. Published Weekly, in wrapper, 1d.; Annual Subscription, post free, 6s. 6d.; Monthly, in wrapper, with coloured plate, 6d.; Annual Subscription, post free, 7s. 6d.

Harrison (Mary) Skilful Cook. New edition, crown 8vo, 5*s*.
Hartshorne (H.) Household Medicine, Surgery, &c. 8vo. 21*s*.
Hatton (Frank) North Borneo. Map and Illust., &c. 18*s*.
Hatton (Joseph) Journalistic London: with Engravings and Portraits of Distinguished Writers of the Day. Fcap. 4to, 12*s*. 6*d*.
—— See also LOW'S STANDARD NOVELS.
Hawthorne (Nathaniel) Life. By JOHN R. LOWELL.
Heath (Francis George) Fern World With Nature-printed Coloured Plates. Crown 8vo, gilt edges, 12*s*. 6*d*. Cheap Edition, 6*s*.
Heath (Gertrude). Tell us Why? The Customs and Ceremonies of the Church of England explained for Children. Cr. 8vo, 2*s*. 6*d*.
Heldmann (B.) Mutiny of the Ship "Leander." Gilt edges, 3*s*. 6*d*.; plainer, 2*s*. 6*d*.
Henty. Winning his Spurs. Cr. 8vo, 3*s*. 6*d*.; plainer, 2*s*. 6*d*.
—— *Cornet of Horse.* Cr. 8vo, 3*s*. 6*d*.; plainer, 2*s*. 6*d*.
—— *Jack Archer.* Illust. 3*s*. 6*d*.; plainer, 2*s*. 6*d*.
Henty (Richmond) Australiana: My Early Life. 5*s*.
Herrick (Robert) Poetry. Preface by AUSTIN DOBSON. With numerous Illustrations by E. A. ABBEY. 4to, gilt edges, 42*s*.
Hetley (Mrs. E.) Native Flowers of New Zealand. Chromos from Drawings. Three Parts, to Subscribers, 63*s*.
Hewitt (James A.) Church History in South Africa, 1795-1848, 12mo, 5*s*.
Hicks (E. S.) Our Boys: How to Enter the Merchant Service. 5*s*.
—— *Yachts, Boats and Canoes.* Illustrated. 8vo, 10*s*. 6*d*.
Hitchman. Public Life of the Earl of Beaconsfield. 3*s*. 6*d*.
Hoey (Mrs. Cashel) See LOW'S STANDARD NOVELS.
Hofmann. Scenes from the Life of our Saviour. 12 mounted plates, 12 × 9 inches, 21*s*.
Holder (C. F.) Marvels of Animal Life. Illustrated. 8*s*. 6*d*.
—— *Ivory King: Elephant and Allies.* Illustrated. 8*s*. 6*d*.
—— *Living Lights: Phosphorescent Animals and Vegetables.* Illustrated. 8vo, 8*s*. 6*d*.
Holmes (O. W.) Before the Curfew, &c. Occasional Poems. 5*s*.
—— *Last Leaf: a Holiday Volume.* 42*s*.
—— *Mortal Antipathy,* 8*s*. 6*d*.; also 2*s*.; paper, 1*s*.
—— *Our Hundred Days in Europe.* 6*s*. Large Paper, 15*s*.
—— *Poetical Works.* 2 vols., 18mo, gilt tops, 10*s*. 6*d*.
Homer, Iliad I.-XII., done into English Verse. By ARTHUR S. WAY. 9*s*.
—— *Odyssey, done into English Verse.* By A. S. WAY. Fcap 4to, 7*s*. 6*d*.

Hopkins (Manley) Treatise on the Cardinal Numbers. 2s. 6d.
Hore (Mrs.) To Lake Tanganyika in a Bath Chair. Cr. 8vo, 7s. 6d.
Howard (Blanche W.) Tony the Maid; a Novelette. Illust., 12mo, 3s. 6d.
Howorth (H. H.) Mammoth and the Flood. 8vo, 18s.
Huet (C. B.) Land of Rubens. For Visitors to Belgium. By VAN DAM. Crown 8vo, 3s. 6d.
Hugo (V.) Notre Dame. With coloured etchings and 150 engravings. 2 vols., 8vo, vellum cloth, 30s.
Hundred Greatest Men (The). 8 portfolios, 21s. each, or 4 vols., half-morocco, gilt edges, 10 guineas. New Ed., 1 vol., royal 8vo, 21s.
Hutchinson (T.) Diary and Letters. Vol. I., 16s.; Vol. II., 16s.
Hygiene and Public Health. Edited by A. H. BUCK, M.D. Illustrated. 2 vols., royal 8vo, 42s.
Hymnal Companion to the Book of Common Prayer. By BISHOP BICKERSTETH. In various styles and bindings from 1d. to 31s. 6d. *Price List and Prospectus will be forwarded on application.*
Hymns and Tunes at St. Thomas', New York. Music by G. W. FARREN. Royal 8vo, 5s.

ILLUSTRATED Text-Books of Art-Education. Edited by EDWARD J. POYNTER, R.A. Illustrated, and strongly bound, 5s. Now ready:—

PAINTING.
Classic and Italian. By HEAD. | **French and Spanish.**
German, Flemish, and Dutch. | **English and American.**

ARCHITECTURE.
Classic and Early Christian.
Gothic and Renaissance. By T. ROGER SMITH.

SCULPTURE.
Antique: Egyptian and Greek.
Renaissance and Modern. By LEADER SCOTT.

Inderwick (F. A.; Q.C.) Side Lights on the Stuarts. Essays. Illustrated, 8vo.
Index to the English Catalogue, Jan., 1874, to Dec., 1880. Royal 8vo, half-morocco, 18s.
Inglis (Hon. James; "Maori") Our New Zealand Cousins. Small post 8vo, 6s.
—— *Tent Life in Tiger Land: Twelve Years a Pioneer Planter.* Col. plates, roy. 8vo, 18s.
Irving (Henry) Impressions of America. 2 vols., 21s.; 1 vol., 6s.
Irving (Washington). Library Edition of his Works in 27 vols., Copyright, with the Author's Latest Revisions. "Geoffrey Crayon" Edition, large square 8vo. 12s. 6d. per vol. *See also* "Little Britain."

JAMES (C.) Curiosities of Law and Lawyers. 8vo, 7s. 6d.

Japan. See ANDERSON, ARTISTIC, AUDSLEY, also MORSE.

Jefferies (Richard) Amaryllis at the Fair. Small 8vo, 7s. 6d.

Jerdon (Gertrude) Key-hole Country. Illustrated. Crown 8vo, cloth, 2s.

Johnston (H. H.) River Congo, from its Mouth to Bolobo. New Edition, 8vo, 21s.

Johnstone (D. Lawson) Land of the Mountain Kingdom. Illust., crown 8vo.

Jones (Major) Heroes of Industry. Biographies with Portraits. 7s. 6d.

―――― *Emigrants' Friend.* Guide to the U.S. N. Ed. 2s. 6d.

Julien (F.) English Student's French Examiner. 16mo, 2s.

―――― *Conversational French Reader.* 16mo, cloth, 2s. 6d.

―――― *French at Home and at School.* Book I., Accidence. 2s.

―――― *First Lessons in Conversational French Grammar.* 1s.

―――― *Petites Leçons de Conversation et de Grammaire.* 3s.

―――― *Phrases of Daily Use.* Limp cloth, 6d.

―――― *" Petites Leçons " and " Phrases " in one.* 3s. 6d.

KARR (H. W. Seton) Shores and Alps of Alaska. 8vo, 16s.

Keats. Endymion. Illust. by W. ST. JOHN HARPER. Imp. 4to, gilt top, 42s.

Kempis (Thomas à) Daily Text-Book. Square 16mo, 2s. 6d.; interleaved as a Birthday Book, 3s. 6d.

Kent's Commentaries : an Abridgment for Students of American Law. By EDEN F. THOMPSON. 10s. 6d.

Kerr (W. M.) Far Interior : Cape of Good Hope, across the Zambesi, to the Lake Regions. Illustrated from Sketches, 2 vols. 8vo, 32s.

Kershaw (S. W.) Protestants from France in their English Home. Crown 8vo, 6s.

King (Henry) Savage London; Riverside Characters, &c. Crown 8vo, 6s.

Kingston (W. H. G.) Works. Illustrated, 16mo, gilt edges, 3s. 6d.; plainer binding, plain edges, 2s. 6d. each.

Captain Mugford, or, Our Salt and Fresh Water Tutors.	Snow-Shoes and Canoes.
Dick Cheveley.	Two Supercargoes.
Heir of Kilfinnan.	With Axe and Rifle.

*Kingsley (Rose) Children of Westminster Abbey: Studies in
English History.* 5s.
Knight (E. J.) Cruise of the "Falcon." New Ed. Cr. 8vo,
7s. 6d.
Knox (Col.) Boy Travellers on the Congo. Illus. Cr. 8vo, 7s. 6d.
Kunhardt (C. B.) Small Yachts: Design and Construction. 35s.
—————— *Steam Yachts and Launches.* Illustrated. 4to, 16s.

*L*AMB *(Charles) Essays of Elia.* Illustrated by C. O.
MURRAY. 6s.
Lanier's Works. Illustrated, crown 8vo, gilt edges, 7s. 6d.
each.
Boy's King Arthur. | Boy's Percy: Ballads of Love and
Boy's Froissart. | Adventure, selected from the
Boy's Knightly Legends of Wales. | "Reliques."
Lansdell (H.) Through Siberia. 2 vols., 8vo, 30s.; 1 vol., 10s. 6d.
—————— *Russia in Central Asia.* Illustrated. 2 vols., 42s.
—————— *Through Central Asia; Russo-Afghan Frontier, &c.*
8vo, 12s.
Larden (W.) School Course on Heat. Second Ed., Illust. 5s.
Laurie (André) Selene Company, Limited. Crown 8vo, 7s. 6d.
Layard (Mrs. Granville) Through the West Indies. Small
post 8vo, 2s. 6d.
Lea (H. C.). History of the Inquisition of the Middle Ages.
3 vols., 8vo, 42s.
Lemon (M.) Small House over the Water, and Stories. Illust.
by Cruikshank, &c. Crown 8vo, 6s.
Leo XIII.: Life. By BERNARD O'REILLY. With Steel
Portrait from Photograph, &c. Large 8vo, 18s.; *édit. de luxe*, 63s.
Leonardo da Vinci's Literary Works. Edited by Dr. JEAN
PAUL RICHTER. Containing his Writings on Painting, Sculpture,
and Architecture, his Philosophical Maxims, Humorous Writings, and
Miscellaneous Notes on Personal Events, on his Contemporaries, on
Literature, &c.; published from Manuscripts. 2 vols., imperial 8vo,
containing about 200 Drawings in Autotype Reproductions, and nu-
merous other Illustrations. Twelve Guineas.
Library of Religious Poetry. Best Poems of all Ages. Edited
by SCHAFF and GILMAN. Royal 8vo, 21s.; cheaper binding, 10s. 6d.
Lindsay (W. S.) History of Merchant Shipping. Over 150
Illustrations, Maps, and Charts. In 4 vols., demy 8vo, cloth extra.
Vols. 1 and 2, 11s. each; vols. 3 and 4, 14s. each. 4 vols., 50s.
*Little (Archibald J.) Through the Yang-tse Gorges: Trade and
Travel in Western China.* New Edition. 8vo, 10s. 6d.

Little Britain, The Spectre Bridegroom, and *Legend of Sleepy Hollow.* By WASHINGTON IRVING. An entirely New *Edition de luxe.* Illustrated by 120 very fine Engravings on Wood, by Mr. J. D. COOPER. Designed by Mr. CHARLES O. MURRAY. Re-issue, square crown 8vo, cloth, 6s.

Longfellow. Maidenhood. With Coloured Plates. Oblong 4to, 2s. 6d.; gilt edges, 3s. 6d.

—— *Courtship of Miles Standish.* Illust. by BROUGHTON, &c. Imp. 4to, 21s.

—— *Nuremberg.* 28 Photogravures. Illum. by M. and A. COMEGYS. 4to, 31s. 6d.

Lowell (J. R.) Vision of Sir Launfal. Illustrated, royal 4to, 63s.

—— *Life of Nathaniel Hawthorne.* Small post 8vo, .

Low's Standard Library of Travel and Adventure. Crown 8vo, uniform in cloth extra, 7s. 6d., except where price is given.

1. **The Great Lone Land.** By Major W. F. BUTLER, C.B.
2. **The Wild North Land.** By Major W. F. BUTLER, C.B.
3. **How I found Livingstone.** By H. M. STANLEY.
4. **Through the Dark Continent.** By H. M. STANLEY. 12s. 6d.
5. **The Threshold of the Unknown Region.** By C. R. MARKHAM. (4th Edition, with Additional Chapters, 10s. 6d.)
6. **Cruise of the Challenger.** By W. J. J. SPRY, R.N.
7. **Burnaby's On Horseback through Asia Minor.** 10s. 6d.
8. **Schweinfurth's Heart of Africa.** 2 vols., 15s.
9. **Through America.** By W. G. MARSHALL.
10. **Through Siberia.** Il. and unabridged, 10s.6d. By H. LANSDELL.
11. **From Home to Home.** By STAVELEY HILL.
12. **Cruise of the Falcon.** By E. J. KNIGHT.
13. **Through Masai Land.** By JOSEPH THOMSON.
14. **To the Central African Lakes.** By JOSEPH THOMSON.
15. **Queen's Highway.** By STUART CUMBERLAND.

Low's Standard Novels. Small post 8vo, cloth extra, 6s. each, unless otherwise stated.

A Daughter of Heth. By W. BLACK.
In Silk Attire. By W. BLACK.
Kilmeny. A Novel. By W. BLACK.
Lady Silverdale's Sweetheart. By W. BLACK.
Sunrise. By W. BLACK.
Three Feathers. By WILLIAM BLACK.
Alice Lorraine. By R. D. BLACKMORE.
Christowell, a Dartmoor Tale. By R. D. BLACKMORE.
Clara Vaughan. By R. D. BLACKMORE.
Cradock Nowell. By R. D. BLACKMORE.
Cripps the Carrier. By R. D. BLACKMORE.
Erema; or, My Father's Sin. By R. D. BLACKMORE.
Lorna Doone. By R. D. BLACKMORE. 25th Edition.
Mary Anerley. By R. D. BLACKMORE.
Tommy Upmore. By R. D. BLACKMORE.

Low's Standard Novels—continued.
Bonaventure. By G. W. CABLE.
An English Squire. By Miss COLERIDGE.
Some One Else. By Mrs. B. M. CROKER.
Under the Stars and Stripes. By E. DE LEON.
Halfway. By Miss BETHAM-EDWARDS.
A Story of the Dragonnades. By Rev. E. GILLIAT, M.A.
A Laodicean. By THOMAS HARDY.
Far from the Madding Crowd. By THOMAS HARDY.
Mayor of Casterbridge. By THOMAS HARDY.
Pair of Blue Eyes. By THOMAS HARDY.
Return of the Native. By THOMAS HARDY.
The Hand of Ethelberta. By THOMAS HARDY.
The Trumpet Major. By THOMAS HARDY.
Two on a Tower. By THOMAS HARDY.
Old House at Sandwich. By JOSEPH HATTON.
Three Recruits. By JOSEPH HATTON.
A Golden Sorrow. By Mrs. CASHEL HOEY. New Edition.
A Stern Chase. By Mrs. CASHEL HOEY.
Out of Court. By Mrs. CASHEL HOEY.
Don John. By JEAN INGELOW.
John Jerome. By JEAN INGELOW. 5s.
Sarah de Berenger. By JEAN INGELOW.
Adela Cathcart. By GEORGE MAC DONALD.
Guild Court. By GEORGE MAC DONALD.
Mary Marston. By GEORGE MAC DONALD.
Stephen Archer. New Ed. of "Gifts." By GEORGE MAC DONALD.
The Vicar's Daughter. By GEORGE MAC DONALD.
Orts. By GEORGE MAC DONALD.
Weighed and Wanting. By GEORGE MAC DONALD.
Diane. By Mrs. MACQUOID.
Elinor Dryden. By Mrs. MACQUOID.
My Lady Greensleeves. By HELEN MATHERS.
Spell of Ashtaroth. By DUFFIELD OSBORNE. 5s.
Alaric Spenceley. By Mrs. J. H. RIDDELL.
Daisies and Buttercups. By Mrs. J. H. RIDDELL.
The Senior Partner. By Mrs. J. H. RIDDELL.
A Struggle for Fame. By Mrs. J. H. RIDDELL.
Frozen Pirate. By W. CLARK RUSSELL.
Jack's Courtship. By W. CLARK RUSSELL.
John Holdsworth. By W. CLARK RUSSELL.
A Sailor's Sweetheart. By W. CLARK RUSSELL.
Sea Queen. By W. CLARK RUSSELL.
Watch Below. By W. CLARK RUSSELL.
Strange Voyage. By W. CLARK RUSSELL.
Wreck of the Grosvenor. By W. CLARK RUSSELL.
The Lady Maud. By W. CLARK RUSSELL.
Little Loo. By W. CLARK RUSSELL.
Bee-man of Orn. By FRANK R. STOCKTON.
My Wife and I. By Mrs. HARRIET B. STOWE.

Low's Standard Novels—*continued.*
  The Late Mrs. Null. By FRANK R. STOCKTON.
  Hundredth Man. By FRANK R. STOCKTON.
  Old Town Folk. By Mrs. HARRIET B. STOWE.
  We and our Neighbours. By Mrs. HARRIET B. STOWE.
  Poganuc People, their Loves and Lives. By Mrs. STOWE.
  Ulu: an African Romance. By JOSEPH THOMSON.
  Ben Hur: a Tale of the Christ. By LEW. WALLACE.
  Anne. By CONSTANCE FENIMORE WOOLSON.
  East Angels. By CONSTANCE FENIMORE WOOLSON.
  For the Major. By CONSTANCE FENIMORE WOOLSON. 5s.
  French Heiress in her own Chateau.

Low's Series of Standard Books for Boys. With numerous Illustrations, 2s. 6d.; gilt edges, 3s. 6d. each.
  Dick Cheveley. By W. H. G. KINGSTON.
  Heir of Kilfinnan. By W. H. G. KINGSTON.
  Off to the Wilds. By G. MANVILLE FENN.
  The Two Supercargoes. By W. H. G. KINGSTON.
  The Silver Cañon. By G. MANVILLE FENN.
  Under the Meteor Flag. By HARRY COLLINGWOOD.
  Jack Archer: a Tale of the Crimea. By G. A. HENTY.
  The Mutiny on Board the Ship Leander. By B. HELDMANN.
  With Axe and Rifle on the Western Prairies. By W. H. G. KINGSTON.
  Red Cloud, the Solitary Sioux: a Tale of the Great Prairie. By Col. Sir WM. BUTLER, K.C.B.
  The Voyage of the Aurora. By HARRY COLLINGWOOD.
  Charmouth Grange: a Tale of the 17th Century. By J. PERCY GROVES.
  Snowshoes and Canoes. By W. H. G. KINGSTON.
  The Son of the Constable of France. By LOUIS ROUSSELET.
  Captain Mugford; or, Our Salt and Fresh Water Tutors. Edited by W. H. G. KINGSTON.
  The Cornet of Horse, a Tale of Marlborough's Wars. By G. A. HENTY.
  The Adventures of Captain Mago. By LEON CAHUN.
  Noble Words and Noble Needs.
  The King of the Tigers. By ROUSSELET.
  Hans Brinker; or, The Silver Skates. By Mrs. DODGE.
  The Drummer-Boy, a Story of the time of Washington. By ROUSSELET.
  Adventures in New Guinea: The Narrative of Louis Tregance.
  The Crusoes of Guiana. By BOUSSENARD.
  The Gold Seekers. A Sequel to the Above. By BOUSSENARD.
  Winning His Spurs, a Tale of the Crusades. By G. A. HENTY.
  The Blue Banner. By LEON CAHUN.

Low's Pocket Encyclopædia: *a Compendium of General Knowledge* for Ready Reference. Upwards of 25,000 References, with Plates. New ed., imp. 32mo, cloth, marbled edges, 3s. 6d.; roan, 4s. 6d.

Low's Handbook to London Charities. Yearly, cloth, 1s. 6d.; paper, 1s.

M^cCORMICK (R.). *Voyages in the Arctic and Antarctic Seas in Search of Sir John Franklin,* &c. With Maps and Lithos. 2 vols., royal 8vo, 52s. 6d.

Mac Donald (George). See LOW'S STANDARD NOVELS.

Macdowall (Alex. B.) Curve Pictures of London for the Social Reformer. 1s.

McGoun's Commercial Correspondence. Crown 8vo, 5s.

Macgregor (John) "*Rob Roy*" *on the Baltic.* 3rd Edition, small post 8vo, 2s. 6d.; cloth, gilt edges, 3s. 6d.

—— *A Thousand Miles in the "Rob Roy" Canoe.* 11th Edition, small post 8vo, 2s. 6d.; cloth, gilt edges, 3s. 6d.

—— *Voyage Alone in the Yawl " Rob Roy."* New Edition, with additions, small post 8vo, 5s.; 3s. 6d. and 2s. 6d.

Mackay (C.) Glossary of Obscure Words in Shakespeare. 21s.

Mackenzie (Sir Morell) Fatal Illness of Frederick the Noble. Crown 8vo, limp cloth, 2s. 6d.

Mackenzie (Rev. John) Austral Africa : Losing it or Ruling it? Illustrations and Maps. 2 vols., 8vo, 32s.

McLellan's Own Story : The War for the Union. Illust. 18s.

McMurdo (Edward) History of Portugal. 8vo, 21s.

Macquoid (Mrs.). See LOW'S STANDARD NOVELS.

Magazine. See ENGLISH ETCHINGS, HARPER.

Maginn (W.) Miscellanies. Prose and Verse. With Memoir. 2 vols., crown 8vo, 24s.

Main (Mrs.; Mrs. Fred Burnaby) High Life and Towers of Silence. Illustrated, square 8vo, 10s. 6d.

Manitoba. See BRYCE.

Manning (E. F.) Delightful Thames. Illustrated. 4to, fancy boards, 5s.

Markham (Clements R.) The Fighting Veres, Sir F. and Sir H. 8vo, 18s.

—— *War between Peru and Chili,* 1879-1881. Third Ed. Crown 8vo, with Maps, 10s. 6d.

—— See also "Foreign Countries," MAURY, and VERES.

Marshall (W. G.) Through America. New Ed., cr. 8vo, 7s. 6d.

Marston (W.) Eminent Recent Actors, Reminiscences Critical, &c. 2 vols. Crown 8vo, 21s.

Martin (J. W.) Float Fishing and Spinning in the Nottingham Style. New Edition. Crown 8vo, 2s. 6d.

Matthews (J. W., M.D.) Incwadi Yami: Twenty years in South Africa. With many Engravings, royal 8vo, 14s.
Maury (Commander) Physical Geography of the Sea, and its Meteorology. New Edition, with Charts and Diagrams, cr. 8vo, 6s.
—— *Life*. By his Daughter. Edited by Mr. CLEMENTS R. MARKHAM. With portrait of Maury. 8vo, 12s. 6d.
Men of Mark: Portraits of the most Eminent Men of the Day. Complete in 7 Vols., 4to, handsomely bound, gilt edges, 25s. each.
Mendelssohn Family (The), 1729—1847. From Letters and Journals. Translated. New Edition, 2 vols., 8vo, 30s.
Mendelssohn. See also "Great Musicians."
Merrifield's Nautical Astronomy. Crown 8vo, 7s. 6d.
Merrylees (J.) Carlsbad and its Environs. 7s. 6d.; roan, 9s.
Milford (P.) Ned Stafford's Experiences in the United States. 5s.
Mills (J.) Alternative Elementary Chemistry. Illust., cr. 8vo.
—— *Alernative Course in Physics*.
Mitchell (D. G.; Ik. Marvel) Works. Uniform Edition, small 8vo, 5s. each.

Bound together.	Reveries of a Bachelor.
Doctor Johns.	Seven Stories, Basement and Attic.
Dream Life.	Wet Days at Edgewood.
Out-of-Town Places.	

Mitford (Mary Russell) Our Village. With 12 full-page and 157 smaller Cuts. Cr. 4to, cloth, gilt edges, 21s.; cheaper binding, 10s. 6d.
Moffatt (W.) Land and Work; Depression, Agricultural and Commercial. Crown 8vo, 5s.
Mohammed Benani: A Story of To-day. 8vo, 10s. 6d.
Mollett (J. W.) Illustrated Dictionary of Words used in Art and Archæology. Illustrated, small 4to, 15s.
Moloney (Governor) Forestry of West Africa. 10s. 6d.
Money (E.) The Truth about America. New Edition. 2s. 6d.
Morlands, The. A Tale of Anglo-Indian Life. By Author of "Sleepy Sketches." Crown 8vo, 6s.
Morley (Henry) English Literature in the Reign of Victoria. 2000th volume of the Tauchnitz Collection of Authors. 18mo, 2s. 6d.
Mormonism. See "Stenhouse."
Morse (E. S.) Japanese Homes and their Surroundings. With more than 300 Illustrations. Re-issue, 10s. 6d.
Morten (Honnor) Sketches of Hospital Life. Cr. 8vo, sewed, 1s.
Morwood. Our Gipsies in City, Tent, and Van. 8vo, 18s.
Moxon (Walter) Pilocereus Senilis. Fcap. 8vo, gilt top, 3s. 6d.
Muller (E.) Noble Words and Noble Deeds. Illustrated, gilt edges, 3s. 6d.; plainer binding, 2s. 6d.

Murray (*E. C. Grenville*) *Memoirs.* By his widow. 2 vols.
Musgrave (*Mrs.*) *Miriam.* Crown 8vo.
Music. See "Great Musicians."

NAPOLEON and Marie Louise: Memoirs. By Madame Durand. 7s. 6d.
Nethercote (*C. B.*) *Pytchley Hunt.* New Ed., cr. 8vo, 8s. 6d.
New Zealand. See Bradshaw.
New Zealand Rulers and Statesmen. See Gisborne.
Nicholls (*J. H. Kerry*) *The King Country: Explorations in New Zealand.* Many Illustrations and Map. New Edition, 8vo, 21s.
Nisbet (*Hume*) *Life and Nature Studies.* With Etching by C. O. Murray. Crown 8vo, 6s.
Nordhoff (*C.*) *California, for Health, Pleasure, and Residence.* New Edition, 8vo, with Maps and Illustrations, 12s. 6d.
Norman (*C. B.*) *Corsairs of France.* With Portraits. 8vo, 18s.
Northbrook Gallery. Edited by Lord Ronald Gower. 36 Permanent Photographs. Imperial 4to, 63s.; large paper, 105s.
Nott (*Major*) *Wild Animals Photographed and Described.* 35s.
Nursery Playmates (*Prince of*). 217 Coloured Pictures for Children by eminent Artists. Folio, in coloured boards, 6s.
Nursing Record. Yearly, 8s.; half-yearly, 4s. 6d.; quarterly, 2s. 6d; weekly, 2d.

O'BRIEN (*R. B.*) *Fifty Years of Concessions to Ireland.* With a Portrait of T. Drummond. Vol. I., 16s., II., 16s.
Orient Line Guide Book. By W. J. Loftie. 5s.
Orvis (*C. F.*) *Fishing with the Fly.* Illustrated. 8vo, 12s. 6d.
Osborne (*Duffield*) *Spell of Ashtaroth.* Crown 8vo, 5s.
Our Little Ones in Heaven. Edited by the Rev. H. Robbins. With Frontispiece after Sir Joshua Reynolds. New Edition, 5s.
Owen (*Douglas*) *Marine Insurance Notes and Clauses.* New Edition, 14s.

PALLISER (*Mrs.*) *A History of Lace.* New Edition, with additional cuts and text. 8vo, 21s.
—— *The China Collector's Pocket Companion.* With upwards of 1000 Illustrations of Marks and Monograms. Small 8vo, 5s.
Parkin (*J.*) *Antidotal Treatment of Epidemic Cholera.* 3s. 6d.
—— *Epidemiology in the Animal and Vegetable Kingdom.* Part I., crown 8vo, 3s. 6d.; Part II., 3s. 6d.
—— *Volcanic Origin of Epidemics.* Popular Edition, crown 8vo, 2s.

Payne (T. O.) Solomon's Temple and Capitol, Ark of the Flood and Tabernacle (four sections at 24s.), extra binding, 105s.
Pennell (H. Cholmondeley) Sporting Fish of Great Britain 15s. ; large paper, 30s.
—— *Modern Improvements in Fishing-tackle.* Crown 8vo, 2s.
Perelaer (M. T. H.) Ran Away from the Dutch; Borneo, &c. Illustrated, square 8vo, 7s. 6d.
Pharmacopœia of the United States of America. 8vo, 21s.
Philpot (H. J.) Diabetes Mellitus. Crown 8vo, 5s.
—— *Diet System.* Tables. I. Diabetes; II. Gout; III. Dyspepsia; IV. Corpulence. In cases, 1s. each.
Plunkett (Major G. T.) Primer of Orthographic Projection. Elementary Solid Geometry. With Problems and Exercises. 2s. 6d.
Poe (E. A.) The Raven. Illustr. by DORÉ. Imperial folio, 63s.
Poems of the Inner Life. Chiefly Modern. Small 8vo, 5s.
Polar Expeditions. See MCCORMICK.
Porcher (A.) Juvenile French Plays. With Notes and a Vocabulary. 18mo, 1s.
Porter (Admiral David D.) Naval History of Civil War. Portraits, Plans, &c. 4to, 25s.
Porter (Noah) Elements of Moral Science. 10s. 6d.
Portraits of Celebrated Race-horses of the Past and Present Centuries. with Pedigrees and Performances. 4 vols., 4to, 126s.
Powles (L. D.) Land of the Pink Pearl: Life in the Bahamas. 8vo, 10s. 6d.
Poynter (Edward J., R.A.). See "Illustrated Text-books."
Pritt (T. E.) North Country Flies. Illustrated from the Author's Drawings. 10s. 6d.
Publishers' Circular (The), and General Record of British and Foreign Literature. Published on the 1st and 15th of every Month, 3d.
Pyle (Howard) Otto of the Silver Hand. Illustrated by the Author. 8vo, 8s. 6d.

RAMBAUD. History of Russia. New Edition, Illustrated. 3 vols., 8vo, 21s.
Reber. History of Mediæval Art. Translated by CLARKE. 422 Illustrations and Glossary. 8vo,
Redford (G.) Ancient Sculpture. New Ed. Crown 8vo, 10s. 6d.
Reed (Sir E. J., M.P.) and Simpson. Modern Ships of War. Illust., royal 8vo, 10s. 6d.
Richards (W.) Aluminium: its History, Occurrence, &c. Illustrated, crown 8vo, 12s. 6d.

Richter (Dr. Jean Paul) Italian Art in the National Gallery.
4to. Illustrated. Cloth gilt, £2 2s.; half-morocco, uncut, £2 12s. 6d.
—— See also LEONARDO DA VINCI.
Riddell (Mrs. J. H.) See LOW'S STANDARD NOVELS.
Robertson (Anne J.) Myself and my Relatives. New Edition, crown 8vo, 5s.
Robin Hood; Merry Adventures of. Written and illustrated by HOWARD PYLE. Imperial 8vo, 15s.
Robinson (Phil.) In my Indian Garden. New Edition, 16mo, limp cloth, 2s.
—— *Noah's Ark. Unnatural History.* Sm. post 8vo, 12s. 6d.
—— *Sinners and Saints: a Tour across the United States of America, and Round them.* Crown 8vo, 10s. 6d.
—— *Under the Punkah.* New Ed., cr. 8vo, limp cloth, 2s.
Rockstro (W. S.) History of Music. New Edition. 8vo, 14s.
Roland, The Story of. Crown 8vo, illustrated, 6s.
Rolfe (Eustace Neville) Pompeii, Popular and Practical. Cr. 8vo, 7s. 6d.
Rome and the Environs. With plans, 3s.
Rose (J.) Complete Practical Machinist. New Ed., 12mo, 12s. 6d.
—— *Key to Engines and Engine-running.* Crown 8vo, 8s. 6d.
—— *Mechanical Drawing.* Illustrated, small 4to, 16s.
—— *Modern Steam Engines.* Illustrated. 31s. 6d.
—— *Steam Boilers. Boiler Construction and Examination.* Illust., 8vo, 12s. 6d.
Rose Library. Each volume, 1s. Many are illustrated—
Little Women. By LOUISA M. ALCOTT.
Little Women Wedded. Forming a Sequel to "Little Women."
Little Women and Little Women Wedded. 1 vol., cloth gilt, 3s. 6d.
Little Men. By L. M. ALCOTT. Double vol., 2s.; cloth gilt, 3s. 6d.
An Old-Fashioned Girl. By LOUISA M. ALCOTT. 2s.; cloth, 3s. 6d.
Work. A Story of Experience. By L. M. ALCOTT. 3s. 6d.; 2 vols., 1s. each.
Stowe (Mrs. H. B.) The Pearl of Orr's Island.
—— **The Minister's Wooing.**
—— **We and our Neighbours.** 2s.; cloth gilt, 6s.
—— **My Wife and I.** 2s.
Hans Brinker; or, the Silver Skates. By Mrs. DODGE. Also 5s.
My Study Windows. By J. R. LOWELL.
The Guardian Angel. By OLIVER WENDELL HOLMES.
My Summer in a Garden. By C. D. WARNER.
Dred. By Mrs. BEECHER STOWE. 2s.; cloth gilt, 3s. 6d.
City Ballads. New Ed. 16mo. By WILL CARLETON.

Rose Library (The)—continued.
   Farm Ballads. By WILL CARLETON. ⎫
   Farm Festivals. By WILL CARLETON. ⎬ 1 vol., cl., gilt ed., 3s. 6d.
   Farm Legends. By WILL CARLETON. ⎭
   The Rose in Bloom. By L. M. ALCOTT. 2s.; cloth gilt, 3s. 6d.
   Eight Cousins. By L. M. ALCOTT. 2s.; cloth gilt, 3s. 6d.
   Under the Lilacs. By L. M. ALCOTT. 2s.; also 3s. 6d.
   Undiscovered Country. By W. D. HOWELLS.
   Clients of Dr. Bernagius. By L. BIART. 2 parts.
   Silver Pitchers. By LOUISA M. ALCOTT. Cloth, 3s. 6d.
   Jimmy's Cruise in the "Pinafore," and other Tales. By LOUISA M. ALCOTT. 2s.; cloth gilt, 3s. 6d.
   Jack and Jill. By LOUISA M. ALCOTT. 2s.; Illustrated, 5s.
   Hitherto. By the Author of the "Gayworthys." 2 vols., 1s. each; 1 vol., cloth gilt, 3s. 6d.
   A Gentleman of Leisure. A Novel. By EDGAR FAWCETT. 1s.

Ross *(Mars) and Stonehewer Cooper. Highlands of Cantabria;* or, Three Days from England. Illustrations and Map, 8vo, 21s.

Rothschilds, the Financial Rulers of Nations. By JOHN REEVES. Crown 8vo, 7s. 6d.

Rousselet (Louis) Son of the Constable of France. Small post 8vo, numerous Illustrations, gilt edges, 3s. 6d.; plainer, 2s. 6d.

—— *King of the Tigers: a Story of Central India.* Illustrated. Small post 8vo, gilt, 3s. 6d.; plainer, 2s. 6d.

—— *Drummer Boy.* Illustrated. Small post 8vo, gilt edges, 3s. 6d.; plainer, 2s. 6d.

Russell (Dora) Strange Message. 3 vols., crown 8vo, 31s. 6d.

Russell (W. Clark) Jack's Courtship. New Ed., small post 8vo, 6s.

—— *English Channel Ports and the Estate of the East* and West India Dock Company. Crown 8vo, 1s.

—— *Frozen Pirate.* New Ed., Illust., small post 8vo, 6s.

—— *Sailor's Language.* Illustrated. Crown 8vo, 3s. 6d.

—— *Sea Queen.* New Ed., small post 8vo, 6s.

—— *Strange Voyage.* New Ed., small post 8vo, 6s.

—— *The Lady Maud.* New Ed., small post 8vo, 6s.

—— *Wreck of the Grosvenor.* Small post 8vo, 6s. 4to, sewed, 6d.

S*AINTS and their Symbols: A Companion in the Churches* and Picture Galleries of Europe. Illustrated. Royal 16mo, 3s. 6d.

Samuels (Capt. J. S.) From Forecastle to Cabin: Autobiography. Illustrated. Crown 8vo, 8s. 6d.; also with fewer Illustrations, cloth, 2s.; paper, 1s.

Sandlands (J. P.) How to Develop Vocal Power. 1s.

Saunders (A.) Our Domestic Birds: Poultry in England and New Zealand. Crown 8vo, 6s.
—— *Our Horses: the Best Muscles controlled by the Best* Brains. 6s.
Scherr (Prof. J.) History of English Literature. Cr. 8vo, 8s. 6d.
Schley. Rescue of Greely. Maps and Illustrations, 8vo, 12s. 6d.
Schuyler (Eugène) American Diplomacy and the Furtherance of Commerce. 12s. 6d.
—— *The Life of Peter the Great.* 2 vols., 8vo, 32s.
Schweinfurth (Georg) Heart of Africa. 2 vols., crown 8vo, 15s.
Scott (Leader) Renaissance of Art in Italy. 4to, 31s. 6d.
—— *Sculpture, Renaissance and Modern.* 5s.
Semmes (Adm. Raphael) Service Afloat: The "Sumter" and the "Alabama." Illustrated. Royal 8vo, 16s.
Senior (W.) Near and Far: an Angler's Sketches of Home Sport and Colonial Life. Crown 8vo, 6s.
—— *Waterside Sketches.* Imp. 32mo, 1s. 6d.; boards, 1s.
Shakespeare. Edited by R. GRANT WHITE. 3 vols., crown 8vo, gilt top, 36s.; *Édition de luxe*, 6 vols., 8vo, cloth extra, 63s.
—— See also CUNDALL, DETHRONING, DONNELLY, MACKAY, and WHITE (R. GRANT).
Shakespeare's Heroines: Studies by Living English Painters. 105s.; artists' proofs, 630s.
—— *Songs and Sonnets.* Illust. by Sir JOHN GILBERT, R.A. 4to, boards, 5s.
Sharpe (R. Bowdler) Birds in Nature. 39 coloured plates and text. 4to, 63s.
Sidney (Sir Philip) Arcadia. New Edition, 6s.
Siegfried, The Story of. Illustrated, crown 8vo, cloth, 6s.
Simon. China: its Social Life. Crown 8vo, 6s.
Simson (A.) Wilds of Ecuador and Exploration of the Putumayor River. Crown 8vo, 8s. 6d.
Sinclair (Mrs.) Indigenous Flowers of the Hawaiian Islands. 44 Plates in Colour. Imp. folio, extra binding, gilt edges, 31s. 6d.
Sloane (T. O.) Home Experiments in Science for Old and Young. Crown 8vo, 6s.
Smith (G.) Assyrian Explorations. Illust. New Ed., 8vo, 18s.
—— *The Chaldean Account of Genesis.* With many Illustrations. 16s. New Ed. By PROFESSOR SAYCE. 8vo, 18s.
Smith (G. Barnett) William I. and the German Empire. New Ed., 8vo, 3s. 6d.
Smith (J. Moyr) Wooing of Æthra. Illustrated. 32mo, 1s.

Smith (Sydney) Life and Times. By STUART J. REID. Illustrated. 8vo, 21s.

Smith (W. R.) Laws concerning Public Health. 8vo, 31s. 6d.

Spiers' French Dictionary. 29th Edition, remodelled. 2 vols., 8vo, 18s.; half bound, 21s.

Spry (W. J. J., R.N., F.R.G.S.) Cruise of H.M.S." Challenger." With Illustrations. 8vo, 18s. Cheap Edit., crown 8vo, 7s. 6d.

Spyri (Joh.) Heidi's Early Experiences: a Story for Children and those who love Children. Illustrated, small post 8vo, 4s. 6d.

—— *Heidi's Further Experiences.* Illust., sm. post 8vo, 4s. 6d.

Stanley (H. M.) Congo, and Founding its Free State. Illustrated, 2 vols., 8vo, 42s.; re-issue, 2 vols. 8vo, 21s.

—— *How I Found Livingstone.* 8vo, 10s. 6d.; cr. 8vo, 7s. 6d.

—— *Through the Dark Continent.* Crown 8vo, 12s. 6d.

Start (J. W. K.) Junior Mensuration Exercises. 8d.

Stenhouse (Mrs.) Tyranny of Mormonism. An Englishwoman in Utah. New ed., cr. 8vo, cloth elegant, 3s. 6d.

Sterry (J. Ashby) Cucumber Chronicles. 5s.

Stevens (E. W.) Fly-Fishing in Maine Lakes. 8s. 6d.

Stevens (T.) Around the World on a Bicycle. Vol. II. 8vo. 16s.

Stockton (Frank R.) Rudder Grange. 3s. 6d.

—— *Bee-Man of Orn, and other Fanciful Tales.* Cr. 8vo, 5s.

—— *The Casting Away of Mrs. Lecks and Mrs. Aleshine.* 1s.

—— *The Dusantes.* Sequel to the above. Sewed, 1s.; this and the preceding book in one volume, cloth, 2s. 6d.

—— *The Hundredth Man.* Small post 8vo, 6s.

—— *The Late Mrs. Null.* Small post 8vo, 6s.

—— *The Story of Viteau.* Illust. Cr. 8vo, 5s.

—— See also LOW'S STANDARD NOVELS.

Stoker (Bram) Under the Sunset. Crown 8vo, 6s.

Storer (Professor F. H.) Agriculture in its Relations to Chemistry. 2 vols., 8vo, 25s.

Stowe (Mrs. Beecher) Dred. Cloth, gilt edges, 3s. 6d.; cloth, 2s.

—— *Flowers and Fruit from her Writings.* Sm. post 8vo, 3s. 6d.

—— *Little Foxes.* Cheap Ed., 1s.; Library Edition, 4s. 6d.

—— *My Wife and I.* Cloth, 2s.

Stowe (Mrs. Beecher) Old Town Folk. 6s.
—— *We and our Neighbours.* 2s.
—— *Poganuc People.* 6s.
—— See also ROSE LIBRARY.
Strachan (J.) Explorations and Adventures in New Guinea.
Illust., crown 8vo, 12s.
Stuttfield (Hugh E. M.) El Maghreb: 1200 *Miles' Ride through Marocco.* 8s. 6d.
Sullivan (A. M.) Nutshell History of Ireland. Paper boards, 6d.

TAINE (H. A.) "Origines." Translated by JOHN DURAND.
   I. The Ancient Regime. Demy 8vo, cloth, 16s.
   II. The French Revolution. Vol. 1. do.
   III. Do. do. Vol. 2. do.
   IV. Do. do. Vol. 3. do.
Tauchnitz's English Editions of German Authors. Each volume, cloth flexible, 2s.; or sewed, 1s. 6d. (Catalogues post free.)
Tauchnitz (B.) German Dictionary. 2s.; paper, 1s. 6d.; roan, 2s. 6d.
—— *French Dictionary.* 2s.; paper, 1s. 6d.; roan, 2s. 6d.
—— *Italian Dictionary.* 2s.; paper, 1s. 6d.; roan, 2s. 6d.
—— *Latin Dictionary.* 2s.; paper, 1s. 6d.; roan, 2s. 6d.
—— *Spanish and English.* 2s.; paper, 1s. 6d.; roan, 2s. 6d.
—— *Spanish and French.* 2s.; paper, 1s. 6d.; roan, 2s. 6d.
Taylor (R. L.) Chemical Analysis Tables. 1s.
—— *Chemistry for Beginners.* Small 8vo, 1s. 6d.
Techno-Chemical Receipt Book. With additions by BRANNT and WAHL. 10s. 6d.
Technological Dictionary. See TOLHAUSEN.
Thausing (Prof.) Malt and the Fabrication of Beer. 8vo, 45s.
Theakston (M.) British Angling Flies. Illustrated. Cr. 8vo, 5s.
Thomson (Jos.) Central African Lakes. New edition, 2 vols. in one, crown 8vo, 7s. 6d.
—— *Through Masai Land.* Illust. 21s.; new edition, 7s. 6d.
—— *and Miss Harris-Smith. Ulu: an African Romance.* crown 8vo, 6s.

Thomson (W.) Algebra for Colleges and Schools. With Answers, 5s. ; without, 4s. 6d. ; Answers separate, 1s. 6d
Tolhausen. Technological German, English, and French Dictionary. Vols. I., II., with Supplement, 12s. 6d. each ; III., 9s. ; Supplement, cr. 8vo, 3s. 6d.
Tromholt (S.) Under the Rays of the Aurora Borealis. By C. SIEWERS. Photographs and Portraits. 2 vols., 8vo, 30s.
Tucker (W. J.) Life and Society in Eastern Europe. 15s.
Tupper (Martin Farquhar) My Life as an Author. 14s.
Turner (Edward) Studies in Russian Literature. Cr. 8vo, 8s. 6d.

UPTON (H.) Manual of Practical Dairy Farming. Cr. 8vo, 2s.

VAN DAM. Land of Rubens; a companion for visitors to Belgium. See HURT.
Vane (Denzil) From the Dead. A Romance. 2 vols., cr. 8vo, 12s.
Vane (Sir Harry Young). By Prof. JAMES K. HOSMER. 8vo, 18s.
Veres. Biography of Sir Francis Vere and Lord Vere, leading Generals in the Netherlands. By CLEMENTS R. MARKHAM. 8vo, 18s.
Victoria (Queen) Life of. By GRACE GREENWOOD. Illust. 6s.
Vincent (Mrs. Howard) Forty Thousand Miles over Land and Water. With Illustrations. New Edit., 3s. 6d.
Viollet-le-Duc (E.) Lectures on Architecture. Translated by BENJAMIN BUCKNALL, Architect. 2 vols., super-royal 8vo, £3 3s.

WAKEFIELD. Aix-les-Bains: Bathing and Attractions. 6d.
Walford (Mrs. L. B.) Her Great Idea, and other Stories. Cr. 8vo, 10s. 6d.
Wallace (L.) Ben Hur: A Tale of the Christ. New Edition, crown 8vo, 6s. ; cheaper edition, 2s.
Waller (Rev. C. H.) The Names on the Gates of Pearl, and other Studies. New Edition. Crown 8vo, cloth extra, 3s. 6d.
—— *Words in the Greek Testament.* Part I. Grammar. Small post 8vo, cloth, 2s. 6d. Part II. Vocabulary, 2s. 6d.

BOOKS BY JULES VERNE.

WORKS. LARGE CROWN 8vo.	Containing 350 to 600 pp. and from 50 to 100 full-page illustrations.		Containing the whole of the text with some illustrations.	
	In very handsome cloth binding, gilt edges.	In plainer binding, plain edges.	In cloth binding, gilt edges, smaller type.	Coloured boards.
	s. d.	s. d.	s. d.	
20,000 Leagues under the Sea. Parts I. and II.	10 6	5 0	3 6	2 vols., 1s. each.
Hector Servadac	10 6	5 0	3 6	2 vols., 1s. each.
The Fur Country	10 6	5 0	3 6	2 vols., 1s. each.
The Earth to the Moon and a Trip round it	10 6	5 0	2 vols., 2s. ea.	2 vols., 1s. each.
Michael Strogoff	10 6	5 0	3 6	2 vols., 1s. each.
Dick Sands, the Boy Captain	10 6	5 0	3 6	2 vols., 1s. each.
Five Weeks in a Balloon	7 6	3 6	2 0	1s. 0d.
Adventures of Three Englishmen and Three Russians	7 6	3 6	2 0	1 0
Round the World in Eighty Days	7 6	3 6	2 0	1 0
A Floating City	7 6	3 6	2 0	1 0
The Blockade Runners			2 0	1 0
Dr. Ox's Experiment	—	—	2 0	1 0
A Winter amid the Ice	—	—	2 0	1 0
Survivors of the "Chancellor"	7 6	3 6	3 6	2 vols., 1s. each.
Martin Paz			2 0	1s. 0d.
The Mysterious Island, 3 vols. :—	22 6	10 6	6 0	3 0
I. Dropped from the Clouds	7 6	3 6	2 0	1 0
II. Abandoned	7 6	3 6	2 0	1 0
III. Secret of the Island	7 6	3 6	2 0	1 0
The Child of the Cavern	7 6	3 6	2 0	1 0
The Begum's Fortune	7 6	3 6	2 0	1 0
The Tribulations of a Chinaman	7 6	3 6	2 0	1 0
The Steam House, 2 vols. :—				
I. Demon of Cawnpore	7 6	3 6	2 0	1 0
II. Tigers and Traitors	7 6	3 6	2 0	1 0
The Giant Raft, 2 vols. :—				
I. 800 Leagues on the Amazon	7 6	3 6	2 0	1 0
II. The Cryptogram	7 6	3 6	2 0	1 0
The Green Ray	6 0	5 0	—	1 0
Godfrey Morgan	7 6	3 6	2 0	1 0
Kéraban the Inflexible :—				
I. Captain of the "Guidara"	7 6	3 6	2 0	1 0
II. Scarpante the Spy	7 6	3 6	2 0	1 0
The Archipelago on Fire	7 6	3 6	2 0	1 0
The Vanished Diamond	7 6	3 6	2 0	1 0
Mathias Sandorf	10 6	5 0		
The Lottery Ticket	7 6			
Clipper of the Clouds	7 6			
North against South	7 6			
Adrift in the Pacific	7 6			
Flight to France	7 6			

CELEBRATED TRAVELS AND TRAVELLERS. 3 vols., 8vo, 600 pp., 100 full-page illustrations, 12s. 6d.; gilt edges, 14s. each :—(1) THE EXPLORATION OF THE WORLD. (2) THE GREAT NAVIGATORS OF THE EIGHTEENTH CENTURY. (3) THE GREAT EXPLORERS OF THE NINETEENTH CENTURY.

Waller (*Rev. C.H.*) *Adoption and the Covenant.* On Confirmation. 2s. 6d.
—— *Silver Sockets; and other Shadows of Redemption.* Sermons at Christ Church, Hampstead. Small post 8vo, 6s.
Walsh (*A. S.*) *Mary, Queen of the House of David.* 8vo, 3s. 6d.
Walton (*Iz.*) *Wallet Book*, CIƆIƆLXXXV. Crown 8vo, half vellum, 21s.; large paper, 42s.
—— *Compleat Angler.* Lea and Dove Edition. Ed. by R. B. MARSTON. With full-page Photogravures on India paper, and the Woodcuts on India paper from blocks. 4to, half-morocco, 105s.; large paper, royal 4to, full dark green morocco, gilt top, 210s.
Walton (*T. H.*) *Coal Mining.* With Illustrations. 4to, 25s.
Wardrop (*O.*) *Kingdom of Georgia.* Illust. and map. 8vo. 14s.
Warner (*C. D.*) *My Summer in a Garden.* Boards, 1s.; leatherette, 1s. 6d.; cloth, 2s.
—— *Their Pilgrimage.* Illustrated by C. S. REINHART. 8vo, 7s. 6d.
Warren (*W. F.*) *Paradise Found; the North Pole the Cradle* of the Human Race. Illustrated. Crown 8vo, 12s. 6d.
Washington Irving's Little Britain. Square crown 8vo, 6s.
Wells (*H. P.*) *American Salmon Fisherman.* 6s.
—— *Fly Rods and Fly Tackle.* Illustrated. 10s. 6d.
Wells (*J. W.*) *Three Thousand Miles through Brazil.* Illustrated from Original Sketches. 2 vols. 8vo, 32s.
Wenzel (*O.*) *Directory of Chemical Products of the German Empire.* 8vo, 25s.
White (*R. Grant*) *England Without and Within.* Crown 8vo, 10s. 6d.
—— *Every-day English.* 10s. 6d.
—— *Fate of Mansfield Humphreys, &c.* Crown 8vo, 6s.
—— *Studies in Shakespeare.* 10s. 6d.
—— *Words and their Uses.* New Edit., crown 8vo, 5s.
Whitney (*Mrs.*) *The Other Girls.* A Sequel to "We Girls." New ed. 12mo, 2s.
—— *We Girls.* New Edition. 2s.
Whittier (*J. G.*) *The King's Missive, and later Poems.* 18mo, choice parchment cover, 3s. 6d.
—— *St. Gregory's Guest, &c.* Recent Poems. 5s.
Wilcox (*Marrion*) *Real People.* Sm. post 8vo, 3s. 6d.
—— *Señora Villena; and Gray, an Oldhaven Romance.* 2 vols. in one, 6s.

William I. and the German Empire. By G. BARNETT SMITH. New Edition, 3s. 6d.
Willis-Bund (J.) Salmon Problems. 3s. 6d.; boards, 2s. 6d.
Wills (Dr. C. J.) Persia as it is. Crown 8vo, 8s. 6d.
Wills, A Few Hints on Proving, without Professional Assistance. By a PROBATE COURT OFFICIAL. 8th Edition, revised, with Forms of Wills, Residuary Accounts, &c. Fcap. 8vo, cloth limp, 1s.
Wilmot (A.) Poetry of South Africa. Collected and arranged. 8vo, 6s.
Wilson (Dr. Andrew) Health for the People. Cr. 8vo, 7s. 6d.
Winsor (Justin) Narrative and Critical History of America. 8 vols., 30s. each; large paper, per vol., 63s.
Woolsey. Introduction to International Law. 5th Ed., 18s.
Woolson (Constance F.) See "Low's Standard Novels."
Wright (H.) Friendship of God. Portrait, &c. Crown 8vo, 6s.
Wright (T.) Town of Cowper, Olney, &c. 6s.
Written to Order; the Journeyings of an Irresponsible Egotist. By the Author of "A Day of my Life at Eton." Crown 8vo, 6s.

YRIARTE (Charles) Florence: its History. Translated by C. B. PITMAN. Illustrated with 500 Engravings. Large imperial 4to, extra binding, gilt edges, 63s.; or 12 Parts, 5s. each.
History; the Medici; the Humanists; letters; arts; the Renaissance; illustrious Florentines; Etruscan art; monuments; sculpture; painting.

London:

SAMPSON LOW, MARSTON, SEARLE, & RIVINGTON, LD.,

St. Dunstan's House,

FETTER LANE, FLEET STREET, E.C.

Gilbert and Rivington, Ld., St. John's House, Clerkenwell Road E.C.

www.ingramcontent.com/pod-product-compliance
Lightning Source LLC
Chambersburg PA
CBHW030347230426
43664CB00007BB/560